FINDING FERRANTE

Finding Ferrante

AUTHORSHIP AND THE POLITICS OF
WORLD LITERATURE

Alessia Ricciardi

Columbia University Press
New York

Columbia University Press
Publishers Since 1893
New York   Chichester, West Sussex
cup.columbia.edu
Copyright © 2021 Columbia University Press
All rights reserved

Library of Congress Cataloging-in-Publication Data
Names: Ricciardi, Alessia, author.
Title: Finding Ferrante : authorship and the politics of world literature / Alessia Ricciardi.
Description: New York : Columbia University Press, [2021] | Includes bibliographical
references and index.
Identifiers: LCCN 2020046756 (print) | LCCN 2020046757 (ebook) | ISBN 9780231200400
(hardback) | ISBN 9780231200417 (trade paperback) | ISBN 9780231553599 (ebook)
Subjects: LCSH: Ferrante, Elena—Criticism and interpretation.
Classification: LCC PQ4866.E6345 Z85 2021 (print) | LCC PQ4866.E6345 (ebook) |
DDC 853/.914—dc23
LC record available at https://lccn.loc.gov/2020046756
LC ebook record available at https://lccn.loc.gov/2020046757

Columbia University Press books are printed on permanent and durable acid-free paper.
Printed in the United States of America

Cover image: Veneranda Biblioteca Ambrosiana, Milan, Italy. De Agostini
Picture Library/Bridgeman Images
Cover design: Chang Jae Lee

For Chris

It is always tricky, the question whether to read an author's work in light of his life or not.

—ANNE CARSON, *THE ALBERTINE WORKOUT*

CONTENTS

ACKNOWLEDGMENTS

As this book has special importance for me, I am very grateful to those who directly or indirectly helped to speed its completion. I was inspired by my students on a continual basis, in particular Eloisa Bressan, with whom I enjoyed many engrossing conversations about both Ferrante and Gramsci, as well as Maïté Marciano, Maureen Winter, and Maria Massucco. While serving as director of Comparative Literary Studies at Northwestern, I found encouragement in the camaraderie of Corey Byrnes, Scott Durham, Harris Feinsod, Nasrin Qader, Domietta Torlasco, Sam Weber, and Tristram Wolff. Most particular thanks are due to Peter Fenves for his exceptionally generous and insightful readings of the manuscript at crucial moments. I am grateful as well to Anne Berger, who gave me invaluable advice at the start of the project. Rebecca Falkoff, with whom I've shared an enthusiasm for Ferrante that dates back years to our first acquaintance in Berkeley, Maria Anna Mariani, and David Kurnick all were happy sources of edification. For the many inexhaustible delights of their friendship, I am indebted to Paola Marrati, Leonore Guénon, Penelope Deutscher, Simona Forti, Patricia Dailey, Isabelle Alfandary, Franca Fraternali, Jens Kleinjung, Chiara Orrei, Laurent Dubreuil, Laurent Ferri, Jared Stark, Armando Solis, and Elaine Golin.

Two anonymous readers of the manuscript shared astute and productive observations that immeasurably clarified the task of readying the book for publication. I have had the great fortune of benefitting from the patience, care, and discernment of Philip Leventhal, whose wise counsel improved the book in innumerable ways. Susan Pensak, Chang Jae Lee, and the entire staff of Columbia University Press were smart and sympathetic collaborators to whom I am deeply grateful.

Invitations to speak about Ferrante's writings from Columbia University, Michigan State University, and the University of Notre Dame gave me opportunities to engage scholars and students from these and other campuses in lively discussions of a number of the questions that I explore in the following pages.

A portion of chapter 3 appeared in somewhat different form in *Estetica: Studi e ricerche* 7, no. 2 (2017).

Once again, my thanks to Chris Yu for his unwavering love and belief in me; to him I dedicate this book.

FINDING FERRANTE

QUESTIONS OF IDENTITY

Among the many surprising aspects of Elena Ferrante's runaway global success, one of the most curious is the diversity of explanations that readers offer for their enthusiasm. Multitudes swoon over the pseudonymous Italian novelist's books, but few agree on the reasons why. To cite only three opinions, her novels have struck critics variously as "a kind of practical *écriture féminine*," "openly autobiographical in form," and "a rich and haunted folk saga."[1] Contemplating the disparity of responses such as these, the scholar David Kurnick has observed that "rarely has such universal agreement about the quality of an aesthetic object coincided with such variation of opinion about what in fact it's like."[2] A blurb from the *Times* of London, with which Ferrante's press in the U.S. has promoted several of her titles, typifies the fog of obfuscation that sometimes swirls around her work when it claims that "Elena Ferrante is best described as Balzac meets *The Sopranos* and rewrites feminist theory."[3] The glibness of this pronouncement in equating the author's densely layered portraits of Italian women and society with a stereotype-laden soap opera about the Jersey mob is almost shocking.

My aim in *Finding Ferrante: Authorship and the Politics of World Literature* is to offer a very different reading of her novels in general and the four volumes that make up the Neapolitan Quartet in particular. Although the female protagonists of her stories often reveal an affinity for literary pursuits whether by profession or inclination, commentators rarely notice that Ferrante's writings are fiercely intellectual. Her novels and essays are not naive slices of life but demanding creative works bristling with ideas, operating as much on an intertextual as on a representational level. They reflect her critical engagement with cultural history, in other words, but in an unexpected way. On the one hand, her fiction, especially as exemplified by the tetralogy, harks back to a notion of energetic and pleasurable story-telling that has its roots in the humanism of the Italian Renaissance ushered in by Boccaccio's *Decameron* in the fourteenth century.[4] Ferrante's "The Story of the Shoes" in *My Brilliant Friend* epitomizes how she handles this mode of storytelling. The episode inverts the Cinderella myth's traditional sexual politics by highlighting the circulation of a desired object, namely the first pair of shoes that results from Lila's idea for a new style of footwear.[5] The men of the neighborhood vie with each other to try on the new design, until the ultimate possessor of the prize turns out to be not a prince but rather Marcello Solara. On the other hand, Ferrante's writing recalls the examples of German literature with equal force of attention and, as I maintain throughout this book, in numerous ways. From incorporating the Faustian theme of a pact with the devil to evoking the genre of the *Bildungsroman* in its portrayal of Elena and Lila's fates or envisioning Lila as a joyful Neapolitan *lazzarella* or female idler, the quartet plainly bears the imprint of Goethe while contesting the gendering of his literary strategies. Walter Benjamin's influence manifests itself in the view of history that the Italian novelist ascribes to the two friends, the language that animates their descriptions of Naples, and the image of Lila's final turn to the life of a scholar. An even more crucial source of inspiration with respect to Ferrante's representation of women is Christa Wolf, whose books provide the Italian novelist with models of character relationships and narrative structure as well as a sense of what feminism's historical depth of field might be. To fathom Ferrante's genius, we must recognize that her imagination lays claim not merely to one but to two cultural legacies: the German and the Italian.

It is high time, then, that we acknowledge Ferrante's apparent identity as the eminent Germanist and translator Anita Raja. As by now is widely known, the journalist Claudio Gatti traced Ferrante back to Raja through public information on her real estate purchases in Rome as well as hacked records of her payments by Ferrante's Italian publisher, Edizioni e/o, which seem to coincide with the novelist's worldwide successes.[6] Clearly determined to promote his conclusions as loudly as possible, he published his findings in October 2016 with *Il Sole 24 Ore*, *Frankfurter Allgemeine Zeitung*, France's *Mediapart*, and the blog of the *New York Review of Books*. Gatti's outing of Raja by methods usually reserved for exposing organized crime and political corruption have looked to many readers callously self-serving.[7] Not content merely with cashing in on his revelation of Raja's connection to Ferrante, the journalist insinuated in a companion piece that she had failed to honor her mother's German Jewish heritage because "none of Ferrante's books gives any indication of the tragedies experienced by Raja's mother and grandparents and their extended family."[8] Willfully denying the premise of her pseudonymity, Gatti betrays in this charge a presumption all the more bizarre if we simply remember that Raja has spent her life translating some of German literature's most famous works.

In the wake of this upheaval, however, I think it no longer makes any sense to suppress the question of Ferrante's identity. Although the means Gatti used to expose Raja as the writer of Ferrante's novels may strike us as repugnant, the evidence of the relation between novelist and translator that he brought to light seems incontrovertible. More important, as I will argue, Ferrante's own writing, particularly as it is exemplified in the epic narrative of Elena and Lila's friendship, bears too many of Raja's intellectual and literary signatures for readers to deny the connection. Of course, any insights that we derive from a storyteller's handling of her ideas and language inevitably are subject to some uncertainty, and many commentators may wish to avoid this difficulty and the residual controversy surrounding Gatti's unmasking of Raja, perhaps out of excessive politeness. Such reticence is the tactic of what might be called the official critical study of the novelist's writings, Tiziana de Rogatis's *Elena Ferrante: Key Words*, which has been issued under the imprimatur of Ferrante's own publishing houses in Italy and the U.S.[9] Although de Rogatis's analysis offers readers many helpful readings, its silence about the novels' authorship at this point simply begs the question.[10] A more productive approach might be to ask how our appreciation of Ferrante's works deepens if we consider the totality of her creative energies, including her possible devotion to a "foreign" literary tradition. Recognizing Raja's voice in these texts not only helps to establish the genealogical specificity of Ferrante's stories but also adds resonance to the critical, political, and feminist views represented by her characters. If we situate Elena Ferrante at the confluence of Italy and Germany's cultural histories, our reading of her place in world literature thankfully can move beyond the topic of her commercial success with a largely anglophone global readership. We may begin to consider in earnest how our knowledge of Ferrante's identity enables us to discern what is original in her writing. For this reason, I take the position in the following pages that the novelist indeed is Anita Raja on the basis of the critical, intertextual linkages between her experiences, statements, and writings as a Germanist and translator and Ferrante's fictive strategies in her novels, while at the same time granting that such indications can never be taken as proof that is conclusive beyond all doubt.

To be sure, Raja's determination not to confirm her authorship of Ferrante's novels has the merit of undercutting the media's attitude that "it's not the book that counts but the aura of its author" (F 271). Her resistance to the publishing industry's constant enforcement of the cult of personality strikes a deeply sympathetic chord. As a result, it is not hard to grasp why so many readers support Raja's continuing refusal to acknowledge her identity as Ferrante. Dayna Tortorici, for example, eloquently makes the case that Ferrante's revolt against the compulsive rituals of our society of spectacle has restored to her readers a nearly forgotten social good because "by protecting her privacy, Ferrante protected ours."[11] As appealing as we may find this argument, the evidence from years of so-called Ferrante Fever would appear to suggest that the victory of the novelist's pseudonymity has been Pyrrhic at best. Ironically, her avoidance of the limelight has thrown fuel on the fire of global readers' fantasies about life in Southern Italy, inviting the transformation of the Neapolitan Quartet into an involuntary tourist guide to the supposedly "colorful" neighborhoods of its settings and a sort of Rorschach test for visitors' stereotypes.[12] Her ongoing demurrals about her life, which recapitulate Roland Barthes's insistence on the death of the author and Michel Foucault's redefinition of the author as a "function," seem somewhat quaint and more than slightly problematic in light of her feminist politics.[13] Without rehashing the convoluted history of poststructuralism, we may ask whether in fact Ferrante is a woman who, as a result of her subject position, has shared the vicissitudes and sufferings of her own sex. Could an Italian man have written about Lila and Elena as Ferrante has done? The question's simplicity does not mean the stakes of answering it are low. Ferrante's gender and politics deserve consideration not because we must satisfy an essentialist impulse but rather because we should not encourage misogynist expectations of our submission.

Assertions of the author's death or relegation to a function aim to diminish the significance of a writer's lived circumstances and historical context. We ought to recall that critics first adopted such positions in the 1960s, when any form of cultural authority looked like an incitement to revolution. In more recent years, interest in world literature and cultural studies has renewed attention to questions of authorial subjectivity. According to theories of intersectionality, or what Christopher L. Miller calls "new identitarianism," if one is not born into a certain identity one should not perform it.[14] It is evident that such positions can risk balkanizing diverse communities when pushed to extremes. We nevertheless gain a measure of self-awareness if we take seriously the risks of cultural and gender appropriation, concerns that it would be wrong to dismiss as matters of exaggerated political correctness. One need not be a self-described new identitarian in order to embrace the creative potential of a literature that demands of both writer and reader outspoken acts of self-questioning rather than evasive retreat into formalist games.

Ferrante's gender and what it means for her writing have been matters of controversy in Italy for years. We may get a sense of how pundits have approached this issue from the interviews that accompanied the DVD release of Roberto Faenza's cinematic dramatization of *The Days of Abandonment* (*I giorni dell'abbandono*) in 2005. The pontifications of the male Italian academics who provided commentary on Ferrante's novel and Faenza's filmed adaptation bring us face to face with an all-too-typical Italian misogyny.[15] Roberto Cotroneo, for example, declares that Ferrante is a very "masculine" writer and seems halfway convinced that Ferrante "c'est moi!" Filippo La Porta contends that the novel and film tell a tale of female masochism with a very specific truth for all of us, which, in his cheerful summary, is "Woman allows herself to be emptied out" ("La donna si fa svuotare"). For years, the writer whom critics most frequently have claimed to glimpse behind the novelist's mask was Anita Raja's husband, Domenico Starnone, although one persistent school of thought has held that the "real" Ferrante might be a collective.[16] This last hypothesis is remarkable mainly for demonstrating to what lengths some readers in Italy will go to avoid concluding that a pseudonymous author who writes about women under a feminine nom de plume might be a woman. Gender appropriation in the sense of men writing in the voice of women has been a literary device for as long as literature has existed. Does this history reassure us that it now would be welcome, satisfying, or interesting for a man to claim to be Madame Bovary, as Flaubert did two centuries ago?

In interviews, Ferrante occasionally has dropped hints about her personal life that give a false impression of who she is. The disinformation has allowed Anita Raja to veil her achievements as a Germanist and translator as well as her marriage to Domenico Starnone under the fantasy of being a Neapolitan seamstress's daughter who lives abroad teaching classics. She has created for herself, in other words, a less comfortably brought-up alter ego with a pseudo-neorealist backstory. As the daughter of a Neapolitan judge and of a German Jewish mother who wrote language textbooks, however, Raja hardly can lay claim to this mantle. The problem is not the threat of appropriating the culturally sacred narratives of less privileged classes; indeed, Ferrante's political critique of modern Italian society is so well honed, especially in the tetralogy, as to warrant Judith Thurman's recent comment that in the story of the two friends we confront "a magisterial social history of class."[17] Rather, the author's subterfuge risks abetting readers too willing to be misled on the subject of Southern Italy's complicated cultural and historical realities. The average anglophone reader will welcome Ferrante's invented biography far more readily than her real one. Thanks to the fable that Raja weaves around the figure of Ferrante, we may lose sight of the extraordinary encounter between Italian and German literatures that she stages in the Neapolitan novels. It is precisely the dynamism of this encounter that challenges us to think outside the provincial rules of national identity.

To hold that the author matters does not necessitate reopening the *querelle* between Proust and Sainte-Beuve in order to privilege the latter's "anecdotalism," as Ferrante calls it, over the former's "stand against positivist biography" (F 179). The aim is not to transform a work of imagination into autobiography but rather to ask how we validate the function of an author who says something new. To borrow an apt call to arms from the Italian literary critic Carla Benedetti, "We must reopen the realm of the possible locked up in the vision of history as a labyrinth."[18] What is at stake is not the personal authenticity of writing but rather its ethical and political imagination. A writer's gender, race, and class remain important, even if her writing amounts to more than a recipe of these conditions.[19] That Karl Ove Knausgaard is celebrated as a radical reinventor of the novel while Ferrante cannot be recognized as Anita Raja is more than puzzling in light of all that is at stake in contemporary discussions of gender. At a moment when women's worldwide outrage at their sexual assault and harassment by men has found its socially mediated voice under the hashtags #MeToo and #TimesUp, the problem of authorship has taken on an undeniable urgency and demands to be historicized. As Rebecca Solnit cogently maintains, "who gets to be the subject of the story is an immensely political question."[20] It might well be added that who gets to be the author of the story is a line of inquiry that is no less politically fraught.

Comparing Ferrante and Knausgaard in fact has become something of a nervous tic among the sort of readers who avidly watch the stock market of authorial prestige.[21] Some commentators like to lump together Ferrante with Knausgaard and, at times, Rachel Cusk as examples of what they view as the defining literary trend of the 2010s, namely the rise of autofiction. According to John Williams, Knausgaard looks like "the sun in this genre's planetary system" due to the inexorable centripetal pull of his six-volume series of novels collectively titled *My Struggle*.[22] If we extend the metaphor to Ferrante, we assimilate her stories to this self-reflecting cosmic order on account of her writing in the first person, giving the name Elena to one of her protagonists in the Neapolitan Quartet and a lesser character in one of her earlier novels, and making Naples a recurring feature of her narratives. These are flimsy reasons for the classification, however, especially given what we know of Raja's background. Although autofiction can encompass different approaches to mixing autobiography and fiction, the category cannot stretch to fit a complete disparity of social and material circumstances between writer and narrator. Insofar as her father belonged to one of the most rigorously educated, highly paid, and socially respected professions in Italy and her mother authored educational texts, Raja clearly grew up in a household of upper-class privilege. Although she may have lived in Rome since early childhood, she can claim to know Naples through her father and his family or her husband, Domenico Starnone, all of whom amassed more firsthand experience of the city. There is little in her novels, in other words, that distinguishes them as autofiction rather than as fiction.

It is important to note on this score that throughout her career Ferrante herself has been unwavering when it comes to championing the primacy of fiction over reality, for instance in this direct answer to a reader who asks which one of her books is the most autobiographical: "I believe that in fiction one pretends much less than one does in reality. In fiction we say and recognize things about ourselves, which, for the sake of propriety, we ignore or do not talk about in reality" (F 213). To believe in fiction as Ferrante advises in this statement is to pay attention above all to the truth expressed by the story itself rather than to look for its explanation in the world outside the text. By taking this position, Raja ironically aligns the specious facts of the life that she has made up for Ferrante with the extraneous "propriety" or "reality" that falsifies the literary work. At the same time, it is Raja's crafting of this imagined biography that has constituted the most playfully appealing invitation for readers to think about the relevance of a writer's life to the interpretation of her works, even if Gatti's response miserably demonstrates the potential price of giving such encouragement. At any rate, to realize that Raja has lived mainly in Rome rather than in Naples and comes from an intellectually and socially rarefied milieu does not mean that there are no biographical elements whatsoever in her novels. Rather, such awareness entails renouncing the wish to define once and for all the ingredients of a pure, authentic connection between author and subject matter and instead reflecting on the more ambiguous lessons of the fictive imagination.

DEGREES OF WORLD LITERATURE

The stunning reception of the Neapolitan novels across more than forty countries is surely one of the great contemporary success stories of world literature. Yet the saga's voracious consumption by global readers also highlights some of the more problematic implications of the category. Most important for the writer's fame and fortune has been the tetralogy's enthusiastic reception in North America, where the books of the series have circulated to the tune of more than two million copies. The critic James Wood helped to hasten the spread of Ferrante Fever in the U.S. with his review of the series' first volume in the *New Yorker* of January 21, 2013. Either he or his editor facetiously titled the essay "Women on the Verge," effectively renaming *My Brilliant Friend* by winking at the title of Pedro Almodóvar's international smash hit, *Women on the Verge of a Nervous Breakdown* (1988). The yoking together of Ferrante's then unknown novel with Almodóvar's already much lionized movie may strike us as more than slightly misleading, as the Italian novelist's feminist epic and the Spanish director's farcical comedy have little in common beyond a diffusely "Latinate" aura that evaporates as soon as one scrutinizes it. More recently, the HBO television series overseen by writer and director Saverio Costanzo has only added to Ferrante's extraordinary worldwide popularity. The novels seem destined to surf the wave of global marketing, especially the tidal current of anglophone publicity, toward the shore of what might be called world literature lite, where readers welcome titles from all nations into a state of slightly exoticized naturalization. Our commodifying of the books raises the risk of imposing stereotypes about the lives of Southern Italians on Elena, Lila, and the characters that inhabit their neighborhood, thus diminishing the novels' potential for critique.[23]

Recognizing the critical influence of the German literary tradition from Goethe to Walter Benjamin and Christa Wolf on Ferrante's writing in this sense helps to problematize the reading of her works as distillations of a middlebrow Italian (or Latinate) cultural essence for the pleasure of a largely Anglo-American readership. For example, we may ask why does Ferrante choose to deploy lines from Goethe's *Faust* as the opening epigraph of *My Brilliant Friend*? Could it be, among other reasons, that the quotation is meant to suggest the novels' inherent resistance to the expectations with which readers approach domestic, and domesticated, literary productions?[24] After all, it is Goethe's declaration in 1827 that "the age of *Weltliteratur* is at hand" that ushers in modern efforts to rethink from a critical perspective the value of literature in light of its cultural specificity and heterogeneity. As Emily Apter points out, Goethean *Weltliteratur* in fact gave rise to the idea of a "situated universalism" that actively reflects on readers' differences, thus standing in opposition to the "flaccid globalisms" of world literature as institutional construct, which invokes otherness while affirming the practices of neoliberalism.[25] Ferrante's quotation of Goethe at the start of *My Brilliant Friend* may signal her rebellion on some level against the threatened obliteration of her writings' artistic and intellectual idiosyncrasies as the cost of their worldwide distribution.

Ferrante's books tell an interesting story, we might conclude, about their own relationship to world literature. In the tetralogy, this narrative ironically begins to take shape when the two friends as little girls choose an American novel for their first-ever book purchase, which they pay for with money that Don Achille has given them as compensation for losing their dolls in his cellar. Of course, the book is Louisa May Alcott's *Little Women*. We may recall that Alcott lived with her family near Emerson and Thoreau in Concord, Massachusetts, and was steeped in the ideas of American transcendentalism. In her portrait of the four March sisters' overcoming of adversity through self-reliance, Lila and Elena recognize something of their own friendship, perhaps begging the question how two poor Neapolitan girls growing up in the middle of the twentieth century could identify with Alcott's heroines. Although the nineteenth-century American sisters are raised in humble conditions, they display genteel manners, are blessed with an even-tempered mother, and, with the exception of Beth, wind up in fortunate situations. If Lila resembles in spirit the rebellious and self-reliant Jo, who is the true heroine of Alcott's saga, she does not manage like Jo to become a writer or teacher, although at times she aspires to be both. In contrast, Elena achieves public success as an author but demonstrates none of Jo's independence or assertiveness. Unlike Elena, Lila personifies a mode of literary genius that is always held in potential. Despite her lack of formal education, for example, she develops pronounced enthusiasms for Beckett and Joyce, both of whom represent modernist anglophone writers whose texts are so demanding that educated but lesser readers such as Nino or Maestra Oliviero cannot make head or tail of them. Lila indeed evinces a distinctly cosmopolitan taste in books as she professes interest only in Latin, Greek, and foreign literatures and never admits to liking any Italian titles, not even Elena's, although she does get excited when she attends a talk by Pier Paolo Pasolini (2:358). Her anglophilia, in other words, is one measure of her fearlessness when it comes to intellectually difficult questions, her modernist affinities, and her openness to cultural differences.

By the time of their publication from 2011 to 2014, Ferrante's Neapolitan novels make clear what a contemporary example of Goethe's prophesied epoch of Weltliteratur might look like. What happens when the mania for global bestsellers collides with the appearance of new experiments in world literature remains an open question. Beyond an academic celebration of transnational narratives that increasingly occurs only through the mediation of anglophone scholarship, what place remains in contemporary fiction for questioning the antagonism between the impulses of cosmopolitan curiosity and identitarian singularity?[26] In this context, reading Ferrante without denying Raja's authorship of her oeuvre offers readers a chance to reassess the logic of the impasse. For if Raja in truth is Ferrante, we have reason to inquire why the quartet enlists readers in the confrontation between Italy and Germany's cultural genealogies, as if to remind us that all our stories eventually reveal mysterious and multifaceted histories of migration. Moreover, paying attention to this confrontation refutes the recurrent charge by hostile Italian critics that Ferrante's style of storytelling amounts to *sceneggiata*, a uniquely Neapolitan form of musical theater in which melodramatic scenes recited in dialect are interspersed with popular songs. Although Ferrante has avowed her lack of shame regarding "the techniques of popular novels" (F 225), Raja's relentless intellectual guile compels us to grapple with the symbolic and philosophical strangeness of the culture depicted in the series, much as the novels' two heroines repeatedly must do.

The inspiration of German culture is vital if we wish to make sense of the specific feminist politics that inform the saga of the two friends. Ferrante has professed enthusiasm in interviews for the theories of Italy's so-called difference feminism of the 1970s (F 59, 77). Given the ingenuity with which she evokes narrative models for Elena and Lila's story from German-language women writers such as Christa Wolf, Ingeborg Bachmann, and Elfriede Jelinek, Ferrante's sympathy for Italian feminism should not be mistaken for a parochial or nostalgic impulse, however. Rather, the author's incorporation in the Neapolitan novels of the ideas of "the thinking of difference" (*il pensiero della differenza*) that originated with the Milan Women's Bookstore Collective (Libreria delle Donne di Milano) highlights the radicalism of Elena and Lila's notions of women's solidarity in contrast to what has become mainstream feminist thinking today. Lorna Finlayson acutely sums up the dominant view of contemporary feminism in North America and Europe when she writes, "It has become the norm for political parties, corporations and academic departments to pledge to improve the proportion of women in 'leadership' positions. As Sarah Banet-Weiser observes, the rhetoric of female 'empowerment' is now a standard marketing tool. Feminism hasn't just acquired establishment approval; it has managed to become voguish."[27]

Ferrante's depiction of women has little in common with a feminism of this sort, which happily acquiesces to the premises and practices of modern-day capitalism, thus encouraging a mood that Lauren Berlant felicitously dubs "cruel optimism."[28] With this turn of phrase, Berlant gives a name to the affective and political dilemma created by the spurious attachments that nowadays promise us access to the supposed good life. In the case of mainstream feminism, work provides an object of such optimistic investment that no imaginative space seems to be left for cultural, political, or social actions beyond the question of equal pay. By contrast, this single-minded ambition is absent from both the Italian feminism of the thinking of difference, which revolves around practices of creative entrustment between women, as well as the German-language feminist tradition represented by authors such as Bachmann, Wolf, and Jelinek, in whose writings it is impossible to distinguish feminist analysis from social and political critique. In this sense, the ambiguous feminist moral of Lila and Elena's saga invites us to contemplate the differences of a feminism in which work never coincides with salvation, especially for working-class women, and all our forms of resistance prove untranslatable into the monocultural argot of global consumerism.

FERRANTE'S INTENSE REALISM

In ways both evident and subtle, Ferrante's first three novels, *Troubling Love*, *The Days of Abandonment*, and *The Lost Daughter*, adopt a different approach to problems of form and style than that taken by the Neapolitan Quartet. The middle-class heroines of these earlier works narrate introverted, somewhat elliptical accounts of their personal conflicts in language that hums with affective or psychological tension. Ferrante adheres in these texts to suppositions of the fragmentariness of subjective experience, of the narrator's solipsism with respect to society and culture, and of the impressionistic indeterminacy of spatial and temporal relationships. The author's allegiance to these articles of faith would appear to signal a writer whose imagination flourishes in the long shadow cast by modernism.

On the sprawling canvas of the Neapolitan novels, however, Ferrante paints an expansive tableau of characters and situations that requires her to venture beyond the limits of the modernist legacy into the light of a new aesthetics. Kurnick astutely captures the significance of this artistic reinvention when he declares that "Ferrante's revivification of realism might be the novels' most surprising achievement."[29] According to this view, the unexpected return of what Roland Barthes long ago defined as "the reality effect" in Elena and Lila's saga ensues from the novels' "unequaled sensitivity to what it feels like to be in and with history."[30] To think of the series as an elongated historical novel, however, risks detracting from the two friends' intensities of thought and feeling in the face of their circumstances, thus threatening to divert the reader's attention from the subjective vicissitudes of Elena and Lila's story, which undercut its claims to historical objectivity, to the events that constitute the plot of the narrative itself. We ought to recognize that it is from the sheer exuberance of storytelling, as Elena and Lila relate their ideas and experiences to one another and to the reader, that any degree of "realism" achieved by Ferrante in the tetralogy originates.

The author dramatizes the antinomies of realist aesthetics in *The Story of the Lost Child* when Lila responds negatively to Elena's third book. Having returned to live in Naples, from where she submits to her publisher the long-suppressed novel chronicling her neighborhood's history of violence, Elena confesses to having succumbed to the grip of a "mania for reality," which has upset the balance between truth and fiction so that "every street, every building had become recognizable, and maybe even the people" (4:283). The result is a thinly disguised rehearsal of the strife between the precinct's Camorrist families that Lila eventually admits to disliking because it succeeds neither as fiction nor as history (4:285). Critics' admiring reviews of the book justify their praises with reasons ranging from the writer's "brutal realism" to her "baroque imagination" and attainment of "a female narrative that was gentle and embracing" (4:287–88). Amusingly, the inconsistency of these verdicts calls to mind the astonishing variety of reactions that Ferrante's own work has provoked.

We might say that in the Neapolitan novels Ferrante takes on the project of revisiting realism in the wake of modernism, which is to say a realism that ironizes and problematizes modernism's presumption of the instability of the subject without entirely repudiating it. Of all the characters in the series, Lila is the one who most explicitly stands for modernist ideas. As we have observed earlier, she names Beckett and Joyce as two of her preferred writers (2:212–13, 2:380–81), intimating that she favors abstraction, difficulty, and disintegration over the polemical and realist impulses that seem to inform Elena's literary tastes. Lila's experiences of *smarginatura* torment her with visions of the destabilization of solid matter along the lines of Francis Bacon's paintings, in which the viewer encounters the figurative subject at moments of shocking deformation. Her own bridal portrait in her wedding dress undergoes a similar distortion when she transforms it into a kind of abstract collage in the Solaras's shop on the Piazza dei Martiri (2:119). The intellectual and emotional dialectic that shapes Elena and Lila's friendship thus is also an aesthetic dichotomy, which the narrative elaborates but never entirely resolves. Both of the two friends embrace modernism's exaltation of the new at some moments and repudiate the ideal at others.

If we were to equate the disruption of reality that Lila names smarginatura with merely one more bout in an ongoing stylistic debate, however, we would fail to do justice to the stakes that Ferrante raises in the depiction of her characters' relations to themselves, their language, and their world. In this sense, the very phenomenon of dissolving margins hints at the inadequacy of aesthetic categories altogether when it comes to determining the limits of representation with respect to our subjectivity. Although Ferrante's characters are never shy in voicing their feelings of happiness, sadness, anger, and so forth, Lila's episodes of what she feels to be the collapse of the very bounds of reality mark her break from the language of emotion and turn toward the logic of affect, which is to say her privileging of enigmatic bodily sensations that cannot signify in conventional terms and, precisely for this reason, paradoxically affirm the Barthesian reality effect or *l'effet de réel*. Barthes, we should recall, argued that, in the absence of a denotative signified, signs of the "real" ultimately could refer only to the concept of realism itself.[31] By contrast, to the extent that affects refer to material, corporeal, or nonverbal states of being, they avow at once a more immediate and more inexplicable relationship to reality than the emotions, in our psychologized understanding of them, can claim. To think of dissolving margins as an affect thus may help us avoid reading Lila's distress at the volatility of the real as another case in the endless series of our prescriptively theorized narratives of trauma, which inevitably define the subject's predicament in terms of her victimization. Rather than portray either of the two friends along such lines, Ferrante instead calls our attention to Lila and Elena's constant invention of new forms of affective resistance to the misogyny of their society. Both women exemplify an attitude that Berlant might view as a reaction to what she calls "crisis ordinariness," which is to say the precariousness of situations, including but also extending far beyond trauma, that require us to survive by means of "the spreading of symbolizations and other inexpressive but life-extending actions throughout the ordinary."[32] As Ferrante views the two friends with neither disinterest nor condescension, she commits to exploring the full breadth and depth of their affective responses to the catastrophe of everyday life, consequently abandoning the rhetoric of emotional or sentimental melodrama.

We may come to the conclusion as a result that, if any principle unites Ferrante's early novels with the Neapolitan Quartet, it is her commitment to a poetics that wholly reflects the intensities of her heroines' subjective lives. The protagonists of her first three novels share a similarly anxious concern for their own self-control that appears to anticipate Lila's fear of the loss or dissolution of the world's margins. In response to this latent threat of disaster, the author's writing crackles with an energy that she holds in reserve only to release at specific turning points like a controlled explosion. If Ferrante affirms a realist viewpoint in the story of the two friends, she gives voice to this attitude in language that fluctuates unpredictably between cool, level-headed description and sudden extremes of heated emotion, keeping the reader in a state of continuous suspense. As she herself laconically describes her method, "I work by contrast: clarity of facts and low emotional reaction alternating with a sort of storm of blood, of frenzied writing. However, I try to avoid dividing lines between the two moments. I tend to make them slide into one another without a break" (F 87). According to Kurnick, the effect of this sliding between clarity and frenzy is to repeatedly challenge readers, compelling them to regain their bearings: "The bland sentences lull us into thinking we know what kind of novel this is, and then the path veers abruptly into more demanding terrain."[33] Ferrante's realism in other words is a practice of sustaining forces that are in perpetual conflict, a way of refraining from the oversimplification of contradictions, as when she remarks of Jane Austen's tone in *Sense and Sensibility* that "the lightness conceals pitiless depths."[34] Although lightness may not be the categorical imperative of Ferrante's critical judgment, her insistence on the tension between lightness and depth in Austen's writing hints at vertiginously multiplying complications that reveal more than a passing resemblance to the questions implicated in Ferrante's own storytelling. All the numerous enigmas that go unsolved by the end of the series—what happened to Tina?, did Pasquale kill the Solaras?, is Lila writing a secret book about Naples?, why does she abandon Elena and vanish from the neighborhood?—leave the reader at every turn on the brink of falling off a new epistemological precipice.

READINGS IN DEPTH

Each chapter that makes up this book investigates one of four different dimensions of Ferrante's writing, focusing specifically on her treatment of sexuality, work, politics, and locality. The first chapter, "Cruel Sexuality," follows Ferrante's evolution from the portrayal in her early novels of women's solipsism, which in *The Days of Abandonment* appears as the potential for an obscenely performative rage recalling the protagonists of Elfriede Jelinek, to the exploration of an ambivalent yet mutually productive form of trust between women in the Neapolitan novels. Although Elena and Lila's saga provides the novelist with an occasion to develop a searing, sustained critique of men's reflexive violence toward women, I argue that her indictment of modern-day Italy's patriarchal culture is all the more compelling for her resistance to depicting women in the role of victims. She recounts the shock of the harassments, sexual assaults, and, in Lila's case, rape that the two friends experience without giving her working-class heroines the terms to describe these incidents as traumas. Instead, Ferrante invents a language of her own to give voice to female anxieties of bodily violation and rupture. This language is encapsulated in Lila's appropriation of the rarely used, practically untranslatable Italian word *smarginatura*—which Ferrante's American translator Ann Goldstein renders as both "dissolving margins" and "dissolving boundaries"—to name her horror at the decomposition of physical reality itself. The author's interest in the energies of words that grow legible at the limits of translation such as *smarginatura* or the emblematic title of her collection of essays and interviews, *Frantumaglia*, reflects Anita Raja's care as a translator for semantic nuance guiding the composition of Ferrante's texts. On this point, the limits of the novels' reception as examples of world literature, especially by anglophone readers, come into sharp focus. In her otherwise perceptive meditation on Ferrante's career in the *New Yorker*, Judith Thurman offers an opinion that only a non-native Italian speaker could propose: "Reading her in English isn't the same experience. Ann Goldstein has translated all of Ferrante's work, and many bilingual readers feel that she has improved the prose."[35] That the commentator has to prop up this claim by vaguely invoking "many bilingual readers" gives away the show. Although Goldstein's English translation is very readable, it is not always faithful to the novelist's challenging and idiosyncratic use of words like *smarginatura*, as I note in greater detail at later points, and thus short-changes her explosive linguistic energy. Thurman's assessment of the relative merits of the Italian original and English translation, in other words, is wrong.

If sex offers Ferrante's protagonists only the provisional and sublimated satisfactions of what Italian feminist theory calls entrustment, work proves to be even more problematic, as I contend in the second chapter, "Working Women." Although her novels envision the lives of vibrant and strong-minded women, their stories cannot be read as parables of self-fulfillment through professional success. One may argue that Elena and Lila's drama ultimately revolves around the struggle to rise above their plebeian origins, but meaningful work in the quartet has less to do with notions of capitalist progress than with an older idea of intellectual *Bildung*. Elena pursues a course of schooling and self-cultivation as a writer that surely belongs more to the German Enlightenment than to the twentieth century. Of course, Lila's financial success as the entrepreneurial force behind Basic Sight, the software company that she starts with her partner, Enzo Scanno, may make her look at first glance like the paradigm of a self-made woman. Following the disappearance of her daughter Tina, however, she loses interest in the business and abandons the venture without a second thought. In a turn of events that takes Elena by surprise, Lila grows preoccupied with the history of Naples in the Biblioteca Nazionale and eventually devotes herself to the toil of the scholarly *vita contemplativa*.

The investigations of gender and class that arise in the first two chapters return with renewed urgency in the third chapter, "Political Cosmologies." It may seem odd to speak of the political consciousness of an author who has said that "I don't have any special passion for politics, it being a never-ending merry-go-round of bosses big and small, all generally mediocre" (F 356). Notwithstanding the disclaimer, the novelist offered a hint as to her partisan sympathies when she took on a weekly column for the left-leaning newspaper the *Guardian* for the year spanning from January 2018 to January 2019.[36] Moreover, her stories and essays, when taken together, amount to no less than a thoroughgoing indictment of the misogynist neoliberalism that prevails in Italy. Her skepticism toward the fundamental premises of this culture grows visible most clearly if we return to our consideration of Anita Raja's relationship to Ferrante's writing. For it is when we examine the novels of Christa Wolf, whose works of fiction and nonfiction Raja has translated throughout her career, that we find the most salient models for the Neapolitan novels regarding their characters and plot structures, their feminist depth of field, which brings to light resemblances between contemporary women and the heroines of classical literature, and their distinct awareness of social and class concerns. At the same time, we should note that Ferrante's attention to the political questions raised by her protagonists' struggles is too easily lost in translation. A clear index of this difficulty, I contend, is visible in her recurrence at numerous points throughout the novels to the politically charged and hard-to-translate Italian word *subalterno* and its variants, which Ann Goldstein's English version renders with ordinary-sounding glosses such as "subordinate" or "inferior" rather than the cognate "subaltern." Although she may be indifferent to the fortunes of specific parties in Italy, Ferrante's seeding of her characters' language with a term borrowed from the thought of the Sardinian Marxist philosopher Antonio Gramsci signals her deep engagement with political ideas and theories. In a larger sense, it is the author's dramatization of Lila and Elena's struggles as women in Italian culture to fulfill their potential as intellectuals, albeit with very different ideas of what such a project might demand of them, that marks the saga as a sort of Gramscian experiment or investigation by literary means. Her approach leads to the elaboration of what we might call an "intimate public sphere" in which the relations of her characters to each other and their critical responses to the vicissitudes of history comprise the most important domain of political action.

Naples as the specific site of confrontation between Ferrante's characters and their social and material conditions is the topic of the fourth chapter, "*Genius Loci.*" The author's representation of the city in the series dialectically opposes the diffuse namelessness of streets and buildings on its east side, where Ferrante situates Lila and Elena's neighborhood (*rione*), to the iconic landmarks on its west side such as Via Chiaia, Via Tasso, and the saga's symbolic epicenter of Piazza dei Martiri. Ferrante's description of these locales cannily draws on a teeming body of writings about Naples including Goethe's observations as a visitor in the eighteenth century, municipal planners' proposals for urban renewal in the nineteenth, and

Benedetto Croce and Anna Maria Ortese's reports on the city's people and structures in the twentieth. However, the literary figure who looms largest over the novelist's vision of the city is Walter Benjamin. As Benjamin did with Paris, Ferrante reimagines the history of Naples as a vast labyrinth of circuitous and unpredictable change that cannot be contained within the logic of rational progress. Accordingly, she visualizes Lila and Elena as simultaneously exhilarated and threatened by the city like spectators of the Kantian sublime. In the equivocation between the splendor and disorder embodied by Naples, the two friends find an echo of the ambivalence of their friendship itself and a final limit to the possibilities of their shared story.

HOW SHE SIGNED HER WORK

Writing about Ferrante's relationship to her global readership, I have proposed that one reason for her prefacing the Neapolitan Quartet with a quote from Goethe may be to signal on some level her allegiance to his notion of Weltliteratur. However, the resonance of the citation throughout the tetralogy as a whole bespeaks a depth of engagement between the Italian novelist and her German predecessor that is more profound than agreement solely on a theory of literary reception. Ferrante indeed risks letting slip her pseudonymous persona and betraying the possibility of Anita Raja's authorship in the epigraph to *My Brilliant Friend*. This inscription consists of lines from the "Prologue in Heaven" to Goethe's *Faust* in which the Lord explains the purpose of Mephistopheles, the spirit whom he characterizes as "ironic." For the sake of clarity, it is worth reviewing both the nineteenth-century American poet Bayard Taylor's translation of Goethe's verse that commences the anglophone edition of *My Brilliant Friend* and the unattributed Italian rendering that begins *L'amica geniale*:

THE LORD: Therein, thou'rt free, according to thy merits:
The like of thee have never moved My hate.
Of all the bold, denying Spirits,
The waggish knave [in German: *der Schalk*] least trouble doth create.
Man's active nature, flagging, seeks too soon the level;
Unqualified repose he learns to crave;

Whence, willingly, the comrade him I gave,
Who works, excites, and must create, as Devil.

IL SIGNORE: Ma sì, fatti vedere quando vuoi;
non ho mai odiato i tuoi simili,
di tutti gli spiriti che dicono di no,
il Beffardo e quello che mi da meno fastidio.
L'agire dell'uomo si sgonfia fin troppo facilmente,
egli presto si invaghisce del riposo assoluto.
Perciò gli do volentieri un compagno
che lo pungoli e che sia tenuto a fare la parte del diavolo.[37]

The reader who checks the three preeminent, modern Italian editions of *Faust*—Barbara Allason's version of 1950, Franco Fortini's of 1970, and Andrea Casalegno's of 1994—will discover that none of them are the source of this version of the Lord's speech that appears in *L'amica geniale*.[38] From Ferrante's avoidance of the major published translations, we can only surmise that the unnamed source of the translation is in fact herself.

The most striking aspect of Ferrante's rendering for Italian readers is its insistence on the colloquial idiom rather than floridly literary rhetoric.[39] Her originality on this score becomes most evident in the third line when she strikes out on her own to avoid magniloquence and rejects Allason, Fortini, and Casalegno's consensus on translating "von allen Geistern, die verneinen" with the formulation "di tutti gli spiriti che negano" (of all the spirits who negate). Instead, she opts for the far more casual expression "di tutti gli spiriti che dicono di no" (of all the spirits who say no). Readers who are not fluent in Italian hopefully nevertheless can appreciate the distinction here between Allason, Fortini, and Casalegno's polysyllabic *negano* and Ferrante's brusque *no*. As for the Lord's crucial epithet for Mephistopheles, *der Schalk* ("rogue" or, as Taylor translates it, "knave"), which occurs in the next line, she sides with Allason and Casalegno in choosing the vernacular *beffardo* over Fortini's more classically latinate *l'ironico*. In the lines that follow, Ferrante continues to insist on a less elevated idiom, utilizing the plainer *sgonfiare* to translate *erschlaffen* instead of Allason's *dormire sugli allori*, Fortini's *rilassarsi*, or Casalegno's *afflosciarsi*, so that the language both resonates in the ear like commonplace Italian speech and remains faithful to the German original.[40]

Ferrante, in other words, makes the passage her own, accomplishing a feat that, given the literary history, we should not underestimate. Her translation of Goethe brims with easy yet vivid turns of phrase that dynamically balance syntax and meaning within the logical demands of the original's metaphysical argument. The effortlessness with which she transmutes Goethe's antiquated German verse into a readable aphorism for twenty-first-century Italian readers epitomizes not only a difficult feat of translation but a telling signature gesture. Answering Eva Ferri's question, "What are the features of your approach to writing?," in one of the interviews collected in *Frantumaglia*, Ferrante replies: "The only thing I know for certain is this: it seems to me that I work well when I start from a flat, dry tone. . . . At the beginning I need curtness, terse, clear formulas that are free of affectations and demonstrations of beautiful form" (F 267–8). For a pseudonymous author, Ferrante's decision to start Elena and Lila's epic narrative with a quotation of the Lord's explanation of Mephistopheles's purpose may seem more than a little improbable inasmuch as the cited speech asserts its speaker's absolutely immanent presence and omniscience while also affirming its addressee's subversive, "denying" temperament. Her choice of epigraph mischievously positions the author as both god and devil of her own imaginative cosmos, setting in motion a tension that runs throughout the novels between reality and fiction, history and storytelling, the conversational and the persuasive, the "flat, dry tone" of divine rationality and the bloody effusiveness of our vital, and potentially infernal, irrationality.

We might say that Ferrante devises the epigraph of *My Brilliant Friend* to appeal more to devotees of literature such as the youthful Lila and Elena than to typical consumers of mass-market bestsellers. Like a cat burglar who cannot refrain from leaving clues at the crime scene, Ferrante in the end endorses the tetralogy with a signature that artfully encodes her likely identity as Anita Raja. In her translations of Christa Wolf's writings, we should note, Raja makes use of both Allason and Fortini's renditions of Goethe when providing Italian equivalents for Wolf's citations of *Faust* throughout her corpus. Yet it seems that in the front matter of her own masterwork she affirms her authorship of the quartet by means of an original act of translation from the German language. The Italian novelist's invocation of Goethe supplies the very *ars poetica* of the Neapolitan novels, which is to say a programmatic declaration of purpose. *My Brilliant*

Friend indeed may be interpreted as a contemporary rewriting of Goethe's *Faust* with Elena playing the part of Faust and Lila that of Mephistopheles. As Goethe did in resuscitating the Faust legend, Ferrante recasts the theme of the scholar's pact with the devil in an original new form.

Throughout the four novels of the series, various characters compare Lila to the devil, whether on account of her character or physiognomy. Lila often takes the role of devil's advocate with Elena, striking a sarcastic note with her more ingenuous friend that goads her to bolder feats of imagination. In one of the rare instances of their discussing religion, the adolescent Lila castigates Elena for devoting her intellectual energies to a labored high school essay on the nature of the Trinity rather than to humanity's very unacademic sufferings:

> You still waste time with those things, Lenù? We are flying over a ball of fire. The part that has cooled floats on the lava. On that part we construct the buildings, the bridges, and the streets, and every so often the lava comes out of Vesuvius or causes an earthquake that destroys everything. There are microbes everywhere that make us sick and die. There are wars. There is a poverty that makes us all cruel. Every second something might happen that will cause you such suffering that you'll never have enough tears. And what are you doing? A theology course in which you struggle to understand what the Holy Spirit is? Forget it, it was the Devil who invented the world, not the Father, the Son, and the Holy Spirit.
>
> (1:261)

This tirade illustrates Lila's prodigious intellectual agility, which manifests itself as a breathtaking capacity for making imaginative leaps from the microbial to the cosmic or, as Elena puts it in *Those Who Leave and Those Who Stay*, "to make connections between very different things" (2:359). At the same time, the speech drives home another crucial point. Insofar as she rebukes Elena for obliviousness to the world's brutality in this diatribe, Lila even when giving voice to her most diabolical opinions cannot be said to affirm a politics of cynicism, if by this word we have in mind something like Peter Sloterdijk's well-known definition of the modern-day cynic as an exemplar of "enlightened false consciousness," which is to say a perpetually self-preserving indifference.[41] To the contrary, Lila embodies an art of life predicated on the courage of truth-telling or *parrhesia*, a practice ironically cultivated by the ancient Greek philosophers known as the Cynics, as Foucault reminds us in his last seminar.[42] Lila's readiness to defy figures who are in positions to threaten her such as Bruno Soccavo or the Solaras thus harks back to the paradigm of Diogenes the Cynic who, when Alexander approached him to ask what wish he might grant the philosopher, famously told the conqueror to stand aside and stop blocking his light.

If Lila at times gives the impression of having a demonic spirit, in other words, she does so to the degree that she shows a fierce willingness to speak truth to power, a recalcitrance that Fredric Jameson, in a gripping essay on Goethe's *Faust,* associates with Mephistopheles's penchant for "the language of satire (distaste for late-feudal bureaucracies but also for petty and provincial Bürgertum, a taste for glamorous, sweeping nihilism and the proud youthful stance of refusal and denial)."[43] According to Jameson, the devil's satirical way of talking stands in contrast to the scholar's language of "passion," which expresses the bourgeois subject's need for fulfillment in terms of love and social status. Considered in such terms, Ferrante's portrayal of Elena and Lila's friendship as a sort of modern, gender-inverted reinterpretation of the dialectic between Faust and Mephistopheles does not look like a casual literary gesture. Ferrante's protagonists' dissimilar habits of speech and writing in this light reflect an exemplary difference of worldviews, a disparity of ethical and political attitudes that corresponds to their divergent positions in relation to history. Precisely as Mephistopheles in *Faust* appears to be a character whose aim is "always to complain" (*immer anzuklagen,* line 294) and whom, as we note earlier, the Lord designates as the play's "rogue" (*der Schalk,* 339), Lila, in the Neapolitan Quartet, reveals a "sharp tongue" in childhood (1:61) that in old age grows into instinctive "screeching, quarreling" (4:340). Her gift for invective at the same time goes hand in hand with an innate eloquence that strikes the adolescent Elena, who on her fifteenth birthday receives a letter from Lila, as a supernatural ability "to speak through writing" while maintaining "the vivid orderliness that I imagined would belong to conversation if one were so fortunate as to be born from the head of Zeus" (1:226–27). Elena herself instead suffers throughout life from a suspicion of her own writing's inadequacy, which culminates in crushing embarrassment when her daughter Elsa reads aloud from her books during a family reunion on Christmas Day of 2002 and exposes their author's "flaws, excesses, tones that were too exclamatory, the aged ideologies that . . . [had looked like] indisputable truths" (4:458). This scene marks a turning point for Elena, after which she increasingly becomes convinced that Lila will produce a book that represents "proof of my failure . . . [showing] how I should have written but had been unable to" (4:459).

Ultimately, we may conclude that Lila's rhetorical similarity to Mephistopheles stems from her resolute hostility to the conditions of subalternity. In her resistance to the status quo, she personifies a dissenting freedom of mind that recalls the devil's own celebrated credo: "I am the spirit who always says no! / And justly so, for all things that exist / Deserve to meet their end" ("ich bin der Geist der stets verneint! / Und das mit Recht; denn alles, was entsteht, / Ist wert, daß es zugrunde geht," 1338–40). Although rarely sharing his destructive inclination, Lila, like Mephistopheles, has a genius for rebellion and nonconformity that threatens to lead Elena, like Faust, to question the foundational premises of her own knowledge.[44] It thus is fitting that *My Brilliant Friend* begins with a citation from the prologue to *Faust* suggesting that the devil's mission is to spur human beings to action through contradiction and critique, hence to fulfill an important pedagogical duty with respect to humanity. Lila herself exemplifies this type of necessary evil insofar as she represents for Elena a tormenting yet productive teacher of hard truths, enabling the quartet to be read as an epic Bildungsroman. On this score, we ought to recall that Mephistopheles describes himself in *Faust 1* as "a part of the power / That always wishes evil and always creates good" ("ein Teil von jener Kraft, / Die stets das Böse will, und stets das Gute schafft," 1336–37). This motto also may be said to sum up Lila's predicament insofar as her fiendish temper inspires fear and anger even though she repeatedly acts in ways that benefit others in the neighborhood.

When they befriend each other as little girls, Elena and Lila reach an understanding that Lila explicitly declares in adulthood: "We made a pact when we were children: I'm the wicked one" (3:144). The bargain seems to be that Lila accepts punishment as the "bad girl" so that Elena can be the "good girl" who gains an education and becomes a celebrated author. That Lila refers to the premise of their relationship as a "pact," as if it were a deal with the devil, is more than a little revealing. On the night before her wedding, she reminds Elena of their arrangement when the other admits doubt about remaining in school: "You're my brilliant friend, you have to be the best of all, boys and girls" (1:312). It is not hard to understand why Elena feels that the writing of her first novel is indebted to Lila's schoolgirl composition, "The Blue Fairy." However, the Neapolitan Quartet cannot be said to run the same risk in relation to *Faust*. Ferrante does not ventriloquize Goethe through acts of stylistic pastiche, whether involuntary or deliberate. She instead directly confronts the literary and cultural legacy represented by Goethe's lyric drama with the purpose of transforming the gender roles that her German precursor affirms. If *Faust* hinges on its hero's idealized desire for Gretchen (2429–40), which the play fulfills in its last lines by celebrating her redemptive mystique as "The Eternal Feminine" (*Das Ewig-Weibliche*, 12110), we may surmise why Ferrante finds Goethe's tragedy to be a clarifying, antithetical point of departure for the saga of Lila and Elena's struggles to lead meaningful lives in the misogynist culture of Southern Italy.

What Ferrante finds in the German literary tradition to inspire the uncompromising voices of feminist and social critique that she raises in the Neapolitan Quartet grows clearer if we consider one more potential link between Ferrante and Anita Raja. If German culture's emphasis on critique supplies Ferrante with a means of exposing the hollow promises of the capitalist and patriarchal order prevailing in Italy, Raja's translations of Christa Wolf specifically show her an end. In my preceding comments, I have suggested that Ferrante's citation of Goethe in the epigraph of *My Brilliant Friend* acts as a kind of signature on the work in which we may detect Raja's handwriting, so to speak. Yet one of Raja's own published essays about Christa Wolf seems to underscore her identity in decisive fashion. To her own prefatory essay for *Che cosa resta* (1991), the Italian edition of Wolf's controversial novel *What Remains* (*Was Bleibt*), which recounts the story of a woman living under the torment of surveillance by the Stasi, Raja gives a title that is telling in its resonance with the Neapolitan Quartet: "City Without Hope" ("La città senza speranza"). The title of Raja's essay is crucial because it so closely foreshadows the idea and even the wording of the theme of "the city without love" that Lila and Elena excitedly develop as schoolgirls in *My Brilliant Friend*. The translator's admiration of Wolf's achievement in depicting the sufferings of a woman who grows utterly estranged from her society thus bears fruit in the novelist's account of the two friends' galvanization on discerning in Dido a tragic example of women's emblematic importance to her city, her people, and her world. Although

Ferrante's reworking of the basic proposition of Raja's essay on Wolf in Elena and Lila's reading of Dido's heroic fate does not quite amount to irrefutable confirmation of the novelist's identity, her fictive reformulation of such a singular critical conceit nevertheless is highly revealing. Of course, it may never be possible to declare with complete certainty who an author is, especially in the sense of understanding the relationship between her life and work, solely on the basis of her imaginative practices. Yet the story of this particular writer's occupation of a specific vantage point between the Italian and German cultural traditions ought to give readers hope of reading her brilliant fictions with keener critical discernment. To the admittedly limited degree that any reading can do, this account should suggest how we might approach the elusive and in the end perhaps impossible task of finding Ferrante.

Chapter One

CRUEL SEXUALITY

SEXUALITY AND INTENSITY

Ferrante's readers are often surprised at her merciless demystification of the experiences of motherhood, especially when it comes to relations between mothers and daughters. For example, James Wood has noted "the savagery with which Ferrante attacks the themes of motherhood and womanhood."[1] Rachel Cusk has nominated "motherhood as it is lived by . . . woman in all her striving" as possibly the most striking of Ferrante's concerns.[2] And in a recent treatise on the subject of maternity Jacqueline Rose remarks that the novelist's treatment of the topic "is like nothing else I have read."[3] That commentators have become so preoccupied with this issue suggests an article of faith well on its way to becoming an interpretative cliché. More important, fascination with the novelist's harsh view of maternity threatens to displace the much bigger picture of her ideas regarding sexuality in general, reducing the complexity of her fictional and critical writings to a slender half-truth. Although motherhood certainly holds an important place in Ferrante's writing, to regard it as her main subject matter is an oversimplification, especially in the Neapolitan Quartet.

To do justice to the originality of Ferrante's writing, in fact, we should start by observing her bluntness regarding women's disenchantment with the realities of sexual experience. Her stories are rooted in the terrain of bad sex, which she begins mapping in her earlier novels, before the epic undertaking of the tetralogy. All of her characters freely speak of the banality, disappointment, pain, and even repugnance of their sexual acts or fantasies, sometimes in excruciating detail.[4] As a result, there is little room in her imaginative universe for sentimental or idealized views of sexuality. In recent Italian literature, no other female author depicts the sexual life of her protagonists in such frank and explicit terms. (Some Italian male novelists may write about sex with equally graphic candor but to much different ends.) In world literature, the figure to whom Ferrante on this score bears the strongest resemblance is Elfriede Jelinek, the Nobel Prize–winning Austrian writer who witheringly diagnoses the violence that men inflict on women under the patriarchal conventions of contemporary Western societies, where the popular mania for sports may encode a gendered threat. Certainly, Jelinek's novels, such as *Women as Lovers* (1975), *Wonderful, Wonderful Times* (1980), *The Piano Teacher* (1983), *Lust* (1989), and *Greed* (2000), often make fearless use of vulgar or obscene language to repudiate the clichés with which the normative misogyny of European culture stifles women's voices. When we consider how Jelinek's example may have come to influence Ferrante and her thinking about sex, the possibility of Anita Raja's authorship of Ferrante's writing grows all the more difficult to avoid, given her wide-ranging expertise as a Germanist.

Ferrante comes closest to embracing Jelinek's unflinching pessimism with respect to women's opportunities for sexual fulfillment in her second novel, *The Days of Abandonment* (2002). The narrative chronicles the heroine Olga's descent into pornographic fantasies and increasingly angry and compulsive acts after her husband leaves her for a younger woman. Yet the story ends with Olga's avowal of having found love with her neighbor Carrano. With this change of heart, she avoids the fates of the forsaken women whom she either implicitly evokes through her actions, such as the protagonists of Jelinek's fictions, or explicitly cites in the course of her account, such as the "poor thing" or *poverella* of her Neapolitan childhood, the titular figure of Simone de Beauvoir's collection of stories, *The Woman Destroyed*, and Tolstoy's Anna Karenina.[5] As we will see in what follows, however, Olga's conversion from rage to hope strikes an unconvincingly saccharine note, casting doubt on the honesty of her claim.

Ferrante takes a notably different approach to the representation of sexuality in the Neapolitan novels. Although Elena and Lila speak of sex with crude honesty when it suits them, neither one obsesses about the topic as Olga does. Moreover, although both Lila and Elena suffer more violent abuses by men than anything that Olga undergoes, neither adopts a received psychological vocabulary to mediate these events or to appeal to our sympathies. Whereas Olga describes herself at various points as "depressed" by Mario's betrayal and her resulting isolation (TDA 38, 132, 155, 166), Elena and Lila never define their responses to the harassments or even sexual assaults they endure in this manner. Perhaps most tellingly, neither resorts to the rhetoric of trauma when recounting their adversities, despite the fact that Elena narrates the saga of their friendship from the vantage of the first decade of the twenty-first century, at a moment when the concepts of trauma, stress, and the uncanny have wide currency. The two friends instead talk about their anxieties either by invoking the everyday lexicon of unhappiness or, on some occasions, by reappropriating the rare and untranslatable word *smarginatura* (or "dissolving margins" as the English translation imprecisely renders it) to name the fears that threaten to shatter their self-control. Lila and Elena's alertness to the ways in which, like forms of pain, words may resist our efforts to absorb and rationalize them reflects Ferrante's own exquisite care with language, which in turn raises once again the specter of Raja's guiding genius as a translator behind the text.

What the story of the two friends ultimately suggests is that the only productive, if not necessarily lasting, response to the limiting ideas of gender that Western culture imposes on our sexuality is to be found in the passionate friendship between women. On this score, the question of the literary and intellectual genealogy of the Neapolitan Quartet and the ensuing issue of Raja's relationship to this legacy acquire crucial significance. Prior to Ferrante's tetralogy, the body of modern fiction devoted to the subject of women's friendships may have looked slight and for the most part unexciting. The exception that stands out in the European tradition is Christa Wolf's *The Quest for Christa T.* (1968), which, we should note, Anita Raja has translated into Italian. As I argue later in this chapter, the characters and narrative structure of Wolf's novel in some respects appear to provide Ferrante with an organizing model for Elena and Lila's epic tale.

In a real sense, the publication of the Neapolitan novels now looks like the supernova that has made more visible the constellation of an entire genre of fiction, which can be seen to include Sheila Heti's *How Should a Person Be* (2010), Zadie Smith's *Swing Time* (2016), and Sally Rooney's *Conversations with Friends* (2017) among many others. Yet, in all these examples, what is missing is the passionate nature of the friendship between the women characters, which represents the hallmark of Wolf and Ferrante's stories. Ferrante's writing in particular repeatedly portrays female protagonists who develop strong emotional attachments to other women, yet whose personal dilemmas are not so much resolved as intensified by their bond. We might say that Ferrante's greatest achievement as a novelist is to make legible the complex ethical intensity of her characters' lives, a vitality that sex may help to affirm but cannot displace as an end in itself.[6]

BAD SEX

In Ferrante's first novel, *Troubling Love* (1992), Delia has sex with Antonio, who displays "an elementary model of virility" (TL 88). Once alone with Delia in a hotel room, he kisses her in a manner devoid of conviction and without embracing her (TL 89). For her part, Delia lies inert on the bed with an air of stoic resignation: "I knew that nothing new would happen" (TL 90). She feels nothing but a diffuse, "not urgent" pleasure, which leaves her body refusing to respond and compliant without interest: "I also noticed that his erection was beginning to recede, like a defective neon light" (TL 92). The mechanical perfunctoriness of their intercourse precludes any genuine attachment from forming between Delia and Antonio. A defective neon light supplies an apt symbol for the characters' inability to seize any possibility of real change, to achieve a moment of intensified feeling.

In *The Days of Abandonment* (2002), Olga makes use of shockingly crude language as if discovering a proto-feminist instrument of rebellion. For Olga, whose husband Mario abandons her for a younger woman, sex represents an arena of control, failure, and revenge. In the pivotal episode of the novel, Olga fantasizes about her husband having sex with his young lover, while she herself coldly seduces her neighbor, Carrano, in an act of imaginary retaliation: "But maybe he (Mario), too, now, in the long night, somewhere else, was spreading Carla's thin legs, letting his gaze rest on her cunt half covered by the underpants, lingering, his heart pounding, on the obscenity of that position, making it more obscene with his fingers. Or, who knows, maybe it was I alone who was obscene now, abandoned to that man who was touching me in secret places, who, in no hurry, was bathing his fingers inside me, with the casual curiosity of one who is not in love" (TDA 84). The narrator underscores the vulgarity of her own words here through triple repetition of the key term *obscenity* and its variants. Olga's compelling ferocity as a storyteller thus results in part from her embrace of a pseudo-pornographic linguistic register.

At first, the obscene appears to promise Olga a means of restitution for her betrayal by Mario, but in fact only when she overcomes the compulsion to think and speak in sexualized terms can she find contentment. Although her change of heart suggests a recovery of emotional equilibrium, the narrator's shift to a mollifying rhetoric strikes a forced note that undermines this possibility. Whereas earlier in the story she gives the impression of being a fearless iconoclast on account of her unsparingly profane imagination, at the end she contrives a happy ending that she herself acknowledges to be an unconvincing falsehood: "I pretended to believe him (Carrano) and so we loved each other for a long time, in the days and months to come, quietly" (TDA 188). If here in the final sentence Olga emphasizes the quiescence of her relationship with the "depressed musician" who lives downstairs (TDA 77), she insists on its monstrous carnality when describing her seduction of Carrano. In her account of their coupling, his tongue "felt animal, an enormous tongue such as I had seen, disgusted, at the butcher ..." (TDA 80–81). When Carrano enters her, she confesses that "I was suddenly afraid, I held my breath. A bestial position, animal liquids and a perfidy utterly human" (TDA 86). Olga's jolting account of their ordeal thwarts any possibility of sentimental reveries and, with its concrete metaphors, vividly evokes the narrator's alienation from her sexual partner.[7]

As readers, we cannot avoid a certain skepticism about Olga's future with Carrano by the time we reach the end of their story. Just as she "pretended to believe" his wordless reassurance, we too can only feign a hopeful stance. In her other novels, Ferrante studiously avoids such impossibly tidy resolutions, aiming instead at a mode of realism that is more provocative than anodyne. Sex plays an important role in the economy of this realist project, where it no longer coincides with the category of the obscene—as it instead does in the first section of *The Days of Abandonment*—but rather represents the object of frequently painful self-analysis. In a sense, Ferrante approaches the riddle of women's subjectivity from the premise that the experience of shame is formative to their psychology. Following her failed encounter with Carrano, Olga enters a phase in which the degradation of this incident promises to lead her to a new perspective, a new sense of herself.

In *The Lost Daughter* (2006), Leda learns to appreciate sex as an "extreme product of the imagination" when she has an extramarital affair with Hardy, the British professor of English literature whom she meets at an academic conference: "The greater the pleasure, the more the other is only a dream, a nocturnal reaction of belly, breasts, mouth, anus—of every isolated inch of skin—to the caresses and thrusts of a vague entity definable according to the necessities of the moment" (TLD 98). She never tells us what Hardy's first name is, an omission that seems fitting for a character whose main role is to provide a blank screen onto which the narrator may project her desires. For Leda, good sex depends on the freedom to invest partial objects—belly, breast, mouth, anus—with her phantasmatic impulses. The "necessities" of pleasure dissuade her from worrying about the tension between desire's metonymic fixation on body parts and the metaphorical "vague entity" to whom the body belongs.

Leda's hedonist bliss, however, gives way to pessimism regarding the possibility of sexual fulfillment as she watches Nina's little girl, Elena, with her doll: "It occurred to me that there was more erotic power in her relationship with the doll, there beside Nina, than in all the eros that she would feel [tutto l'eros che avrebbe sperimentato] as she grew up and grew older" (TLD 93; LFO 98). The force of Leda's prophecy in Italian hinges on the idea that, as she advances into womanhood, the girl self-consciously will experiment—*avrebbe sperimentato*—with sex. Rendering the original assertion with the passive-sounding "would feel," the English translation blunts Ferrante's emphasis on Elena's active thinking as a subject who relentlessly, if vainly, strives to recover the infantile libidinal spontaneity of play. Eros offers us the greatest happiness in childhood, the novelist ironically implies, when our polymorphous desires still may be satisfied by purely symbolic expression. The doll thus represents an ideal point of convergence for the metonymic and metaphoric dimensions of desire, an embodiment that exacts no cost on the imagination.

HARASSMENT

In Italian, Ferrante's debut novel bears the title *L'amore molesto*, which the English-language edition renders as *Troubling Love*. The translation does not quite do justice to the original's range of nuances. Etymologically, the adjective *molesto* is related to the verb *molestare* and encompasses meanings that stretch from "troubling" or "worrisome" to "harassed" and "molested." Although ostensibly the story revolves around the tormented relationship between a mother and daughter, Amalia and Delia, Naples takes on the importance of a third character in their narrative. The city comes to represent a monumental embodiment of the patriarchal history looming over the characters' past and present. For women who live in its environs, getting on a bus or the *funicolare* means braving real, specific risks. To be ogled and groped by men are ordinary occurrences, as are slappings, beatings, and other forms of so-called domestic violence.

Of course, Naples is by no means the only city in which Italy's belligerent sexism has flourished in the open. For example, we may recall photographer Ruth Orkin's iconic snapshot, *American Girl in Italy* (1951), which captures the leering of an all-male crowd of loiterers at a young woman tourist who walks past them on a street corner in Florence. A decade later, the cinematic auteur Michelangelo Antonioni dramatizes a similar phenomenon in his watershed film *L'avventura* (1960), where in one scene he depicts the protagonist Claudia (Monica Vitti) surrounded by a growing number of men who follow her with insistent and threatening curiosity as she strolls through the Sicilian city of Noto.

Ferrante dedicates considerable attention in the Neapolitan Quartet to men's cruelty toward women. It is commonplace for husbands to beat their wives, as Stefano Carracci does with Lila and Michele Solara does with Gigliola. As young men, the Solara brothers lure young girls like Ada into their Fiat 1100 in order to bully them into sexual acts, unsuccessfully trying to force themselves in this manner on Elena and Lila (1:113, 134–36). Lila is hurled through a window by her father, raped by her husband Stefano, and groped by male coworkers at the Soccavo salami factory. Already beautiful by her early teens, she captivates grown men whenever she goes out to explore the city, from a pizza maker on the Rettifilo to a middle-aged father with his wife and three boys who floridly compares her to "a Boticelli Venus" (1:144, 146). Harassment is an everyday fact of life; as

Elena puts it, "on the street the men looked at all of us . . . [we] had learned instinctively to lower our eyes, pretend not to hear the obscenities they directed at us, and keep going" (1:145). Indeed, Elena herself routinely endures mistreatment from men not only among her proletarian neighbors in Naples but also among the well-bred bourgeoisie of Milan. Her mother-in-law's friend, Professor Tarratano, who disingenuously advises her not to be defensive about the "obscenity" of her first novel, does not refrain from making "unseemly" sexual advances on Elena in an elevator after one of her readings (3:65–66).

All these events in the Neapolitan Quartet are narrated in a dispassionate, matter-of-fact tone. Ferrante carefully avoids using the terms in which we typically couch discussions of harassment. Her women characters, for example, never speak of "trauma," "assault," "rape," their human or civil "rights," or even "harassment" itself to describe their experiences of abuse and violence. In this sense, she confronts us with a narrative that deliberately resists prevailing wisdom regarding such outrages. Ferrante systematically eschews psychoanalytic explanations of women's distress as well as legal notions of justice for survivors of sexual aggression, both of which would have been unthinkable in Elena and Lila's neighborhood. At the same time, she exposes the lasting consequences of abuse in the ordinary language not only of women's habitual stoicism but also their denials, self-doubts, flashes of anger, and occasional acts of compliance.

At the start of *My Brilliant Friend*, Elena looks back on the events of her life from the perspective of a sixty-six-year-old writer who lives in Turin in the year 2010. Consequently, she must be well aware of the pervasiveness of the psychological and legalistic terms in which stories of misogyny tend to be framed in contemporary culture. However, she avoids any hint of retrospective knowingness as she narrates episodes of violence against women that occurred in earlier decades. Contemporary readers, especially those in the U.S., may find it unsettling to encounter the seemingly blasé indifference with which Ferrante's characters accept these acts as quotidian realities of life in Italy. As a young girl, Elena's truancy from school to visit the sea with Lila earns her a beating from her father that leaves her covered in bruises, prompting Lila to exclaim in incredulity, "All they did was beat you" (1:79)? At the same age, Lila winds up with a broken arm from being thrown by her father through a window, which Elena remarks with nonchalance: "Fathers could do that and other things to impudent girls" (1:82). And when the sixteen-year-old Lila returns from her horrific honeymoon in Amalfi after having been beaten and raped by Stefano, "no one, not even her mother, who was silent during the entire visit, seemed to notice her swollen, black right eye, the cut on her lower lip, the bruises on her arms" (2:44).

One story, however, stands out among all the others, namely Donato Sarratore's molestation of Elena on the night of her fifteenth birthday. Donato is one of the most reviled characters of the neighborhood, whom even his son Nino seems to hold in righteous contempt until the son ultimately turns out to be as compulsive a womanizer as the father. The fact that Donato is a train conductor who has published a book of poems loftily titled *Attempts at Serenity*, copies of which he likes to present as gifts to women who have caught his eye, does little to recommend him as a model of seriousness when it comes to either literature or sex (1:129, 212). Bearing some resemblance to the character of Federico in Domenico Starnone's *Via Gemito*, who is another immoderate man that works on the railroad while aspiring to an artistic vocation (in Federico's case that of painter), Donato is introduced to us in *My Brilliant Friend* as the craven seducer of Melina Cappuccio, the emotionally unstable mother of Antonio and Ada who is related to Lila through her mother's side of the family. He begins to interest Elena when as a middle-school student she learns that, following the Sarratores' move out of the neighborhood, Donato sent his book to Melina, leading Elena to confess that "what continued to excite me more than anything else was the fact that Donato Sarratore had published a book" (1:127). When Elena encounters Donato in person some two years later, she is on summer vacation in Ischia after her first year in high school, living away from her family for the first time in the care of Maestra Oliviero's cousin Nella, and learning to appreciate "the joy of the new" (1:211). She also has fallen in love with the tall, moody, and precocious Nino, whose charming volubility she finds can give way to sudden outbursts of hatred for his father.

During the dog days of summer, Elena spends time in conversations with Nino but also repeatedly winds up in the company of Donato, who gets into the habit of reading aloud to her the opinion pages of the right-wing newspaper *Roma*, including his own article "written in high-flown sentences" on the ludicrous topic of how much faster it is to travel by train than by horse or foot (1:225). With a naivety that is both touching and dismaying, Elena at one point tells Nino that Donato and Melina's affair is inspired by an emotion as overwhelming as Aeneas and Dido's passion, concluding improbably that Donato is "the father that every girl, every boy should want" (1:221). The primal scene of sexual assault takes place in Nella's kitchen, where Elena's bed is situated. Because she does not have her own bedroom and has to sleep in a communal space of the house, Donato can enter in the middle of the night on the pretext of needing a drink of water before approaching her. What follows is Elena's disturbingly specific account of being forced to endure Donato's predatory ministrations:

> I was immobilized. He pushed the sheet aside, continuing to kiss me with care, with passion, and he sought my breast with his hands, he caressed me under the nightgown. Then he let go, descended between my legs, pressed two fingers hard over my underpants. I said nothing, did nothing, I was terrified by that behavior, by the horror it created, by the pleasure I nevertheless felt.
>
> (1:232)

That Elena feels a contradictory mix of pleasure and horror starkly underscores the violence of an ordeal so disorienting as to rob her of movement and speech. From her narration, we eventually learn that she and Lila grew up "in small houses, without our own rooms, without a place to study" and consequently both girls lacked the privacy in which they may have learned to gratify themselves (1:289). It becomes clear in fact that, when Donato attacks her, she finds the very sensation of sexual pleasure so shocking in its unfamiliarity that she has no idea how to respond: ". . . As long as I could remember until that night I had never given myself pleasure, I didn't know about it, to feel it surprised me" (1:232). In this sense, the violation that Elena suffers at Donato's hands is made worse by a degree of sexual inexperience that directly results from her belonging to a disadvantaged class.

While Donato, in Elena's words, "squatted beside me" (*mi si accucciò* or literally "crouched like a dog"), he grotesquely declaims to her, "I love you," using a formulation in Italian—*ti voglio molto bene*—that ambiguously could connote either intimate desire or familial attachment and thus suggests his own perverse ambivalence between the impulses of lover and father (1:232 EN; 1:227–28 IT). By her own account filled with "an uncontrollable hatred for Donato Sarratore and disgust for myself" (1:232), Elena encounters for the first time the possibility of an incommensurable split between desire and pleasure, harboring desire for the delicate son while exploring pleasure with the repulsive father. She moreover realizes that, although her violation by Donato has given her "a story that Lila could not match," she cannot share this episode with her friend because of her anger and sense of shame about it: "I knew immediately that the disgust I felt for Sarratore and the revulsion that I had toward myself would keep me from saying anything" (1:233). She then adds, "In fact this is the first time I've sought words for that unexpected end to my vacation" (1:233), revealingly switching to the present tense of a sixty-six-year-old in the twenty-first century. It is worth noting on this score that Elena's account of the incident is not what we might expect from a well-educated, successful author in later life who has achieved significant mastery over her narrative or even autonomy in relation to it. She avoids any self-conscious representation of what happened as a trauma, describing the occurrence phenomenologically in terms of her feelings of "horror," "pleasure," "hatred," "disgust," and "revulsion." By refusing to apply to her adolescent experience the rhetoric that we have grown accustomed to use in reporting acts of sexual violence, Elena subtly obliges us to relive her own defenselessness in the face of her assault. That is to say, she withholds the apparatus needed to put her anguish in critical perspective. Referring to her coercion as a trauma would be an intellectual luxury, a possibility for girls from more privileged classes but not for a poor girl such as Elena. It ultimately becomes apparent that her first encounter with Donato, which forces pleasure on her and silences her afterward, is more troubling for Elena than her astonishing second liaison with him, which actually represents her real loss of virginity and provides the subject of her debut novel.

Elena's second assignation with Donato takes place on a return visit to Ischia three years later. She has persuaded Lila to accompany her to the island for the summer in the hope of coming across Nino, only to face the prospect, when they do meet, of Nino and Lila falling madly in love with each other. On the evening that Lila and Nino arrange with Elena's help for an overnight rendezvous, Elena chances upon Donato on the beach and, instead of refusing his entreaties, welcomes his overtures as a way of distracting herself from "the frenzied thoughts of girlish disappointment" that have preoccupied her (2:290). Now eighteen, Elena is in a steady relationship with Antonio but still a virgin. Donato announces his presence by calling her "Lena" (2:290), a name that he is the only one to utter in the entire saga, as if laying claim to her attention by means of a private language. On this score, it is noteworthy that he avoids her childhood nickname of "Lenù," which features the comfortingly vernacular *accento grave* on the final syllable and tends to be used by her immediate family members and intimate friends such as Lila.[8] Sitting down next to her, Donato begins to praise the natural beauty of their surroundings with such bombastic gusto that Elena cannot help noticing "the ridiculousness of his trained voice . . . the sleazy lyricizing behind which he concealed his eagerness to put his hands on me" (2:290). Yet instead of recoiling from his bungling attempts at seduction, she comes to the glum conclusion that "maybe we really are condemned, blameless, to the same, identical mediocrity" (2:290). When she finally does acquiesce to his desires, she finds Donato to be an unexpectedly adept lover who helps her to acknowledge an aspect of herself that previously has been obscure even to her:

> He therefore knew much more about me than Antonio had ever learned . . . in fact he knew what I myself didn't know. I had a hidden me—I realized— that fingers, mouth, teeth, tongue were able to discover. The entire time I did not once regret having accepted what was happening. I had no second thoughts and was proud of myself, I wanted it to be like that, I imposed it on myself.
> (2:291)

In spite of the unsettling circumstances, Elena's initiation into sexual adulthood gives her pleasure and, more important, an opportunity to reframe her earlier, passive experience of abuse into an active choice. Elena shows every sign of being swept up by manic feelings of triumph, reveling in her abject submission to Donato's lust as a means of denying her sense of loss regarding Nino's love.

The morning after, when she goes to pick up Lila from her friend's night of passion with Nino, Elena is unable to resist comparing her own "sensation of alienness" from Donato to Lila's engrossment in thoughts of Nino, admitting morosely that "this difference between us made me sad" (2:296). Yet some five years later, while preparing to complete her degree at the Scuola Normale Superiore in Pisa, she reasserts her will over her loss of sexual innocence by transforming the event into the fictionalized basis of her first book, which, as she notes, she is careful to write "in the third person" (2:433). Elena perhaps comes closest to recognizing how uncannily productive her rivalry with Lila has been when she accidentally finds her friend's grade school composition, "The Blue Fairy," among some mementos left to her by Maestra Oliviero after the teacher's death and realizes with a stomach-churning shock that "Lila's childish pages were the heart of my book" (2:455). In an ironic twist, she learns over time that none of her readers feels the same enthusiasm for her work that she felt as a child for "The Blue Fairy," instead responding either in scandalized or approving tones only to the "titillating pages" of her history with her older seducer, the "episode of sex on the beach," or the "dirty stuff," as Lila bluntly sums it up, "that men don't want to hear and women know but are afraid to say" (3:55, 65, 175). Adding insult to injury, Donato himself pans Elena's book in the pages of *Roma*, where he accuses her of writing an "indecent novel" (3:56).

Of her two encounters with Donato in Ischia, the first episode indisputably has a traumatic effect on Elena. The conditions of her assault by Donato in Nella's kitchen—her muteness and paralysis, her lack of linguistic or imaginative resources adequate to her heightened state of arousal, her very fear of sex itself or *Sexualschreck*, to use the Freudian term— correspond to the classic definition of trauma provided by Freud in *Studies on Hysteria* (*Studien über Hysterie*), which he published in 1895 at the beginning of his career. Returning to the topic around 1920, Freud modified his earlier economic interpretation of trauma by focusing on the importance of the repetition compulsion and the death drive, which he viewed as specific threats to the integrity of the subject. In the third chapter of *Beyond the Pleasure Principle*, Freud crucially analyzes the repetitive logic or pattern of suffering manifested by subjects who have been exposed to trauma, which gives them the appearance of being possessed by a catastrophic fate.[9] In Freud's account, the repetition of trauma can seem accidental or coincidental to the traumatized subject, as in Tancredi's unintentional double-killing of Clorinda in *Gerusalemme Liberata*. Although Elena never uses the word *trauma* in the Neapolitan Quartet, her narration vividly enacts the structure and rhythm of an accidental yet traumatic repetition. Not coincidentally, commentators on Ferrante's writings, as exemplified both by her earlier novels and the books of the

Neapolitan Quartet, often invoke the notion of "the uncanny," which is based on the return of the repressed.

Elena's complex tangle of feelings for Donato, which encompasses not only disgust and contempt but also the pliancy of the seduced, resurfaces again in a sort of coda to their story that takes place twenty years later. Now a celebrated author who is pregnant with a daughter by Nino, Elena agrees to accompany her partner on a visit to his parents' home for Sunday lunch. Her first sight of the aging Donato, as she suggests with droll under- statement, makes "an impression on me" (4:145). A bloated parody of "a man of the world," Donato sports a receding hairline that he dyes "a vaguely reddish color," brandishes stubby hands disfigured by liver spots and dirty fingernails, and flashes missing teeth whenever he smiles (4:146). Elena thinks to herself that what happened at the Maronti between her as a girl and the "foul man" before her is not possible, insisting that she is "so very different from the me of Ischia" and drawing a hard line between the "now" of the present and the "then" of the past (4:146). Yet we may well have reason to doubt her claims of adult self-control. During her Sunday reunion with the Sarratore family, Elena slips with unnerving ease back into an attitude of complicity with Donato's manipulative ploys.

He calls her over to him and begins boasting to everyone that she, "a writer who has no equal anywhere in the world," owes her discovery of literature to the inspiration of his poetry (4:146). More disturbingly, he stresses that he has known Elena since she was "a girl" (*una bambina*) and claims to have observed that when she visited Ischia as "a child [*una raga- zzina*] . . . she read my book before going to sleep" (4:146 EN; 4:134 IT). At this point, he looks at her hesitantly "like a supplicant," and Elena discon- certingly chooses to play along with his ruse, affirming his mythical, Pygmalion-like power over her: "And I said yes, it's true, as a girl I couldn't believe that I knew personally someone who had written a book of poetry and whose thoughts were printed in the newspaper. I thanked him for the review that a dozen years earlier he had given my first book, I said it had been very useful. And Donato turned red with joy, he took off, he began to celebrate himself" (4:146–47). Elena's "yes" strikes a jarring note, bizarrely suggesting a conspiratorial rapport with her former assailant and demon- strating that she is not as different from her pubescent self of Ischia as she pretends to be. In the epithet "red with joy, he took off" (*rosso di gioia, prese quota;* 4:134 IT) that Elena applies to Donato, she inscribes the traces of his latest violation and enjoyment of her. Notwithstanding Elena's claims, the story of Donato and Elena is in fact a chronicle of repetition, of successive acts of compliance with her aggressor's desires.

Perhaps the most alarming example of her compulsiveness along these lines, however, is, in the end, her blindness toward Nino. Elena plunges into her love affair with him despite knowing how cravenly as a young man he leaves Lila in the lurch. Reappearing in Elena's life first in Milan and then in Florence, Nino comes over many years to look like the return of what has been repressed in Donato. Stubbornly, Elena remains blind to his frequent betrayals in spite of Lila's warnings and her own intuition that he devotes time to women only to indulge what Elena herself acknowledges is "his penchant for seductive behavior" (4:230). In fact, she cannot overcome her own denial of reality until she arrives home unexpectedly one day and witnesses Nino copulating with her housekeeper Silvana in the bathroom. At that moment, Elena has a flash of insight in which she recognizes in Nino's expression an upsetting link between her past and present: "It was the expression of his father, Donato, not when he deflowered me on the Maronti but when he touched me between the legs, under the sheet, in Nella's kitchen" (4:239). Although the son's education and worldliness once seemed to distinguish him from the father, Nino turns out to be "nothing alien, then, but much that was ugly," as Elena aptly puts it, adding sadly that in the end he "was what he wouldn't have wanted to be and yet always had been" (4:239).

Over the course of the entire narrative, Nino indeed reveals himself to be even more self-serving, cowardly, and destructive than his father. As a deputy of the Italian Socialist Party (Partito Socialista Italiano or PSI), he not only supports the policies of "gangs of looters who make laws against the looting of others," to quote Elena's exclamation of dismay, but also actively exchanges political favors for bribes and kickbacks until, as a result of the *Mani Pulite* investigations of the 1990s, he winds up on the judiciary's "increasingly crowded list of corrupters and corrupt" and is jailed (4:432, 435). At the end of the Neapolitan Quartet, something strange takes place. Elena returns to Naples as a sixty-six-year-old woman for the funerals of her father and Nino's mother Lidia. Donato already has died, she tells us, but she was not present at his memorial service. She asserts that she had to miss his funeral "not out of bitterness, only because I was abroad" (4:469–70). Why does Elena explicitly tell us that she harbors no bitterness toward her abuser? On this score, she clearly does not reflect the outlook that we have come to expect of women who endure sexual harassment, espousing the spirit rather than the letter of contemporary feminism. We may conclude that Elena's almost offhand remark indicates the extent of her indifference to Donato, his ultimate lack of significance in her imagination.

However, Elena's disavowal of anger toward her harasser perhaps encodes a deeper truth. When Elena briefly reunites with Nino at Lidia's funeral, he seems physically to have metamorphosed into his father, giving the appearance of being "large, bloated, a big ruddy man with thinning hair who was constantly celebrating himself" (4:470). As Ferrante's epic tetralogy nears its conclusion, Nino takes over the role originally played by Donato in Elena's imagination, enabling her gradually to transfer her bitterness and anger over her mistreatment as a girl from her older seducer to her younger partner. The son thus comes to represent the living sublimation of the father and leaves her at the end of the saga with nothing more than "an impression of wasted time" (4:470). As he is eclipsed by the more powerfully criminal figure of Nino, Donato's menace as a sexual predator apparently recedes into the background, paradoxically allowing him to recover a relative measure of innocence.

If the narrative of the Neapolitan novels draws some of its energies from Freud's ideas regarding traumatic repetition, we may find it useful to consider what, if anything, literature can do to help us deflect, contain, or resolve trauma. During an interview with Sandra Ozzola, Sandro Ferri, and Eva Ferri that first appeared in the *Paris Review* and is reprinted in *Frantumaglia,* Ferrante casually remarks that "it very often happens that women, in moments of crisis, try to calm ourselves by writing" (F 285). This attempt at self-mollification may be what Elena is after when she authors her first book. Narrated in the third person, this fictionalized retelling of her history with Donato seems to offer a potential means of redeeming the past from her anger and shame in the present. Yet the novel's reception never quite goes as planned, as we already know. Even switching to the first person, as Elena presumably does for her last book, *A Friendship,* cannot rescue the act of writing from its inherent hypocrisy. Elena regains success with the release of this title, which retells the story of her bond with Lila and Lila's grief at losing her daughter Tina, but in the process provokes Lila to cut off all contact with her (4:339). In the vertiginous circuit of trauma and writing, the letter of the written word always arrives too late, raising the risk of renewed shock and anguish. Replying in an interview to the Turkish journalist Yasemin Çongar's question, "what is the untamed truth of your writing?," the author elaborates a beautiful, telling metaphor that intimates both the radical potential and radical cost of writing for women: "I describe common experiences, common wounds, and my biggest worry—not the only one—is to find a tone in writing that can remove layer by layer the gauze that binds the wound and reach the true story of the wound. The more deeply hidden the wound seems—by stereotypes, by the fictions that the characters themselves have tacked on to protect themselves; in other words, the more resistant it seems to the story—the harder I insist" (F 308).

SMARGINATURA

At various moments in this book, I ask how the knowledge that Ferrante may be Anita Raja ought to influence the ways in which we read her writings. Given with what care Ferrante pays attention to women's experiences including especially the language in which they voice their thoughts and feelings, Raja's vocation as a translator offers a useful point of departure when it comes to understanding Ferrante's novels. For it is in relation to whether or not her ideas are translatable that readers may appreciate the full significance of Ferrante's most idiosyncratic and essential achievements as a creator of literature. Notwithstanding her exceptional international success, her writing poses a unique intellectual problem for global readers. In chapter 3, where I discuss the politics of the Neapolitan Quartet, the author's persistent recourse to the concept of the subaltern provides a crucial example of this problem. In this chapter, I wish to examine what is arguably the most elusive notion in the series, and certainly one of the most important for any consideration of how Ferrante represents feminine subjectivity, namely the overwhelming fear of the mutability of reality that Lila calls *smarginatura*. Why does Ferrante ascribe this odd, rare word in Italian to Lila's ruminations on her anxiety rather than any of the more common terms for trauma or panic? What implications does Lila's verbalizing of her distress have for the question of how Ferrante views the gendering of different subject positions in Italian culture?

In its first occurrence in the Neapolitan novels, at the start of the section of *My Brilliant Friend* entitled "Adolescence," the translator Ann Goldstein renders *smarginatura* with the two words that conclude the following sentence: "On December 31st of 1958 Lila had her first episode of dissolving margins" (1:89). Faced with the difficulty of finding an exact equivalent in English for an esoteric Italian concept, she solves the problem by combining a participial adjective with a plural noun, inserting a modifier where none exists in Italian in order to telegraph the gist of the idea to readers. Her perfectly good reason for this decision, one might suppose, is to reinforce the text's intelligibility. Certainly, Goldstein's fellow translators have taken a variety of approaches, each of which illustrates its own calculus of merits and drawbacks. Elsa Damien opts in French for *délimitation*, which like its cognate in English suggests at face value the opposite of *smarginatura* inasmuch as it primarily signifies a fixing or circumscribing of limits rather than their removal.[10] For the German edition, Karin Krieger chooses *Auflösung*, which encompasses among its several definitions the sense both of the dissolving of form and of the resolution of a puzzle, mathematical problem, or musical dissonance.[11] Celia Filipetto Isicato elects to go with the Spanish *desbordamiento*, whose primary meaning suggests the overflowing or bursting out of a liquid, which the original does not imply.[12] Goldstein's "dissolving margins" has the advantage of being plainspoken. Yet the formula also normalizes the strangeness with which *smarginatura* strikes a native speaker's ear, thus sacrificing the incantatory power that it acquires in Ferrante's writing.

What a closer look reveals in this case is that Ferrante rescues a term that otherwise appears only in specialized professional discussions from narrow areas of relevance and gives it new life. In the Treccani dictionary we find two restrictively technical senses. With respect to book production, the first designates the work of trimming excess margins from printed pages. With respect to botany, the second refers to a small notch at the tip of a leaf or some other part of the plant.[13] The first sense clearly stresses a certain force, perhaps even a sort of violence, involved in the process of publishing books, which is to say that it emphasizes the labor resulting from the commercialization and professionalization of writing.[14] Such a connotation has no small relevance for readers of the Neapolitan Quartet, given to what a high degree Elena and Lila both define satisfaction with their lives in terms of literary ability, what supreme importance each places on her fluency with the written word. It is a bleak irony that, when Elena publishes *A Friendship*, she provokes Lila to end their actual friendship by falling silent and vanishing from sight. What makes this turn of events even more painful is Elena's admission at the end of *The Story of the Lost Child* that her latest work of writing, which apparently constitutes the narrative of the Neapolitan Quartet itself, is an attempt to make amends to Lila by easing her greatest fear: "It's only and always the two of us who are involved: she who wants me to give what her nature and circumstances kept her from giving, I who can't give what she demands; she who gets angry at my inadequacy and out of spite wants to reduce me to nothing, as she has done with herself, I who have written for months and months and months to give her a form whose boundaries won't dissolve [una forma che non si smargini] and defeat her, and calm her, and so in turn calm myself" (4:466 EN; 4:444 IT). Smarginatura in this light seems to represent the very antithesis of a well-organized story, which is to say an unstable "form" whose outlines inevitably will dissolve or disintegrate, thus necessitating the asymmetrical, conflicted, yet ultimately structuring exchange of language between women.

By adopting this little-used Italian noun and redeploying it in such cunning and provocative ways, Ferrante deliberately introduces an untranslatable element into her language. On this score, the presence of Anita Raja as Ferrante's apparent alter ego looms as a pointed question. Why does the novelist inscribe in Lila's explanation of her innermost fear a term that stubbornly resists communication? If Ferrante views her own writing through a translator's eyes, is her refashioning of the word meant as a gesture of rebellion against the idea that language can be made transparent, a reminder that "what is unsayable is the task of literature" (F 325)? Does her insistence on the impossibility of naming her protagonists' motivations help to privilege the intimacy of their private language over its potential to be shared publicly and quickly acculturated, not only among readers of other countries but even, in a sense, among Italian readers as well? In spite of the global circulation of the Neapolitan novels, Ferrante's reappropriation of *smarginatura* has defied the efforts of Raja's professional peers to reproduce its effect in other languages. The author mobilizes the term not only in the two friends' saga but also in a number of her interviews, giving the conceit an unusual gravitational pull in her writing. Her association of *smarginatura* with the irrational and fragmentary places the word in close semantic proximity to *frantumaglia*, the coined name that Ferrante claims to have learned from her mother for the "disquiet not otherwise definable" arising from "a miscellaneous crowd of things in her head, debris in a muddy water of the brain" (F 99). Whereas the latter idea appears to focus on the results of this mood seen from a third-person perspective, however, the former seems to center on the process of dissolution experienced from a first-person point of view. At any rate, the fabricated, made-up quality of both words implies an extraordinary richness of personal significance, as if each becomes a kind of talisman for the women who assimilate it into their speech.

Lila's first, full-blown episode of dissolving margins occurs, as we know, on New Year's Eve of 1958 while watching the fireworks over Naples at a party with Elena. She breaks out in a sweat and feels that everybody around her is screaming too loudly and moving too fast: "This sensation was accompanied by nausea, and she had the impression that something absolutely material, which had been present around her and around everyone and everything forever, but imperceptible, was breaking down the outlines of persons and things and revealing itself" (1:90). At first glance, we might consider Lila's feeling to be the result of a panic attack. Yet Lila's perception of the "absolutely material" nature of the occurrence does not support this theory, as the very essence of a panic attack consists in its subjectivity, whereas *smarginatura* maintains at all times its rootedness for Lila in the objective. The irregular meaning that the term gains as she adapts it to her need reflects the disruptive claims asserted by the event itself on the "material" of reality. Her world, we might say, is one of astonishing forces and energies that can only be evoked by a new, invented word. One crucial incident in *My Brilliant Friend* implies that the earliest sign of Lila's fear emerges in childhood, before she even can find the right label for it. When her father throws her through the window of the family's apartment at the age of ten, she thinks to herself while falling to the asphalt that "the small, very friendly reddish animals were dissolving the composition of the street, transforming it into a smooth, soft material" (1:91). The link between Lila's first intuition of the disorder of things and the violence inflicted on her as a child hints at an explanation that has grown familiar from the popularization of trauma theory, which suggests why at least one of Ferrante's interviewers equates dissolving boundaries with "emotional breakdown" (F 356). Yet Ferrante herself consistently denies her two heroines the luxury of psychological explanations when discussing their states of mind. According to conventional wisdom, our defensive instincts block out the full, subjective comprehension of trauma, making it impossible to metabolize. Because the two friends run the risk of violence on a regular basis, however, the idea that they can shut its effects out of consciousness seems improbable. Instead, Lila comes to terms with her own "style of being overwhelmed," to borrow Lauren Berlant's apt phrase, by giving it the enigmatic name of *smarginatura*.[15]

Ferrante's avoidance of the discourse with which we customarily talk about the irrational or enigmatic perhaps has something to do with the wish of a writer who has stated that "the search for the right tone is for the me the synthesis of every possible experiment" (F 310) to avoid the glib claims to self-consciousness that words such as *trauma* inevitably assert, claims that may appear even more incongruous in relation to her protagonists' lower-class backgrounds. By contrast, "dissolving margins" places emphasis on the loss of the exterior outlines of the world and other people, mainly men, rather than on the interior life of a subject who happens to be a woman. It is hardly accidental that the only time when Lila discusses her condition with Elena is during the earthquake of 1980, although Elena herself remains so conscious of its latent threat that, as we know, she tries to "calm" her friend by writing the definitive account of their story.[16] On the occurrence of the natural disaster, Lila undergoes an unnerving metamorphosis before Elena's startled eyes: writhing, trembling, emitting what Elena calls "a death rattle," and immediately growing convinced that Enzo and Gennaro have been "destroyed" (4:174). She seems paralyzed by the sight of people running or shouting and reacts in terror when she spots Marcello driving his car, because she envisions man and machine flowing into each other and mixing like liquids:

> She used that term: *dissolving boundaries*. It was on that occasion that she resorted to it for the first time; she struggled to elucidate the meaning, she wanted me to understand what the dissolution of boundaries meant and how much it frightened her. She was still holding my hand tight, breathing hard. She said that the outlines of things and people were delicate, that they broke like cotton thread. She whispered that for her it had always been that way, an object lost its edges and poured into another, into a solution of heterogeneous materials, a merging and mixing. . . . She would be plunged

into a sticky, jumbled reality and would never again be able to give sensations clear outlines. . . . If she didn't stay alert, if she didn't pay attention to the boundaries, the waters would break through, a flood would rise, carrying everything off in clots of menstrual blood, in cancerous polyps, in bits of yellowish fiber.

(4:175–76)

In this passage, Goldstein noticeably revises the turn of phrase that she has used at earlier points in the narrative to translate *smarginatura.* By replacing *margins,* which is a cognate of the Italian, with the word *boundaries,* she invokes one of the most ubiquitous notions in contemporary discussions of psychological matters. Particularly in the U.S., we are barraged with the idea that all we need to do in order to assure healthy relationships is to set and respect clear boundaries between ourselves and others. However, nothing of this association, which is unavoidable in English, is implied in Italian, as the original term has no connection to the language of psychology. The rhetoric of selfhood, boundaries, trauma, and panic attacks, which generally is more available to members of the middle and upper classes, does not truthfully represent the understanding that Ferrante's characters have of their own affects and relation to the world.

On this score, we may find it helpful to remember Lila's annoyance with the proposal that she contemplate a course of psychological care after braving unbearable punishments at work. After reaching a point of total exhaustion from mistreatment at the Soccavo salami factory, Lila visits an eminent cardiologist with whom Elena has made an appointment through the influence of Adele, the mother of her fiancée Pietro Airota. After finding nothing wrong with her heart, the doctor suggests to Lila "a neurological examination." Peeved, Lila growls that she does not have a "nervous illness," distinguishing what she regards as a problem only "for ladies" from her own situation by bringing up a familiar figure:

A relative of mine, a cousin of my mother's was unhappy, she had been unhappy her whole life. In the summer, when I was little, I would hear her through the open window, shouting, laughing. Or I would see her on the street doing slightly crazy things. But it was unhappiness, and so she never went to a neurologist, in fact she never went to any doctor.

(3:192)

Lila of course is talking about Melina, with whom she has felt a secret solidarity ever since childhood and whose "slightly crazy" aspect she increasingly seems to share after Tina vanishes. By insisting on the everyday
notion of "unhappiness," she makes evident her reluctance to explain
Melina's behavior in medical or therapeutic jargon. Moreover, we may
have reason to suspect that her distaste for clinical terminology arises in
no small measure from an unspoken feminist sympathy. As Sara Ahmed
has pointed out, feminism can be looked at precisely as "the cultivation of
sympathy for women who are unhappy," insofar as sadness is gendered in
problematic ways that must be contested by the "unhappy archive" of feminist thought.[17] As Ahmed clarifies, unhappiness has always been regarded
as a socially inappropriate affect, especially for women, who often are
compelled instead to perform happiness as a form of emotional labor. In
retelling Melina's story, Lila makes a point of recognizing a woman's right
to unhappiness, of asserting that class and gender inequities should neither be denied nor sublimated by recasting them as the psychoanalytic
burden of the individual.

We should note that Ferrante's use of the name Melina for Lila's
unhappy maternal relative most likely pays homage to the unsettling Italian poet Amelia Rosselli (1930–1996), whose work has inspired Ferrante's
vocal admiration.[18] As more than one critical account has documented,
Rosselli's family called the poet "Melina" at home.[19] The daughter of Carlo
Rosselli, who fought fascism and was a hero of the Resistance, Amelia suffered psychological difficulties throughout her life and underwent a variety of treatments including electroshock therapy. Yet she succeeded in
writing and publishing poetry not only in Italian but also in English and
French that brought her into the company of writers such as Pier Paolo
Pasolini and John Ashbery. Although Melina Cappuccio's passion for Donato
Sarratore in the Neapolitan Quartet repeatedly devolves into what look like
scenes from an overwrought melodrama, Ferrante invests her character
with unexpected dignity through the invocation of Melina Rosselli, whose
own anguish puts her namesake's troubles in an ironic new light. Insofar as
her forename conjures up the figure of the poet, thus underscoring the contrast between real literary genius and Donato's pathetic scribblings, Melina
Cappuccio has the ultimate revenge on her faithless lover.

Like the names they reserve mainly for use with each other, Lenù and
Lila, smarginatura illustrates the two friends' preference at times for their

own personal lexicon over the vocabulary that their culture foists on them. In this case, their private habit of speech subtly repudiates the subaltern general acceptance of the theories of pop psychology. Can we say, however, that smarginatura represents a feminist concept in the way that, for instance, Ahmed argues we should view unhappiness? It is telling that Lila's own explanation to Elena of her fear of dissolving margins culminates in the vision of an apocalyptic flood of menstrual blood and cancerous growths that clearly bespeaks anxiety of the female body's susceptibility to change and disease. Such a worry is familiar to Ferrante's characters. In *Troubling Love*, the arrival of her period adds to Delia's confusion on the day of her mother's funeral. In *The Lost Daughter*, Nina's swelling pregnancy and the infusion of her daughter's hollow doll with wet sand, saltwater, and worms together represent an unspoken link for Leda between the world's chaotic disorder and the discomforts of being a woman. In *The Story of the Lost Child*, the threat or reality of loss for women is signaled repeatedly by the appearance of blood: the approaching death of Immacolata, Elena's mother, manifests itself in a pool of blood, while Lila, after losing Tina, finds herself constantly menstruating (4:372). A dictum that Ferrante attributes to Amelia Rosselli helps to clarify the symbolic connection between the enigma of dissolving margins in the largest sense and women's biological differences:

> We, all of us women, need to build a genealogy of our own, one that will embolden us, define us, allow us to see ourselves outside the tradition through which men have viewed, represented, evaluated, and catalogued us—for millennia.... To narrate thoroughly, freely—even provocatively—our own "more than this" is important: it contributes to the drawing of a map of what we are or what we want to be. There's a quote from Amelia Rosselli—one of the most innovative and unsettling Italian poets of the twentieth century—that dates from the nineteen-sixties. Years ago I adopted it as a literary manifesto that is at once ironic and dead serious. It's an exclamation: "What black deep activism there is in my menstruation!"
> (F 361–62)

Ferrante affirms here the idea of a feminist genealogy that enables women "to see ourselves outside the tradition" in which men have confined them and, by dissolving margins that have shaped patriarchal culture, to draw "a map of what we are or what we want to be." Implicated in her call for women to narrate their own stories "freely" and "provocatively" is the awareness that to think, speak, and act outside the gendered lines of authority necessitates acceptance of both uncertainty and vulnerability. Citing Rosselli's call to arms, the novelist embraces the poet's metonymic association of the adversities that women risk in activism with the pains and indeterminacies that they confront in relation to their bodies. What both Rosselli and Ferrante assert is that smarginatura in the sense of a woman's anguish at her own sexual difference is the necessary complement of the work of dissolving margins with respect to the social and cultural conventions that define patriarchy. From this perspective, smarginatura can be thought of as an example of what Ahmed calls a "sweaty concept," which is to say a notion "that comes out of a description of a body that is not at home in the world" and specifically originates in "the practical experience of coming up against a world, or the practical experience of trying to transform a world."[20]

The antagonism between women and a world in which their bodies have no home entails the horror of physical disintegration that Lila calls smarginatura in one other concrete sense. What becomes clear as we encounter successive examples of dissolving margins in the narrative is that the characters who undergo the annihilating loss of form that so alarms Lila are all men. During the occurrence on New Year's Eve of 1958, her "disgust, who knows why, was concentrated in particular on her brother Rino" (1:90), then leads in the next instance to "the disintegration of Stefano in the passage from fiancé to husband" (2:355–56), and, finally, when the earthquake strikes, engulfs Michele Solara in his car (4:175). Elena's identification of the formlessness that unnerves Lila with "disgust" hardly seems casual. It almost seems as if, at the level of the narrative's own unconscious, Ferrante pictures Lila's revulsion at a world that leaves women homeless magically obliterating all the patriarchal bodies that call it home. Indeed, Elena discovers belatedly that one of Lila's most harrowing episodes of *smarginatura* appears to have been provoked by Stefano's enraged beatings of her after their wedding: "I learned only from her notebooks how much her wedding night had scarred her and how she feared the potential distortion of her husband's body, his disfigurement by the internal impulses of desire and rage. . . . Especially at night she was afraid of waking up and finding him formless in the bed, transformed into excrescences that burst out of too much fluid, the flesh melted and drip-ping, and with it everything around, the furniture, the entire apartment and she herself, his wife, broken, sucked into that stream polluted by living matter" (2:356). In the end, however, Lila herself is the personage who dis-appears completely from the saga, leaving no trace behind, as if to compel the process of smarginatura to its logical conclusion. With this final ges-ture, she brings to mind the female narrator of Ingeborg Bachmann's novel, *Malina*, who magically and mysteriously vanishes through a crack in the wall, as she claims at the novel's end. Lila's final erasure of herself from Naples leaves Elena bewildered at the end of the two friends' story and starkly demonstrates the limits of Ferrante's respect for the margins of realism or reason. Her characters embody a self-contradictory intensity of energies, an ethical smarginatura, that threatens to eradicate all obstacles, including even themselves, in their efforts to find or to create a home of their own.

In the same interview with Yasemin Çongar that we cite earlier, which is reprinted in *Frantumaglia*, Ferrante expounds on the project of the Nea-politan Quartet, which as she summarizes it, is to elicit "the collision between staying within the boundaries and dissolving the boundaries" (F 310). The writer in search of truth—real truth and not merely its stylized, "realist" simulation—on this account must relinquish the consolations of genre and form and instead take on "the job of describing what escapes the story, what escapes the narrative order" (F 312). To tell the stories of the women whose shadowy lives and friendships escape the narrative order of our increasingly global contemporary culture requires, we might say, a translator's talent for dissolving margins. As Ferrante eloquently puts it at another point in *Frantumaglia*, during her exchange with Ruth Joos: "Bor-ders make us feel stable. At the first hint of conflict, at the least threat, we close them. . . . But it's purely an appearance. A story begins when, one after another, our borders collapse" (F 326).

LILA'S DESIRES

With Lila, we witness a complete divergence between desire and pleasure, a separation that seems to leave her forever unable to enjoy sex. In an interview with Deborah Orr, Ferrante notes that men's monopolization of culture poses an obstacle to an honest view of women's sexuality: "I think our sexuality is all yet to be recounted and that, especially in this context, the rich male literary tradition constitutes a huge obstacle. The way Elena and Lila behave are just two different aspects of the same arduous and almost always unhappy adjustment to men and their sexuality" (F 358). Lila indeed seems to be the character least interested in sex in the quartet. Her disdain is intrinsic to her own unique mode of nonchalance or *sprezzatura*, the fascinating mix of insightfulness and contempt that makes her so compelling to other characters. Elena learns how to enjoy sex with both Antonio and Nino (at least for a while), notwithstanding her shameful indoctrination into physical pleasure by Donato. By contrast, Lila seems only to feel desire with Nino, during the love affair they begin in Ischia, and otherwise may not take any pleasure from sex at all.

In *Those Who Leave and Those Who Stay*, Nino meets Elena in Milan while she is on a book tour and, with "a grimace of displeasure," tells her that Lila is "really made badly: in her mind and in everything, even when it comes to sex" (3:36). Nino's disparagement of Lila on grounds that include her attractions as a sexual partner disturbs Elena to the point of causing her "anxiety" at his indifference to her friendship with his former lover (3:36–37). On the one hand, the fact that he talks about Lila as "no one in the neighborhood would have in speaking of the woman he loved" endears Nino neither to Elena nor to the reader (3:37). On the other hand, Elena's own narration later confirms the fact that Lila takes no gratification from sexual relations: "She had truly loved Nino. She had desired him deeply, she had desired to please him and for his pleasure had done willingly everything that with her husband she had to do by force, overcoming disgust, in order not to be killed. But she had never felt what it was said she was supposed to feel when she was penetrated, that she was sure of, and not only with Stefano but also with Nino" (3:146). When Lila confesses to her friend in the bluntest terms that "fucking had never given her the pleasure she had expected as a girl, that in fact she had almost never felt anything, that after Stefano, after Nino, to do it really annoyed her" (3:174), Elena can only respond somewhat noncommittally that for her it is different. Lila trenchantly observes in reply that Elena wrote in her first novel about "stuff that men don't want to hear and women know but are afraid to say" and therefore clearly recognizes what she herself calls "*the bother of fucking*" (3:176).

In her notebook entries, as Elena recounts them, Lila describes her love for Nino as salvation from being "on the point of dying," an escape from the feeling that she was "crossing the *stradone* just as a truck was coming and (she would) be hit, dragged away" (2:295). At the height of her affair with Nino, she seems to have a premonition of the worst tragedy of her life. Her recollection of her prior unhappiness eerily foreshadows the disappearance of her daughter Tina, whose vanishing as Lila nears middle age is linked to a truck that passes by while she animatedly converses with Nino and holds in her arms Imma, his daughter with Elena. For all of the ardor that Lila voices in her notebooks, her image of herself being run over implies a nihilist wish that she sadly fulfills in later life, albeit only symbolically. Once Nino abandons her, Lila loses the ability to feel sexual desire for many years. She instead settles for an affectionate but initially celibate relationship with the stocky and ungainly Enzo: "I've had great respect for you, Enzo, since we were children. . . . But I can't sleep with you. It is not because we've seen each other alone at most two or three times. And it's not that I do not like you. It's that I have no feelings, I am like this wall or that table" (2:441). Although Stefano's reflexive aggression toward her may contribute to Lila's sexually inanimate state, nothing in her behavior suggests that the continual brutality of their marriage is the cause of her lack of interest in sex. As I have observed with respect to the notion of dissolving margins, Ferrante indeed resists dramatizing events by means of the language of trauma in the Neapolitan novels, refusing to make it the key to whatever sexual or emotional pathologies her protagonists suffer. If anything, the author instead emphasizes the ordinariness of acts of violence among the lower classes, which precludes the characters from engaging in the satisfaction of self-reflection. After Tina goes missing, when Lila reverts to sleeping alone despite having slept with Enzo for years, she responds with a shrug to Elena's proposal that she see a therapist: "Enough with doctors . . . I am fine like this. Fucking is overrated" (4:380).[21] Elena clarifies that she is thinking of Lila's need for love, but Lila replies that she has Tina on her mind. The theater of trauma in Ferrante's Naples appears to be a luxury that her heroines cannot afford. Lila in this sense never becomes an entirely tragic character in the narrative. An aura of possibility always emanates from her. If she renounces carnal pleasures, she proves over and over again that one can desire productively in other ways, that desire should not be reduced merely to sex.

Desire finds expression for Lila in forms that are evocative less of our customary ideas of eros or romance than of French philosopher Gilles

Deleuze's notion of *agencement* or "assemblage," as it is usually translated into English, meaning the connection and arrangement of bodies, concepts, and contexts in new relationships to create sense.[22] From her youthful interests of books, shoes, and visual design to her later curiosity for computer programming and the city of Naples, her desire seems to circulate within and spread to her surroundings, to be constantly "deterritorialized," as Deleuze and his collaborator Félix Guattari would have put it. Her desires, in this sense, are rarely manifestations of narcissistic wishes. They manage instead to "assemble" or organize social continuums that encompass her brother, her father, Stefano, the Solaras, and the entire neighborhood in the case of Cerullo shoes, or Enzo, Alfonso, Ada, Michele Solara, and her brother in the case of her software company, Basic Sight. Her ultimate passion, the city of Naples itself in all of its social, historical, and architectural grandeur, is the most prominent example of her knack for acts of critical agencement that map the present through the past. Poignantly, Lila's love for Naples and fascination with its mysteries come to light only in the wake of Tina's disappearance. Following the loss of her daughter, Lila becomes a nocturnal flaneur through the streets of the city, haunting its darkened spaces in order to chart the constellations of Naples's monuments, inhabitants, and events in new and unexpected ways. Like Walter Benjamin, who sought to assemble a panoply of insights about the Parisian arcades in his unfinished masterpiece known today as the *Arcades Project* (*Passagenwerk*), she acquires encyclopedic knowledge of the city through her wanderings, which I discuss more fully in chapter 4, "*Genius Loci*." Her compulsive fear of the dissolution of margins or smarginatura might be viewed as the price of her determination to explore her ever-changing desires to their limits, to pursue imaginative lines of flight that cannot be reversed.[23]

The creative relationship to love and desire that is embodied by Lila exerts a lasting influence on other characters in the saga. Of course, Elena responds to Lila's example continually from childhood through old age: her ferocious intellect, her virtuosity as a writer, her marriage and initiation into sex with Stefano, her *amour fou* with Nino, her skill as a mother, etc. When Enzo and Lila move in together in San Giovanni a Teduccio, she discovers a "new passion" for computational languages, which eventually blossoms into a talent "for innovation and for profit" so dynamic that it makes her the Solaras' equal in power in the neighborhood (2:465, 4:129–30).[24] In middle age, Elena realizes that Nino still regards Lila, decades after their liaison, as "the highest example of female intelligence," whose memory means that "the season of Ischia would always remain radiant for him" (4:235–36). Yet perhaps the most remarkable sign of Lila's hold over others, oddly enough, is Michele Solara's tortured but chaste attachment to her. Although he is utterly enthralled by Lila, he does not really want to make love to her. During a confrontation with him in the Soccavo salami factory, she thinks to herself: "Once . . . he asked me to become his lover. But that's not what he really wants, there's something else, something that doesn't have to do with sex and that not even he can explain. He is obsessed, it is like a superstition. Maybe he thinks that I have a power and that power is indispensable to him" (3:167). Michele himself confirms Lila's suspicion when he declares that what he actually wants is to own her gift for imaginative leaps, to purchase her vivacity of mind: "Lina has something alive in her mind that no one else has, something strong, that jumps here and there and nothing can stop it. . . . Well, for a long time I have wanted to buy this distinctive aspect of her" (3:333–34). His demure, if possessive, curiosity about her intellect seems all the more incongruous given his identity as a macho *camorrista* who feels obliged to boast of having slept with hundreds of women to no less than Elena's professorial husband, Pietro. More typically, Michele treats his wife, Gigliola, like a slave, with the utmost contempt and violence. Psychologically, however, his compulsion to sublimate his feelings for Lila seems fitting insofar as this strategy, which is to say the mimicry of her desire, represents his only chance of raising her interest.

ELENA'S PLEASURES

If Lila noticeably adopts a certain coolness and even cynicism toward sex in the Neapolitan novels, she is far from being alone on this score. Several of Ferrante's women characters confess to each other the insignificance of sex in their daily lives. When Elena assumes responsibility for the care of her aging mother, Immacolata, and manages to establish a more open dialogue between them, for example, she is forced to endure an "embarrassing" revelation about her parents' relationship.[25] Summing up her life for her daughter, Immacolata reveals that she always remained faithful to her husband despite his being "perfunctory" in bed and more like a brother to her than a lover: "She could not remember if sleeping with him had ever truly given her pleasure" (4:151). She confides that her only moment of joy in the marriage occurred when she gave birth to Elena. Here Ferrante poignantly illuminates a lower-class woman's disenchantment with the prevailing ideology of married life and sexuality, which, it might be said, is a subject that the contemporary Italian novel is far from exhausting. From her mother's disclosure, Elena gains a clarifying insight into Immacolata's anguish. As a result, she recognizes that her mother's occasional encouragement of her father's public bragging about their sex life was "pure show" (4:202). In the absence of desire and pleasure, her parents' vulgar banter sustains the performance of their gender roles in accordance with heteronormative social expectations.

When they become the topic of candid conversation between women, most marriages in the quartet look more or less like case studies in sexual frustration. After the death of Lila's brother, Rino, his wife, Pinuccia, unexpectedly reveals to Elena in a "low voice" that he had been a "real husband" to her only for a brief time and "otherwise . . . had behaved like a boy: even in bed, one minute and off he got, sometimes not even the minute" (4:358). Against this chorus of unfulfilled women, Elena stands out as a relative exception. Although her sentimental education certainly provides its share of pain and dismay, she differs from most of her women friends, including Lila, insofar as she resists cynicism when it comes to the possibility of sexual pleasure. We may find her optimism on this score somewhat surprising, as she agonizes throughout childhood and adolescence over her unrequited passion for Nino. Yet she never becomes jaded about sex, despite the fact that gratification often proves to be elusive, especially in adulthood, during the years of her marriage to Pietro. Remarkably, she even couches her description of her repugnant encounters as a teenager with Donato Sarratore in Ischia in terms of enjoyment. When Elena reflects the next day on the loss of her virginity to Donato on the beach at Maronti, she improbably refers to the event in her own thoughts as "my pleasure," albeit while refusing to tell her story to Lila, who has just returned from making love to Nino and "would have recognized in her fulfillment the reverse of my emptiness" (2:296).

Although as a twenty-two-year-old the memory of her night with Donato elicits "long crying spells" and shame at her "degrading" experience, Elena in the end strikes a thoughtful balance between the claims of conscience and desire. Reconsidering even fulfilling relationships such as her liaison with Franco Mari, she asks herself: "Is it possible that even happy moments of pleasure never stand up to a rigorous examination? Possible" (2:430–31, 433). Yet she neither withdraws from the pursuit of such "happy moments," like Lila, nor does she subscribe to the mythical ideal of the "unmediated orgasm" made popular during the cultural upheaval of 1968. While staying with her sister-in-law Mariarosa in Milan, for example, Elena rebuffs the advances of Juan, a Venezuelan painter who claims to be an exponent of free love. Elena rapidly grows indignant, making clear that she does not share the ideology of "diffuse erotic excitement" that appears to be in the air (3:82–83). In this respect, Elena to some extent appears to be one of the more mature characters in the Neapolitan Quartet. Between matter-of-fact pragmatism with respect to the "sticky" rewards of sexuality and romantic idealism with respect to the imaginative and physical intimacies of erotic love, she moves back and forth with relative ease as circumstances permit.

In a seminal essay occasioned by the publication of Michel Foucault's *The Will to Knowledge* in 1977, Deleuze explains why he privileges the notion of desire over that of pleasure, in contrast to the position held by Foucault: "I cannot give any positive value to pleasure, because pleasure seems to me to interrupt the immanent process of desire; pleasure seems to me to be on the side of strata and organization."[26] Deleuze premises his judgment on the conviction that desire coincides with "an *assemblage* of heterogeneous elements that function . . . it is affect, as opposed to sentiment; it is '*haec*-ceity' (the individuality of a day, a season, a life), as opposed to subjectivity; it is event, as opposed to a thing or a person."[27] For him, the operations of desire presume movements of deterritorialization that lead to the constitution of a "body without organs," a difficult notion that derives from Artaud and aims primarily at rejecting structural, hierarchical views of "the body" in both the biological and political senses. Without delving into all the complexities of Deleuze's philosophy of desire, which he and Guattari elaborate in *Anti-Oedipus* and *A Thousand Plateaus*, we may find it useful to look at how he frames the dichotomy between desire and pleasure as we reflect on the fortunes of Ferrante's protagonists. Elena's pragmatism when it comes to making decisions—her ability to deterritorialize and reterritorialize her life—connects her to the laws of pleasure, which, as we have seen, is a frequently recurring word in her vocabulary. Her pubescent relationship with Antonio, in which she first learns the joys of sexual excitement and satisfaction, appears to be literally circumscribed within the territory of the ponds near the abandoned canning factory on the outskirts of the neighborhood. In other words, the site of pleasure is the obverse of a space of the imagination for her. Instead, she evidently associates gratification with the most derelict quarter of the neighborhood, a wild, waterlogged, unpopulated setting that bears the mark of once having been a thriving place of industry but is now forsaken and gone to seed.

Antonio is not especially smart or handsome and, like his mother Melina, develops some kind of psychological incapacity when he reaches maturity. As young teenagers, he and Elena get involved with each other practically by accident. Elena takes increasing comfort and pleasure in their sexual experiments together, although they never take the step of losing their virginity with each other. Decades later, on the day that she finally ends her adult love affair with Nino, Elena has her first and only full sexual experience with the now middle-aged Antonio, confessing to him that she has never felt the same need for anyone else:

> "I never desired anyone the way I desired you, not even him." I talked for a long time, I told him the truth, the truth of the moment and the truth of the faraway time of the ponds. He was the discovery of excitement, he was the pit of the stomach that grew warm, that opened up, that turned liquid. . . . Franco, Pietro, Nino had stumbled on that expectation but had never managed to satisfy it, because it was an expectation without a definite object, it was the hope of pleasure, the hardest to fulfill. The taste of Antonio's mouth, the perfume of his desire, his hands, the large sex taut between his thighs constituted a before that could not be matched. The after had never been truly equal to our afternoons hidden by the skeleton of the canning factory, although they consisted of love without penetration and often without orgasm.
>
> (4:256)

Clearly, the "desire" at stake in Elena's profession of feeling for Antonio is consistent with the hope of pleasure. It is a desire that is unshackled from the imagination and reterritorialized among other ways in terms of class, since Antonio, in his lack of prospects and ambition, represents for Elena the point of departure from her plebeian origins that Nino does not.

However, her revelation comes as news to us readers, who have grown accustomed to her seemingly inexhaustible reveries about Nino. Should we believe Elena? Does her statement betray an affinity for the exquisite nostalgia with which, say, Flaubert concludes *Sentimental Education*? The ending of Flaubert's novel depicts the protagonist Frédéric recounting to his friend Deslauriers his memory of a supposedly "minor" moment of their past and famously concluding: "That was the best time we ever had" ("C'est là que nous avons eu du meilleur").

Perhaps it is more likely that, in her customarily well-organized way, Elena as a grown woman comes to value not the snobbery of melancholic remembrance but rather the avoidance of the emotional chaos ensuing from pleasure. At the same time, there may also be an implicit critical point to her praise of Antonio. Revisiting Carla Lonzi's *Let's Spit on Hegel*, the treatise that inspires Elena's embrace of feminism during the initial years of her marriage to Pietro, we find that the author extols at length the advantages of clitoral over vaginal orgasm. The distinction between the two types of pleasure was crucial for Italian proponents of women's sexual difference, as they held that clitoral orgasm emancipated the subject from marital coitus and released her into the domain of specific, yet polymorphous pleasure. Whereas Lila derides this suggestion, Elena is not as dismissive and in fact appears to put the theory into practice with both Antonio and Franco. Before marriage, she advances in her sexual self-discovery through her relationship with Franco and learns to take pleasure from him via more circuitous routes than she found with previous lovers: "Franco . . . before entering me and afterward let me rub against one of his legs, against his stomach . . . this was nice and sometimes made the penetration nice, too" (3:175).

With Pietro, coitus becomes a tedious, painful, and darkly comic occurrence, during which her husband "strained for a time that seemed endless" (3:231). Unlike her two previous boyfriends, Pietro is both obsessively goal oriented and overly quick, and his laborious performances leave Elena "hurting and unsatisfied" (3:231). While he may be a mild-mannered intellectual in public, he turns out to be inadvertently callous in private, insofar as his entire repertoire of lovemaking consists of "deliberate thrusting" and "monotonous insistence": "He was covered with sweat from his long exertions, maybe from suffering, and when I saw his damp face and neck, touched his wet back, desire disappeared completely"

(3:231). Touchingly, Elena does not initially respond with despair, but rather with patience and resignation. Over time, though, the absence of either desire or pleasure from the routine of marriage wears her down and leads Elena to fantasies of emulating her sister-in-law Mariarosa's freedom as a "liberated woman" as well as to a few, futile diversions that seem more sentimental than sexual: "A couple of times it seemed to me that I was falling in love" (3:256).

Fortunately for Elena, Nino resurfaces in her life after years of obscurity, thanks to a chance encounter with Pietro's father that leads to an unlikely friendship between Pietro and Nino. As Elena becomes reacquainted with Nino, she is surprised by his interest in women writers (3:361) and finds herself writing "in a state of pleasurable intellectual overexcitement" to win his approval (3:364). This "pleasurable" intellectual exchange gives way to Elena sleeping with Nino during one of his visits to Florence and thus initiating their love affair. With him, she appears for the first time in her adult life to feel the complete convergence of desire and pleasure: "I was amazed at how much I wanted him. . . . We embraced with a fury that I had never known, as if our bodies were crashing against each other with the intention of breaking. So pleasure was this: breaking, mixing, no longer knowing what was mine and what was his" (3:388). For a period of roughly six years, Elena and Nino sustain a passionate, fulfilling romance throughout their various movements between Florence and Naples as well as travels to France, West Germany and Austria, the Monte Argentario peninsula of Tuscany, and New York.[28] Yet even the happy symmetry between bodily and imaginative impulses that they achieve cannot last. As Elena herself aptly puts it: "Daily life frequently erupted, like a slap, making irrelevant if not ridiculous every meandering little fantasy" (4:237).

Indeed, Elena suffers a blow that dispels all her fantasies involving Nino when she returns home to their apartment on Via Tasso and catches him making love *more ferarum* to the maid, Silvana, while "holding her heavy stomach with his arm" (4:238).[29] The degraded compulsiveness of Nino and the maid in this scenario bears some resemblance to Olga's angry seduction of Carrano, which also ends with the man positioned behind the woman, in *The Days of Abandonment* (TDA 84–85). In his famous case study entitled *The Wolfman*, Freud theorizes that when his patient witnesses his parents' *coitus a tergo*, he encounters a traumatic "primal scene" that has potentially pathogenic consequences. Ferrante almost seems to transmute this idea into a sort of "feminized primal scene," ascribing a decisive symbolic meaning to the arrangement of man posterior to woman insofar as it enacts the raw, animalistic, and disappointing nature of sex for many women. After fleeing from this primal scene, Elena in later years has other flings, whom she mentions in such clinical terms as to suggest a certain detachment. Toward the end of *The Story of the Lost Child*, for example, she briskly depicts her "most recent lover" as a nameless "professor at the Polytechnic, eight years younger than me, twice divorced, with a son" (4:459).

Ultimately, Elena's most direct, uncomplicated source of pleasure may be her own writing. After she finishes her second novel, her editor praises her for being able to awaken her reader to the "pure pleasure of narration" (4:258). Lila, however, does not like Elena's books, because they possess neither the imaginative freedom of fiction nor the true-to-life veracity of history and so lack courage. As Lila herself puts it, "Things are told or not told: you remained in the middle" (4:285). An enthusiast of the writings of James Joyce and Samuel Beckett, she does not appear to be swayed by the pure pleasure of narration. On this point, it is fascinating to peruse Ferrante's deliberations on writing in *Frantumaglia*, where she argues that it is the writer's ability to give the reader pleasure by demonstrating breadth of tone, texture, point of view, etc. that determines whether the story is memorable. We may imagine that this conviction places her squarely in Elena's camp when we come across statements such as this one from her interview with Sandra Ozzola, Sandro Ferri, and Eva Ferri:

> An ambitious writer has a duty, even more than in the past, to have a vast literary culture. . . . I renounce nothing that can give pleasure to the reader, not even what is considered old, trite, vulgar. As I was saying, what makes everything new and acceptable is literary truth; whether a text is short, long, or endless, what counts above all is richness, complexity, the fascination of the literary texture.
>
> (F 269–70)

Ferrante's willingness to welcome the "vulgar" in the name of pleasure practically invites comparison to Elena's readiness to take on risqué and controversial literary projects. Yet the turn that Ferrante makes toward "literary truth" in the last sentence of this citation reinforces Lila's distinction between the fictive and the factual, the things that are told and those that are not told, especially as she concludes by avowing the ideals of "richness, complexity, the fascination of the literary texture." Tantalizingly, the author's defense of pleasure as a means to literary truth suggests an identification with both Elena and Lila, as if each of the two friends dialectically represented a different aspect of her own sensibility.

WOMEN AS LOVERS

The women characters who inhabit Ferrante's stories often become very close and feel the pull of mutual attraction but never enter into sexual relationships with each other. Why, we may ask, does the novelist take such strong, consistent interest in the affinity between women without ever granting their potential for erotic love with each other as well?

The book in which Ferrante perhaps comes closest to portraying same-sex desire is *The Lost Daughter*. As we note earlier, the novel tells the story of a middle-aged woman, Leda, who becomes fascinated by a younger woman, Nina. Leda is aroused by Nina while at the same time identifying with Nina's maternal affection for her daughter, Elena. One day, when Nina loses sight of Elena on the beach, Leda finds the little girl and returns her to her family, but steals Elena's doll, Nani, for reasons that she cannot explain even to herself. When the theft is revealed sometime later, Nina angrily stabs Leda with a hatpin that the older woman bought for her as a gift. With this vengeful gesture, Nina clearly rejects Leda's token of friendship. More important, she rebuffs Leda's ill-conceived attempt, just before returning Nani, to persuade Nina to abandon her husband and family in order to complete her education in Florence where Leda lives and teaches. A narrative that appears to toy with the idea of a homosocial bond between the main characters thus delivers in the end a sharply observed portrait of the inconceivability of queer relations between women in contemporary Italy.

Before reaching this conclusion, however, the novel clearly entertains the possibility of women's same-sex desire. It is quite obvious that Leda is excited at every level both by Nina and by the recollected figure of Brenda, a young Englishwoman who left her husband for another man and whom Leda befriended in Calabria. Male characters instead represent pale figures at the margins of the narrative, lacking in charisma. Even the famous scholar for whom Leda leaves her own family after welcoming his advances at an academic conference, Professor Hardy, is described by Leda's adviser as "old, bored" (TLD 98) and only goes by his last name in her retelling of their affair, giving the impression of a distant and detached presence. By contrast, Leda exclusively refers to Nina and Brenda by their first names, both of which are subtly assonant with her own, as if this echoic similarity encapsulated the women's intimacy.

After Leda and her husband, Gianni, take Brenda and her lover into their home for the night, Leda comes to a surprising realization. Brenda's passion and freedom stir Leda to admit how dull her life with Gianni and their two daughters has become: "Yet that morning when I stripped the bed where Brenda and her lover had slept, when I opened the window to get rid of their odor, I had seemed to discover in my body a call for pleasure that had nothing to do with that of my early sexual experiences, at the age of sixteen, with the uncomfortable and unsatisfying sex with my future husband, with our conjugal habits before and especially after the birth of our children" (TLD 94). Instead, when she pictures Brenda naked, Leda feels a "liquid excitement between her legs that was mine" (TLD 83). The same excitement seems to come over Leda when she recalls the accidental sight of a young beach attendant, Gino, kissing Nina: "Their kiss still burned, warmed my stomach, my mouth had a taste of warm saliva" (TLD 92). When she runs into Nina at the village fair and answers her questions about what it was like to leave and return to her family, Leda senses in her "an emotion of gratitude that manifested itself as an urgent need of contact," which Nina makes overt by kissing her goodbye "on the lips with a light embarrassed kiss" (TLD 119). *The Lost Daughter* may be Ferrante's most fearless book insofar as it is the one in which she most fully questions the cultural ideals of marriage and motherhood and contemplates the horizon of women's longing for each other. Although the ostensible turning point of Leda's life, which she reveals midway through the novel, is the story of her desertion of husband and daughters for an ultimately pointless affair with Hardy, Leda's transformation into a modern-day Anna Karenina takes up little space in the narrative and is displaced rapidly by the more enigmatic events surrounding her rapport with Nina.

Between Leda and Brenda as well as Leda and Nina there are also relations of what Italian feminists of the 1970s would have called "entrustment" (*affidamento*). This theory holds that one woman entrusting herself to another can lead to new political opportunities through the asymmetrical combination of their knowledge and talents. In the next chapter, I discuss the concept at greater length, but suffice it to say for now that what and how women learn from one another may be the most crucial questions of *The Lost Daughter*. Thanks to Brenda's interest in reading her work, Leda publishes the article that Hardy admiringly cites during his lecture at the conference, and thanks to Leda's candor in discussing her own personal decisions, Nina imagines what it could mean to change her life. The current of erotic desire between the women galvanizes the possibility of their entrustment, strategically linking the work of studying each other to their libidinal drives and attachments.

Although Olga in *The Days of Abandonment* supposedly busies herself with trying to forget Mario, the ex-husband who has left her, she apparently reserves her deepest passion for fantasizing about, and at one point overheatedly confronting, Mario's younger lover, Carla.[30] The suggestion that jealousy can give way to attraction toward another woman perhaps is not by itself shocking, but what Olga's chronicle of her struggles with her separation conveys in devastatingly brusque terms is the ugliness of the men who remain within reach of her attention. Her descriptions of their bodies and her own physical reactions to them are particularly unappealing. At one point, Olga characterizes Mario's smell as striking her "like the memory of the odor of an old man who, on a bus, has rubbed off on us the desires of his dying flesh" (TDA 155). Not even the courtesy, modesty, and kindness of Carrano, the "depressed musician" whom she seduces to prove she is still attractive to men, can erase the indelible image of his "gray flesh" or the sound of his moan "like braying" during sex (TDA 86). Surprisingly, she later encounters him by accident at a concert where he plays the cello so beautifully that he seems transformed into "a body full of seductive anomalies" (TDA 174). This description is so ludicrously incongruous that it can only put us in a skeptical mood when, at the end of the narrative, Olga claims to have found with Carrano "a feeling of fullness and joy" (TDA 188).

Readers of the Neapolitan Quartet may well expect some kind of romantic intrigue to occur between the two protagonists. Certainly, Elena is captivated by Lila from an early age and professes to love her in later life. Yet it is clear that, in the quartet, Ferrante is not telling a story along the lines of Patricia Highsmith's *Carol* or Dorothy Strachey's *Olivia*, where sexual desire between women is the main focus. Nonetheless, Elena admits as a teenager to feeling "the force of seduction that Lila had given off since she was a child" (2:16), and even for Lila it is never in doubt that, at least emotionally, Elena comes first in her life. Reflecting on the day of Lila's wedding to Stefano, Elena makes a telling confession as she recalls helping to bathe her friend: "I had never seen her naked, I was embarrassed. Today I can say that it was the embarrassment of gazing with pleasure at her body, of being the not impartial witness of her sixteen-year-old beauty a few hours before Stefano touched her, penetrated her, disfigured her, perhaps, by making her pregnant" (1:312–13). Gazing at Lila's nudity, Elena feels that her own heart is "agitated," her veins "inflamed" (1:313). There is no question that their friendship is passionate and difficult to define, especially for Elena. Although Lila does not return her gaze while bathing, she seizes the moment to dub Elena "my brilliant friend," underlining the symbolic importance of the moment for both of them (1:312). About that moment Elena writes: "I had a confusion of feelings and thoughts . . . in the end there was only the hostile thought that I was washing her, from her hair to her feet, early in the morning, just so that Stefano could sully her in the course of the night. I imagined her naked as she was at the moment, entwined with her husband, in the bed in the new house, while the train clattered under their windows and his violent flesh entered her with a sharp blow, like the cork pushed by the palm into the neck of the wine bottle" (1:313). The final vulgar metaphor of the cork and the bottle emblematizes Elena's raw feelings for Lila, while eerily anticipating in metaphorical terms the all-too-literal violence of the wedding night that lies ahead for her friend.

When Marcello Solara makes his entrance at the wedding party like a vicious Cinderella in the shoes that Lila designed, Elena momentarily fantasizes that, in her rage at Stefano for having given the shoes to the Solaras, Lila will run away with her: "Yes, yes, I felt that I wanted that. . . . An end of love and of that intolerable celebration, no embraces in the bed in Amalfi. Immediately shatter everything and every person in the neighborhood, tear them to pieces, Lila and I, go and live far away, lightheartedly descending together all the steps of humiliation, alone, in unknown cities" (2:19). Elena's daydream of eloping with Lila provides the most evanescently tender image of the bond between the two friends in the entire saga.

In Italian, we should note, the last sentence is far more sexually suggestive with respect to the nature of Elena's romantic dream of life with Lila than in English. Goldstein paraphrases the original's *allegro sciupio* as "light-heartedly," but a more literal rendering might be "with cheerful wasteful-ness," while she describes the two friends as bearing a "humiliation" that seems notably weaker than the Italian *abiezione*, which could be trans-lated more precisely as "abjection" (2:19 EN, 2:19 IT). In other words, the impression that Ferrante gives in her own prose is of Lila and Elena's imagined excess of enjoyment or pleasure, which clearly runs the risk of stigmatization if they do not escape to live "in unknown cities."

Notwithstanding the fact that Elena and Lila never become lovers, they are so emotionally bonded to one another that they adopt communal forms of life not just once but twice in their shared narrative: at first as adolescents in Ischia and then as adults in Naples, after Elena's separation from Nino.[31] Shortly before Nino's ruinous betrayal of Elena with their maid, Lila and Elena simultaneously become pregnant at the age of thirty-six. The coincidence almost suggests a miraculous, reciprocal insemina-tion that launches the happiest days of their friendship. With her acute gaze, Lila discerns her friend's wish to have a child with Nino so that, when Elena later returns from a visit to the U.S. with the news that she is expecting, Lila can surprise her with her own revelation. Yet Elena and Lila perceive the passage of time during their pregnancies very differently, with dissimilar feelings of anticipation; as Elena puts it, "The months of pregnancy passed quickly for me . . . and very slowly for Lila" (4:154). Despite having divergent views of their experiences of pregnancy, they find that their joint visits to the gynecologist become "a rare hour of joy" for both of them:

> Now we went together for our examinations, and had arranged to see her at the same time: when it was my turn, she stood quietly in a corner, and when it was her turn, I held her hand, because doctors still made her nervous. But the best part was in the waiting room. In those moments I forgot about my mother's suffering and we became girls again. We liked sitting next to each other, I fair, she dark, I calm, she anxious, I likable, she malicious, the two of us opposite and united, and separate from the other pregnant women, whom we observed ironically.
>
> (4:157)

After Elena and Lila respectively give birth to Imma and Tina and name each of their newborn daughters for their mothers, Elena makes the wrenching discovery of Nino coupling with Silvana in the bathroom, submits for publication her third book—which in the chronology of her efforts was actually the second manuscript that she wrote—and finally decides to move back to the old neighborhood, taking the apartment above the one where Lila and Enzo live (4:260).

This choice transports the two friends into an uncanny situation, which Elena recognizes as soon as she settles in: "The dusty light that had always struggled to penetrate the windows had the effect of an evocative childhood memory" (4:260). We may imagine that for each of the two women the other's presence in the vertically contiguous apartment represents a kind of unconscious, constant reminder of their shared past. The communal form of life that Lila and Elena organize for themselves offers a creative solution to their most pressing pragmatic needs, as they are able to take turns looking after each other and each other's families. Even more fundamentally, their proximity enables them at will to conjure up and take comfort in each other's disembodied presence through the sound of their voices and the voices of their children. On a day in the autumn of 1984 when Nino returns to the neighborhood to visit the two friends, Elena seizes on her connectedness to Lila in order to reassure herself: "Separating us was only a layer of floor, and yet she could shorten the distance further or expand it according to her mood and convenience and the movements of her mind, which shifted like the sea when the moon seizes it whole and pulls it upward. I tidied, I cooked, I thought Lila—below—was doing the same. We were both waiting to hear again the voices of our daughters, the steps of the man we had loved" (4:329). Whereas the thought of Elena and Lila listening with the same sense of expectation for Nino's approach hints at the antagonistic potential of their friendship, the idea of their related anticipation for the return of their daughters emphasizes its reparative possibility. In fact, their close living arrangement inaugurates a uniquely shared form of life in which the two young girls wonder which of the two friends is their mother and often receive from Enzo identical gifts (4:287, 323). Tina and Imma begin to resemble their mothers to the point of reproducing the two women's unequal division of power. In Elena's words, Imma "was the slave of Tina's joyful expansiveness, of her elevated capacity for verbalization, of the way she aroused tenderness, admiration, affection in everyone, especially me" (4:321). Inhabiting a shared history that threatens to repeat itself in their daughters, Lila and Elena construct a sort of everyday fantasy in which they live together as if in a single, extended family, thus entrusting their children—and especially the little girls—to one another. In Italian, the primary meaning of entrustment or affidamento is the act of an adult guardian in assuming legal custody of a child. At pivotal moments, in fact, the two friends entrust each other with their daughters as if to symbolize the legal act: Tina is entrusted to Elena in the photo published by the magazine *Panorama* and Imma is entrusted to Lila when Nino returns to Naples in 1984. Tragically, in the latter case it may be because Lila becomes engrossed in talking to Nino while holding Imma that she loses sight of Tina, precipitating the little girl's mysterious vanishing from the neighborhood without a trace.

Ferrante does not explore a possible erotic life between the two friends, but her decision hardly seems like a failure of nerve when considered from the perspective of the story's architecture as a whole. By not resolving Lila and Elena's narrative so definitively, the author in fact is able to pursue questions that are more open-ended and ambiguous. Ferrante experiments with a complicated scenario in which passionate friendship neither acquiesces to the norms of contemporary capitalism nor is predicated on sexual repression but comes to represent a new form of life that transforms or sublimates the two friends' libidinal energies into a subversive, utopian space of shared dependence. Tina's removal from their lives brings to an end the fragile idyll of the two women's intimacy and returns Lila, who eventually disappears as well, to her childhood role for Elena of the elusive and wounding object of mournful desire.

Throughout their lives, Lila and Elena waver ambivalently between hatred and love for each other and share an anxious need to repair one another's injuries. Their mutual dependence is so strong that it may be said to resemble the emotional bonds between mothers and children. According to the theory proposed by the celebrated psychoanalyst Melanie Klein, the complicated first bond between mother and child sets in motion our most extreme emotions—that is, both our worst impulses of envy and aggression and our best instincts of affection and reparation. Elena and Lila live their friendship in a way that is strikingly suggestive of the first bond. This is why, above all other experiences, the event of the two friends simultaneously becoming pregnant in *The Story of the Lost Child* marks their closeness in both pragmatic and symbolic terms.

Other women of the neighborhood make peace readily with the oppressive conditions of their culture. Whether members of the older generation such as Melina, Nunzia, and Immacolata or of the younger such as Gigliola, Carmela, Marisa, and Pinuccia, examples of "born" women who accept received ideas of their gender and cultural identity without argument abound in the quartet. Lila and Elena instead try to become women in the sense of thinking critically about their alternatives. Elena sums up this ambition when she recognizes that Lila's "absolute freedom" perpetually has spurred her to declare to herself: "*I wanted to become*, even though I had never known what" (3:346). The fear of *smarginatura* that haunts Lila may signify, among other things, the cost of her efforts to achieve this freedom as a woman in Naples. Indeed, both friends endure real pains for resisting the expectations that others impose on them. Lila succumbs to the sheer stress of the working conditions at the Soccavo salami factory, while Elena struggles with poverty when, at different times, her relationships with Pietro and Nino turn cool. Yet as they try to help each other overcome their sufferings, even those that are mutually inflicted, the two friends demonstrate how trust may develop from a shared sense of purpose rather than a fantasy of unconditional love.

GENDER TROUBLE

In an interview published in *El País* and reprinted in *Frantumaglia*, Ferrante responds to the question who in the Neapolitan Quartet is her favorite male character by naming Alfonso (F 345). Her answer is more than a little ironic, as our perception of Alfonso's gender identification changes dramatically over the course of the narrative. Yet the reason for Ferrante's preference is not hard to surmise, as other men in the novels adhere to roles that circumscribe their imaginations within a rigid code of gender, class, and violence. As we have noted earlier, Elena is fascinated by the activity of "becoming," although she cannot quite define what it is.[32] Ferrante indeed allows some women in the quartet to "become," to evolve and transform themselves, and even to try what Judith Butler calls "undoing gender," which is to say to question the role and function that society assigns them.[33] The men, however, appear to be condemned invariably to suffocate beneath the weight of their own cultural burdens.

Alfonso's brother, Stefano, is the perfect archetype of the Neapolitan male in this sense. As a young man, he apparently wishes to repudiate his legacy as son of the feared Don Achille by cultivating a genteel air. After marrying Lila, however, he proves to be a thug all the same, beating her during their honeymoon and later raping her when she resists sex. Most male characters in Ferrante's saga are "at the margins," to borrow Kaja Silverman's expression,[34] meaning that they are consumed by the symbolic order, always on the verge of irrelevance. Although Lila's brother, Rino, tries to protect her as a child, he squanders his life on drug addiction, beats his wife, Pina, and eventually dies of an overdose in an abandoned railway car that stinks of "shit and pee" (4:357). Elena's younger brothers, Peppe and Gianni, do not fare much better, selling drugs for the Solaras and living so much at the margins that when Lila offers them a way out, they refuse her offer (4:219). Lila's son, Gennaro, also proves to be a weak and subaltern character, who, disoriented and confused, is unable to find his way in life.

Even the male characters who are less obviously brutal tend to be trapped within the rules of their gender. Nino devotes time to women only in order to indulge what Elena calls "his penchant for seductive behavior" (4:230). Although, in contrast to Nino, Pietro enjoys the advantages of a polished upbringing and education, he does not refrain from relegating Elena to a subaltern space. The lone exception to the rule appears to be Enzo, who sells fruits and vegetables as a boy and becomes Lila's companion in adulthood. A patient and responsible man, Enzo carefully builds a prosperous career in the new field of software engineering, where he seems able to forget the Camorra and his exploitation as a worker in San Giovanni a Teduccio. However, he pays a price for escaping the dominant symbolic economy in his powerlessness when it comes to self-expression, his inability to relax into a more expansive attitude.

At the core of the Neapolitan novels' portrait of Italian men are the Solara brothers. Just as Don Achille does during Elena and Lila's early childhood, during the two friends' adolescence and adulthood the Solaras seem to play the symbolic part of ogres in fairy tales. Ferrante indeed playfully defines Don Achille as the neighborhood "ogre" (*l'orco*) in the index of characters of *My Brilliant Friend*. She thereby highlights the cultural construction of a symbolic order in which men hold sovereign authority, but not without a strong air of grotesquerie. The Solaras are violent and predatory even as teenagers, abducting Antonio's sister, Ada, in their car and trying to do the same with Elena and Lila. Lila's readiness to do violence to them in return keeps the brothers at bay, yet both Marcello and Michele fall in love with her, only to be rebuked and humiliated repeatedly over time. Michele, who represents one of the most complex characters in the saga, projects an especially paradoxical image of masculinity. On the one hand, he exemplifies the violence of Italian men to perfection, not only in his criminal dealings but also in the way that he abuses Gigliola, his long-suffering wife. On the other, he appears to be so mesmerized by Lila's ingenuity that he surrenders to Alfonso's desire for him, once Alfonso begins impersonating her, as a means of expressing his own for Lila.

One might say that Alfonso in fact represents the blind spot in the gender economy of Ferrante's Naples. Even before Elena understands through neighborhood rumors and innuendoes that he is gay, Alfonso seems unusual. His childhood habit of playing with dolls provokes his father's derision, while his gentleness and intelligence as a student set him apart from the other boys of the neighborhood. As an adult, Elena realizes that as a youngster she must have intuited Alfonso's sexual difference without acknowledging it (4:187). Often anxious about both family and schoolwork as a girl, she walks home with him after classes on most days and finds in him a trustworthy friend and confidant. It is hardly accidental that Alfonso is one of only two boys from the neighborhood who attend the *liceo classico* or classical high school with Elena, the other being Nino. The rest of their generation, Pasquale, Enzo, Antonio, Rino, and Stefano, give up before acquiring all but the rudiments of an education, let alone hope for a professional career. We are left to conclude that in their eyes it looks too farfetched to take on the difficulties not only of schooling but also of defying the expectations that Italian society forces on young men and women of the Neapolitan lower classes.

While Elena as a grown woman writes her second book, which criticizes the myth of woman's invention by man, Lila occupies herself with the project of "extracting" her own likeness from Alfonso, of reinventing him in her own image (4:57). On a brief visit to Naples following her graduation from the Scuola Normale, Elena describes Alfonso as having become as beautiful, cultured, and well-spoken as a "Spanish nobleman" (2:439). Years later, when she returns to the neighborhood after the collapse of her marriage to Pietro, she finds Alfonso's looks and mannerisms to be "disorienting," until she is struck by his resemblance to Lila (4:51, 55). By her own admission, she is startled to see him "so refined, so delicate, as good looking in my eyes as Lila and more" (4:146). What does Elena mean here by "and more?" Does she intend this turn of phrase to acknowledge Alfonso's excessive physical beauty or rather the intangible *je ne sais quoi* that makes up his identity? As she herself observes, what she finds most compelling about Alfonso is his nonconformism to Southern Italian norms of masculinity: "I was fond of him precisely because he was not like the other boys, precisely because of that peculiar alienation from the male behaviors of the neighborhood" (4:188–89).

In defiance of the neighborhood's rigid symbolic code, Alfonso indeed embodies a rare spirit of adventure toward gender. The world of Ferrante's Neapolitan saga is far removed from, say, that of Proust's *In Search of Lost Time*, where the sexual "inversions" of several characters—from Charlus to Saint Loup, Albertine, and the *jeunes filles* of the narrator's adolescence— reveal the primordial mutability of their identities. Alfonso's narrative also offers no evidence to suggest that his identification with Lila qualifies him as a *femminiello*, the hermaphroditic figure to whom Neapolitan tradition has granted social legitimacy and even the status of conferring good luck. The origin of the *femminielli* dates back to their role in cult rituals that derive from classical Greek mythology. In Ferrante's Naples, Alfonso's willed transformation instead appears to be a very personal form of play that turns increasingly perilous. When Elena and Lila, during their simultaneous pregnancies, take him along with them on a shopping excursion, Lila asks Alfonso to model a dress for her, so she can see how it will look on "me" (4:164). His chameleonic act of cross-gender mimicry is so perfect that it leaves Elena speechless: Alfonso becomes a "copy of Lila" and maybe "even handsomer, more beautiful than she" (4:164). Elena's insistence on Alfonso's superlative beauty while in drag foretells the later revelation that he has seduced Michele Solara, who, after years of yearning for Lila, is evidently willing to satisfy his desire with "a shadow of a shadow" (4:167). As a "male-female" type, Alfonso performs an impersonation or "doing" of

Lila that transcends the mere expression of female identification and rein-scribes same-sex desire in the power structure of Naples with almost Machiavellian guile.[35]

What quickly becomes clear is that the neighborhood cannot tolerate Alfonso and Lila's phantasmatic experiments in identification. Lila grows worried that Alfonso has precipitated a dissolving or *smarginatura* of sexual conventions that makes him increasingly likely to break like a "cotton thread" (4:177). When Elena by chance runs into Alfonso and Michele at Basic Sight and finally understands Alfonso's identification as a gay man and furtive affair with Michele, she is surprised by their secrecy even in front of her, a worldly member of the intelligentsia (4:187). Yet the two lovers are surely correct in surmising that Elena, for all her sophistication of learning, has never intuited the truth of Alfonso's sexuality on her own. Alfonso is by no means exempt from the unforgiving rules of the game of gender relations in Southern Italy, however. Soon enough, those rules reassert themselves through the actions of Michele (and perhaps of Marcello and the Solaras' underlings), as Alfonso shows signs of beatings: "a black eye, a split lip" (4:272). He reverts in sadness to his masculine aspect, putting on weight and increasingly coming to resemble his father, Don Achille (4:304). Eventually, he vanishes without warning from Elena and Lila's view, and his disappearance chillingly anticipates the sudden, enigmatic loss of Lila and Enzo's young daughter, Tina. When Alfonso's body finally washes up on the beach at Coroglio, on the side of Posillipo where Elena learned to swim as a girl, the two friends are overwhelmed by grief. Alfonso, it becomes clear, was beaten senseless and thrown into the sea, suffering a tragic death that redirects the trajectory of the narrative. At first, Elena seems to hold Lila responsible for their friend's murder, suggesting that she goaded him into ever riskier transgressions: "Lila's fault, I thought in the heat of the moment: with her mania for forcing others by mixing everything up, she overwhelmed him" (4:304–5). On seeing Lila collapse in sorrow, however, she rapidly changes her mind: "Between her and Alfonso there must have been a more complex relationship than I had imagined. She must have looked at him as at a mirror and seen herself in him and had wanted to draw out of his body a part of herself. The complete opposite, I thought uneasily, of what I had narrated in my second book" (4:305). By encouraging Alfonso's performances of gender, Lila ultimately teaches Elena to recognize her own blind spot as a feminist, her narrow idea of who a woman is.

As she does in a few other episodes, Elena revises her initial reading of Lila's actions by working through her own resistance to her friend's motivations. In the end, she admits that she herself was unable to grasp the "complex" reality of Lila and Alfonso's singular bond. At the funeral, Lila confronts the Solaras, Michele in particular, whom she holds responsible for Alfonso's death. In return, Michele threatens her with a vow to "take away everything you have," before punching her hard in the face (4:306–7). Reconsidering this scene after Tina goes missing, we may well suspect that Michele's hitting of Lila betrays his responsibility for the little girl's disappearance; ironically, Lila rebuffs his threat at the time by warning him not to touch Enzo or Gennaro, failing to imagine that he may have even Tina in mind. Like an image in the infinite regress between facing mirrors, the uncertainty regarding who is "guilty" of Alfonso's death reflects forward on the mystery of Tina's fate and thus on Lila's eventual withdrawal from Elena. Each loss suffered by the two friends in the quartet raises the ghostly specter of the next.

The importance of Alfonso's story is that it not only makes clear the plight of a gay man in Southern Italy but also helps us envision how solidarity between gay men, women, and other oppressed groups may lead to new forms of freedom, however fleetingly. As Elena belatedly realizes, Alfonso and Lila can express their creative desires together through their friendship in ways that neither can do without the other. Lila confesses her dread of smarginatura to Elena at various points, most conspicuously during the Neapolitan earthquake of 1980. As she describes it, her anxiety does not represent panic brought on by everyday stress so much as a terror of ontological instability. Yet it seems that her preoccupation with the material world's unreliability in some sense frees her to act and speak without fear in the arena of politics. Generally scornful of the results of capitalism in Italy, Lila stands out like a heretic for her readiness to flout society's conventional rules. When Alfonso begins blurring the lines of his own sexuality, Lila, like a female Pygmalion, teaches him to remake himself until he becomes indistinguishable from her. When we consider her role in this episode alongside her influence over Enzo, Nino, and even

Michele and Marcello Solara, we may well conclude that Lila provides the sole example in the narrative of a woman who exerts real power over men. The task of literary criticism that Elena performs in her second book by debunking the myth of man's creation of woman pales in comparison.

ISCHIA

If the passionate friendship that leads to entrustment represents the only real opportunity in the Neapolitan novels for women to reinterpret their gender roles in important and productive ways, Ferrante seems to allow, albeit briefly, the idea that such friendship may encompass the terms of sexual fulfillment for women under some circumstances. This suggestion arises during Elena's second sojourn on Ischia as an adolescent, in the days leading to a fevered love affair between Lila and Nino, which Elena helps them to consummate. The triangular romance that develops on the island between the teenaged Elena, Lila, and Nino for a moment appears to promise happiness through something like "free love," which is to say sexual and romantic gratification that neither conforms to society's norms nor risks self-destruction through transgression. The episode describes an amorous space of transference between the two friends, an emotional domain that in Ischia almost crystallizes into a beautiful utopia of polyamory, as the scholar Massimo Fusillo aptly characterizes it.[36]

On the island, Elena refuses to author a *sceneggiata* (or musical melodrama) of jealousy and betrayal and, even though she herself is in love with Nino, helps Lila to fulfill her desire with him in the name of the two friends' passionate devotion to each other. While at times introducing into her narration a note of jaded melancholy reminiscent of the novels of Françoise Sagan, who wrote *Bonjour Tristesse* (1954) at the age of eighteen, the decision also provides Elena with genuine and meaningful satisfactions. Not only does she recognize that she could "become necessary to both" Lila and Nino (2:241) but she also concludes in the end that "I loved them both" (*li amavo entrambi;* 2:284 EN, 2:284 IT). Elena's resolute declaration of her love for Lila and Nino occurs just a few pages after she observes the difference in Italian between *amare* (to love someone) and *voler bene* (to feel affection or fondness for someone; 2:273). What in fact prompts Elena to notice this distinction is her surprise when Lila uses the more elevated verb, *amare*, in place of the more common expression, *voler bene*, to describe her feelings for Nino. Elena's sensitivity to the nuances of these two terms makes all the more telling her own choice of *amare* to name her love for Lila and Nino instead of *voler bene* to connote a more everyday attachment.

This episode is one of several in the Neapolitan Quartet in which the potential for melodrama is commingled with and ultimately deflected by other possibilities. Spontaneously erupting from a stolen kiss, Lila and Nino's mutual attraction looks to Elena's eyes more like a natural event than conscious deliberation: "It hadn't been a decision, it had happened" (2:237). She, in other words, perceives their relationship as a force along the lines of Goethe's notion of "chemical" attraction, which he dramatizes in his novel, *Elective Affinities* (1809), the title of which Elena in fact invokes, perhaps with a touch of irony, to define her friends' fascination with each other: "In their history there was something intense, sublime: elective affinities" (2:237). The island appears to raise the possibility of experimentation with an open-minded attitude toward sex that readers have come to associate more readily with European artists and intellectuals, as if the trio of Lila, Elena, and Nino could end up in a *ménage à trois* along the lines of *Jules et Jim*, Henri-Pierre Roché's novel about his relationship with both the German writer Franz Hessel and Helen Grund. Yet this idyll of shared love cannot last. Because he has heard rumor of his wife's entanglement with Nino, Stefano soon arrives and beats Lila with unrestrained brutality, prompting Elena to confess that "the excessive violence he repressed behind his polite manners and his meek face terrified me" (2:302). On their return to Naples, the spell cast by the island evaporates, leading Elena to resolve that "from that moment on I would live for myself only" (2:304) and Lila to run away with Nino in a doomed attempt at building a new life that collapses after twenty-three days when he abandons her. The realities of society and culture quickly catch up to the two friends, attaching a dispiriting coda to the dream of shared pleasure that they create on their island retreat.

Chapter Two

WORKING WOMEN

POINTS OF INCOHERENCE

Ferrante's fiction introduces us to a series of women who are in her own words "strong, educated, self-aware" (F 251). Prior to the Neapolitan Quartet, her stories always revolve around middle-class main characters with unambiguous *curricula vitae*. Yet it never seems that work is what gives them happiness, galvanizes them with purpose, or shapes their being. In the author's first novel, *Troubling Love*, Delia is so mesmerized by her mother Amalia that we learn next to nothing about her own job as a cartoonist, which is mentioned only once, toward the end of the book (TL 120).[1] Olga, the protagonist of *The Days of Abandonment*, is not only willful but ruthlessly "vigilant" in circumscribing her "obligatory daily tasks" (TDA 28). As a young woman, she initially answers customer complaints for an airline in Rome and then writes and publishes "a long story set in Naples," but drops both occupations as marriage and motherhood consume her energy, leaving her "reduced to nothing" (TDA 30). When she starts to write again, after her husband leaves her, the activity clearly becomes another occasion for pragmatic vigilance, rather than for gratification of artistic or intellectual ambition (TDA 162–63). Indeed, she manages to make ends meet by handling international correspondence for a car rental agency in Turin.

Given her skepticism toward the dignifying ideal of labor, Ferrante's feminism cannot be described as ready-made for contemporary readers. At the same time, we cannot characterize her attitude as either premodern or resembling that of first-generation feminists. As I note in the previous chapter, Olga defies the example not only of the poverella, the ghostly figure of the forsaken woman from her childhood in Naples, but also the lachrymose paradigm of women's victimization by men that Simone de Beauvoir developed in her collection of short stories, *The Woman Destroyed* (1967). Thanks to her critical intelligence and self-awareness, Olga eventually fashions for herself a different, more ambiguous fate. Leda in *The Lost Daughter* holds the job of a professor of literature, but her erratic early career suggests ambivalence and even her mature responsibilities are modest, offering readers few clues as to her true ambitions. On the evidence of these examples, it may seem somewhat incongruous that Ferrante's Neapolitan novels strike such a chord with readers, especially in the U.S. Feminism of the popular sort increasingly ties itself to a neoliberal agenda that inevitably regards a woman's profession as the justification of her existence. For Ferrante, however, work in the sense of one's job does not in and of itself ennoble her characters' lives. Why, then, do Ferrante's readers feel that her books are so irresistible, that her writings speak so compellingly to them? This question casts a long shadow over the epic chronicle of Elena and Lila's friendship.

What makes the subject of work so compelling in her novels in other words is Ferrante's willingness to disrupt the paradigm according to which women must seek their fulfillment in work, thereby affirming through their ambition the supposed historical victory of capitalism. In the Neapolitan Quartet, Elena's narrative undermines the celebratory view of work as a means to happiness with unmistakable pointedness, especially when we consider the symbolic correspondences between her story and its antecedents in German literature. We may believe at first glance that her success as a writer in fact exemplifies the social ascent that the invisible hand of the market holds out like a gift, yet the Faustian pact that enables her advancement introduces a fundamental feeling of ambivalence and an eventual sense of defeat into her opinion of her own achievements. She becomes an author only thanks to the Mephistophelean influence of Lila and, as is the case with Goethe's Faust and the protagonist of Thomas Mann's *Doctor Faustus*, Adrian Leverkühn, the bargain that Elena strikes with Lila comes at a high price.

As telling as the arc of Elena's life may be, Lila's own destiny proves no less exemplary as a point of departure for criticizing the capitalist idealization of work and also recalls a form of life that derives from a German cultural source. When she needs to make money after her affair with Nino collapses and she moves to San Giovanni a Teduccio with Enzo, Lila takes a job requiring manual labor at the Soccavo salami factory, where she encounters brutally dangerous working conditions and suffers abuse at the hands of both managers and coworkers. Exhausted by the degradation of the factory, she magically transforms herself into a virtuosic computer programmer and entrepreneur, only to renounce without a moment's hesitation the software company that she starts with Enzo. Her final metamorphosis into a reclusive scholar, who alternates between days shut in the Biblioteca Nazionale and nights wandering the streets of Naples to learn the city's history by heart, seems oddly fitting. As I contend at greater length in chapter 4, "*Genius Loci*," both Lila's studious vocation and Elena's conviction that Lila's researches will yield the definitive chronicle of Naples call to mind the figure of Walter Benjamin and the fixation of his devotees with his never-finished project on the *passages couverts* of Paris. Consideration of the Faustian allegory that imbues the Neapolitan Quartet as a whole adds a further irony. For at the end of the saga, we discover that it is Mephistopheles's turn rather than Faust's to acquire knowledge through an unbearable loss.

It is true that the Neapolitan novels brim with images of women and men at work. Glimpses of blue- and white-collar workers, pastry chefs, dressmakers, teachers and professors, writers and editors, sales clerks, gas station attendants, and even computer programmers crowd Ferrante's pages. In one sense, it seems like the author sets out to write a phenomenology of contemporary labor from its most mind-numbing to its most creative aspects. In another sense, the characters' jobs as such never seem truly enough to absorb or define them, to explain their most important choices. This is evident for Lila in particular. She develops and loses enthusiasm for new challenges with equal abandon, concluding with each new accomplishment, according to Elena, that "she doesn't care about it anymore" (2:315). Lila's anarchic spirit, her Mephistophelian personality as a "waggish knave," clearly manifests itself in her indifference to work as a means to an end. Her genius comes to life in the scholarly pursuit of knowledge as a schoolgirl at the start of the saga and as a middle-aged woman at its end, when she devotes herself to studying Naples's cultural and historical treasures in the Biblioteca Nazionale. Only half surprisingly, her true mission in life turns out to be that of vita contemplativa.

Ferrante's protagonists may be said to affirm an original, creative mode of feminism, in other words. Rather than equate their emancipation with higher wages as supposedly feminist neoliberals do, her characters relish exercising their intellectual and imaginative freedom in ways that call into question the conventional identification of a woman's life with her job. Given Elena and Lila's shared love of intellectual competition as young girls in *My Brilliant Friend*, we may expect the question of work to play a pivotal role in their lives and in any feminist interpretation of their stories. By the time we reach the conclusion of *The Story of the Lost Child*, however, we realize that this problem ultimately occupies an ambivalent space in the Neapolitan Quartet, a territory that for both Elena and Lila becomes increasingly confining over the course of the saga.

The author in fact does not treat the topic as an important focus of her two main characters' psychological energies, dedicating more attention to Lila and Elena's friendships, loves, family relations, and even political loyalties. Yet the emphasis never appears to be linked to nostalgia for a bygone era or apathy toward the marginalization of women in Southern Italian culture. *Pace* Vivian Gornick, who has proclaimed the demise of the novel of love in contemporary literature, Ferrante explores the possibility of the genre's reinvention in her oeuvre.[2] It is all the more significant, then, that the heroines of her narratives find little possibility of harmony between love and career. Mostly relegated to the background of the characters' thoughts and concerns, labor does not represent for them a means of redeeming their circumstances. This disenchanted view of their employment does not signal a premodern wish to deny the socioeconomic disadvantages faced by women, but rather critical wariness regarding the bromides that we typically attach to such inequities.

Ferrante's feminism, we should observe, is never ideologically straightforward or clear-cut. When Elena tries to explain her own zeal for the ideas of radical feminist theorists such as Carla Lonzi, Lila comically responds in Neapolitan dialect with a vulgarity (3:282). Yet as a schoolgirl, Lila ferociously defends Elena from the threatening attentions of the much bigger Marcello Solara by holding a knife to his throat, thus supplying the most electrifying image of solidarity between women in the quartet (1:135). If Ferrante's exact gender politics remains an open question beyond her acknowledged sympathy for Italian difference feminism of the 1970s (F 59, 77), the author's elusive point of view bespeaks not apathy toward feminist concerns but rather a conviction that women's fight for genuine emotional and political freedom entails far more provisional victories than those resulting from any theoretical skirmish. In one of the interviews collected in *Frantumaglia*, Ferrante astutely voices this conviction as a preference for "points of incoherence" over "the linearity of militant causes" (F 309).

When the teenaged Elena learns that Nino, after passing his high school exams, has gone to England to travel and learn the language, she excitedly asks Lila why he can feel free to follow his impulses while young women like the two of them cannot (2:106). Lila, however, seems unmoved by the prospect of such adventure. Symbolic equality holds little appeal for her, as she seems more aware than Elena that for women the real cost of acquiring cultural capital too often tends to be violence suffered at the hands of men. When Michele Solara reveals his ownership of the Soccavo factory where Lila has endured extremes of abuse merely to hold a job, he taunts her by comparing her unfavorably to a woman whom he claims to have taught how to whistle after a two-hour liaison, because, as he puts it, "a real man can make a woman do everything" (3:169). Lila surmises that he has staged her hiring at the factory in order to keep her in a subaltern position—that he wishes to control her, because he thinks she possesses a "power [that] is indispensable to him" (3:167)—and rebuffs him with the contemptuous reply, "I've known how to whistle since I was five years old" (3:170).

By contrast, the person whom Lila most admires is Elena's eventual ex-husband, Pietro, because he appears to have read "a hundred thousand" books yet speaks without the stiffness of a text (4:266). We might think that Lila's liking for Pietro represents a transference of old feelings for Nino, with whom she had "lively discussions" in which all her thoughts found voice (2:358). Yet Pietro has none of Nino's narcissism or worldly ambition. Even after Elena and Pietro's divorce and Tina's disappearance, Lila confides to him alone that she has devoted herself in her middle age to studying Naples in the Biblioteca Nazionale. That she discovers in this scholarly occupation a new calling or what Pietro calls a way "to engage her mind" (4:395) may strike us initially as surprising. In fact, however, her intellectual reawakening provides a horizon in which to understand the precise itinerary of Lila and Elena's relationships to work, culture, and each other.

LAZZARELLA

Naples's problematic cultural mythology may be said to hinge on the figure of the *lazzaro* or *lazzarone*, which emerges during the era of the revolt against Habsburg Spain led by Tommaso Aniello, who was popularly known as "Masaniello," in the seventeenth century. Benedetto Croce proposes in an essay written in 1895 that the name derives from the Spanish *laceria*, connoting both "leprosy" and "misery." Moreover, he notes that the term applied generally to Neapolitans of the lowest plebeian ranks, designating a character of anarchy, rebellion, and laziness that was viewed as not only an economic but also a psychological affliction.[3] On a more positive note, the *lazzaro* also was associated with a joyful cynicism and wily flair for improvisation. The word even makes an appearance in Hegel's *Elements of the Philosophy of Right* (1820), where the German philosopher invoked it as a term of censure for the shiftlessness of men who resign themselves to chance, shunning work like the *lazzaroni* of Naples.[4]

Not all German intellectuals, however, were so quick to embrace this stereotype of the idle Neapolitan. Goethe, for example, offered quite the opposite view of the city and its people. In the account of his travels through Italy between 1786 and 1788, which he published under the title *Italian Journey* (*Italienische Reise*, 1816–1817), he emphatically rejects the northern prejudice against Southern Italians, arguing that what counts in Naples is not material production so much as the spirit of industriousness (*operosità*). In an entry on the city dated May 28, 1787, he declares that *lazzaroni* do not work merely to endure but rather to enjoy life and adds that they often perform a task as if business were a sport.[5] He furthermore explains Neapolitans' notorious lack of planning as a result of the city's felicitous natural situation, maintaining that the warm and fertile climate encourages improvisation.

As we might expect of a novelist whose understanding of the historical intersection of German and Neapolitan culture is as sophisticated as Anita Raja's, Ferrante takes a discerning position on the question of the lazzarone, apparently sympathizing more with the Goethean than the

Hegelian notion while being careful not to romanticize her portrayal of Naples's working class. In the rione of Elena and Lila's childhood, both men and women have to work hard if they wish to survive and, as a result, grow old and tired before their time. Melina's husband may have died of "weariness" from unloading fruit baskets at the market, and Melina, who cleans the stairways of the buildings in the neighborhood, has the gray hair of an "old woman" by the age of thirty (1:38). Elena's grandfather dies after falling from a scaffolding at a building site, while her friend Pasquale Peluso's grandfather is missing an arm from an accident with a lathe (1:32). Even before we encounter the cruelty of the Soccavo factory in *The Story of a New Name* and *Those Who Leave and Those Who Stay*, we find many examples in the quartet of the relentless struggles of the people of Naples to eke out a living. Enzo Scanno, who eventually becomes Lila's companion, epitomizes the fortitude of the blue-collar laborer, starting in childhood to sell fruits and vegetables from a cart, rising before dawn every day, braving the streets in every season and type of weather, and even fending off threats from the Camorra (1:148). His body becomes strong and compact from the relentless grind of his trade. Despite his obvious intelligence when it comes to math, the class prejudice of Italy's educational system forces him to drop out of school. As an adult he nevertheless persists in studying both on his own and through nightly conversations with Lila, eventually managing to refashion himself into a computer systems engineer working on IBM mainframes (3:262). The effort of will required to establish a successful career, however, leaves him in a state of nearly mute indifference to small talk and everyday social exchanges. When Elena mentions in *The Story of the Lost Child* that he "spoke a lot to his daughter, and often sang to her" (4:265), we may feel a pang of surprise at the revelation of Enzo's tender volubility with Tina.

If any character resembles the figure of the lazzarone in the Neapolitan Quartet, it is Lila. In many respects, she embodies the lack of constancy, genius for improvisation, playfulness with respect to work, and rebellious impulses that are typical of lazzaroni, especially in their more positive, Goethian instances. It is hardly coincidental that, at her wedding dinner, the band plays the popular song "Lazzarella," which relates the story of an amorous female incarnation of the archetypally male Neapolitan rogue (1:330). After forcing Lila for financial reasons to abandon her schooling at the age of ten despite her evident intellectual genius, her father sends her to a trade school to learn a hodgepodge of "stenography, bookkeeping, home economics," but she mutinies against the tediousness of the curriculum and flunks out within a year (1:91). She nevertheless quickly embraces a new project, namely the design of an unprecedented style of shoe that for a time enriches her family's fortunes and places her own creative brilliance in an entirely different light.

"The Story of the Shoes," as Ferrante herself calls it in the subtitle of the second section of *My Brilliant Friend*, reads like a modern-day fairy tale. The subplot pointedly inverts the gender roles of the myth of Cinderella by depicting a chain of male characters that includes Lila's father Fernando, Stefano, Antonio, and Marcello Solara all trying to fit into the fabulously lightweight shoes designed by Lila. Moreover, Lila in this retelling of the legend symbolically metamorphoses not into a princess but rather into the figure of an inventor, a sort of female *homo faber*. She suggests a Cinderella-like ability to overcome her lowly class origins, but on the strength of sheer ingenuity rather than a long-hidden secret of birth. As I observe in chapter 3 in relation to the question of subalternity, the neighborhood's residents generally address Fernando by means of the disparaging epithet of *scarparo* (e.g., 1:61 EN, 1:100 IT). In fact, he is the only character in *My Brilliant Friend* whose profession is designated with a name in vulgar Neapolitan dialect rather than with a synonym in standard Italian such as *calzolaio* or the humbler *ciabattino*. In *The Story of a New Name*, Fernando in fact graduates to the more respectable *calzolaio*, but both Lila and Rino end up tagged with the dismissive label of *scarpari*. *Scarparo*, we should note, has a derogatory connotation in Neapolitan insofar as the noun signifies someone who performs a job without suitable preparation or professionalism. The fact that the term so closely resembles in morphology the Italian word for "shoe" (*scarpa*) itself appears to enact a kind of lexical laziness, which is to say a failure of imagination. However, there is nothing slapdash or dull-witted when it comes to Lila's shoe designs. She draws patterns from which she and Rino craft men's shoes that, as their father is forced to admit, turn out to be magically "light but also strong" (1:181), eventually persuading Stefano to invest in their manufacture. Commerce in this case derives immediately from creative vision. What makes the business possible is Lila's force of invention. By transforming the menial labor of shoe repair performed by her father into a profitable line of work making beautiful goods out of original ideas, Lila infuses the family livelihood with the value of craftwork and even that of art.[6]

Rino has none of her talent for innovation but supports Lila because he recognizes her gifts, albeit at times with some envy. By contrast, Fernando for a long time angrily resists her influence, as he suffers from a reflexive fatalism about his life and occupation that amounts to little more than lack of nerve. As a young man, he briefly ran away from the cobbler's shop owned by his grandfather to work in a factory in Casoria where he learned how to use the machines required for mass production. Although he pursued this adventure out of a youthful longing "to be free," he soon returned to the quiet and soothing familiarity of the family shop (1:98). His violence toward Lila, whom he throws out of a window of the family's apartment when she is ten, erupts with particular ferocity during the period when she turns "unreasonable and mean" because she has to give up her education (1:80). Clearly, Fernando grows furious at his daughter because of her dissatisfaction with the family's self-imposed limitations, which we may surmise aggravates his feeling of shame at settling for less when he was young and renouncing all hope of progress. Elena's narration of the episode, which culminates in Lila's breaking her arm after being flung through the window, compares the logic of Fernando and Lila's clash of wills to arguments between Elena's own parents over money, while distinguishing Fernando's excessive degree of anger with the observation that "his rage fed on itself" (1:82). The narrator's account, in other words, helps to illuminate the psychology of men and women who are relegated to subaltern social classes as well as the symbolic importance of work within this emotional order.

As a result of Stefano's investment, Lila is able to give "slow, elaborate, rancorous birth" to the dream of Cerullo shoes, but this birth comes at a horrific cost (1:287). When she sees the shoes as a finished product for the first time, she feels a surge of emotion "as if a fairy had appeared" to make her wish come true (1:304). Pinuccia also calls attention to the shoes' magical strangeness by praising in paradoxical terms the "sturdy lightness" and "dissonant harmony" of their design (1:304). Her response hints at the shock value that avant-garde or nonconformist thinking possesses for the people of the neighborhood. The shock is all the greater when such thinking cannily grasps the desires of "the wealthy, those who casually

reached for their wallets," as Elena puts it when she reports on the shoes'
eventual commercial triumph (2:138). Lila's shoes indeed have to be sold
in the posh district of Piazza dei Martiri because they cannot be mar-
keted in the rione, despite Fernando's attempts to normalize their design
by adding ridiculous, clichéd embellishments such as visible stitching, a
gilded pin, and fringe: "Even with Fernando's modifications, they were
the shoes of our childish dreams, not invented for the reality of the neighborhood" (1:305). The opening of a store in the Piazza dei Martiri, however, necessitates the Solaras's involvement in its financing, which in turn
means that "Solara" displaces the name "Cerullo" on the storefront, effectively bringing to an end the era of childish reveries (2:127). When Lila
realizes the degree to which Rino and Stefano have put themselves in debt
to the Solaras, she tells Rino "from now on, every man for himself" and
provocatively walks around the piazza with Michele Solara "in a playfully
flirtatious way" to reassert the sway that she holds in the world of adult
negotiations (2:128). Immediately after her promenade with Michele,
however, she has to shut herself in the bathroom of the shop. When she
emerges looking "very pale," Lila admits to Elena that she has lost blood
because the unborn child with Stefano that she has been carrying has
died in her womb (2:128).

After being disappointed by Rino and Stefano and suffering the loss of
her pregnancy, Lila loses enthusiasm for developing new shoe styles and
irrevocably breaks with the enterprise. Elena explains this turn of events
to Pinuccia by insisting on their friend's volatility: "Lina gets curious
about a thing and she's utterly caught up in it. But once she's done it, the
desire goes away, she doesn't care about it anymore" (2:315). This summary,
however, too hastily glosses over Lila's true state of mind. When Michele
tells Stefano that Lila must take on the responsibility of designing new
"chic" models for the store in Piazza dei Martiri, she flatly refuses, vowing
"that she wouldn't design anything, not even a sandal, not even a slipper"
(2:142). Discussing her decision with Elena, Lila confesses that her family's
newfound prosperity has brought with it a disturbing sense of estrangement not only from the satisfactions of the work itself but even from each
other and from their friends.

> The shoes . . . had come out of her brain only that one time. . . . That game
> was over, she didn't know how to start it again. . . . And then everything

had changed. Fernando's small shop had been consumed by the new spaces, by the workers' benches, by three machines. Her father had as it were grown smaller, he didn't even quarrel with his oldest son, he worked and that was all. Even affections were as if deflated . . . she could no longer feel the bond with Rino. Ruined, broken. The need to help and protect him had diminished. Thus the motivations for the fantasy of the shoes had vanished, the soil in which they had germinated was arid.

(2:143)

That Lila uses the word *gioco*, or "game," to describe the project of devising Cerullo shoes makes clear how much weight she gives to the results of her own labor. For her, the purpose of the venture was neither to amass riches beyond what was needed for her family's well-being nor to see her ideas realized on the scale of mass commerce. Lila's hope was to find a means of self-expression that in fact might strengthen the ties between herself and her community, might enlarge rather than reduce her affections. In this light, her penchant for elegant forms of inoperativity, her affinity for modes of playing rather than of working, may be understood as a poignant reaffirmation of the conclusion that she reached as a little girl on reading the *Aeneid* that without love the life of a city and those who inhabit it grows barren (1:160).

If designing luxury goods loses its thrill for Lila, she eventually abandons the game because she comes to regard it as empty of social meaning. Her brief stint as a shoemaker thus conjures up the rags-to-riches stories of many historical Italian fashion moguls while at the same time debunking the uncritical celebration of their achievement as capitalists. As I note in chapter 4, *"Genius Loci,"* the shoe designer whose fame is linked most conspicuously to Naples and especially to the Piazza dei Martiri is Salvatore Ferragamo. Ferragamo was born in 1898 into a poor family in the Neapolitan area and studied shoemaking in Naples before emigrating at first to Boston and then to California, where he built a lucrative business as Hollywood's preferred "Shoemaker to the Stars." After cultivating his reputation in the U.S., he returned to Italy to set up his company's operations in Florence in 1927, which over the years grew to include, among many other locations throughout Italy, two boutiques in the Piazza dei Martiri: a store for women at number 56 and a store for men at number 60. "The Story of the Shoes" in the Neapolitan Quartet easily could have adhered to a narrative structure more closely resembling Ferragamo's life and career. Ferrante, however, carefully resists the urge to fulfill the fairy-tale promise of this subplot by invoking a readily available historical model. Lila's entry into the world of fashion does not catapult her to the heights of glamour and affluence, and the moral of her story is not that making money leads to emancipation. Although she eventually becomes a self-made woman by founding a profitable software start-up called Basic Sight, she proves willing to give up all her gains with a casual gesture when, a few years after Tina's disappearance, she tells Elena simply that "she didn't want to work anymore" (4:379).

In the days surrounding the death of her unborn child, Lila shows a flair for orchestrating to proper effect all the businesses in which her in-laws, the Carraccis, are involved: the old grocery from which they first turn a profit, the new grocery with which they hope to add to their means, and the shoe salon in Piazza dei Martiri in which they take a stake with the Solaras. Yet no matter how much she throws herself into these pur-suits, she cannot seem to shake off "an increasingly ungovernable unhap-piness" (2:145). For a while, she works as a sales clerk in the old grocery, where Stefano shows her how to cheat customers by manipulating the scale. Although she fumes at him for his dishonesty, she cannot restrain her competitive impulses and starts to concoct new ways to deceive their clients (2:144). At the age of seventeen, she rearranges the new grocery and the store in Piazza dei Martiri to make everything "easier and more effi-cient," gaining control to the point that she can tell Stefano to give Ada a bigger, higher-paid role (2:109). She freely takes cash from the register to help Pasquale pay for dental work, to give Antonio support as he enters the army, and to buy Elena the textbooks she needs for school, handing out cash among her friends like "waste paper" (2:110–11). After losing her baby, Lila dedicates herself to seeing that the new grocery thrives, assuring that "by Christmastime the profits had risen and within a few months sur-passed those of the grocery in the old neighborhood" (2:129).

Even when bringing "disorder to Piazza dei Martiri" by intervening in preparations for the opening of the shoe store, Lila wins the endorsement of Michele Solara, who "seemed to grasp most readily the advantages of Lila's suggestions" and only half-jokingly claims he will pay her to reno-vate the Bar Solara too (2:108). Michele's appreciation in due course grows into the certitude that she is the person best suited to run the business and, after some negotiation, Lila accepts the Solaras's offer to manage the shop. She makes changes to its decor and sets a different tone when dealing with customers, inventing in the process what we might call a "concept store," which promotes its own site-specific, material mise-en-scène rather than a list of products: "She devoted herself to the new job. And soon sales rose sharply. The shop became a place where people went to buy, but also to chat with that lively, very pretty young woman, whose conversation sparkled, who kept books among the shoes, who read those books, and who, moreover, never seemed to want to sell Cerullo shoes or Solara shoes" (2:348). Lila's preference for chatting with visitors over hawking shoes is less a refined sales method than a reflection of her desire to create something unique and her indifference to the bottom line. Yet as she decorates the walls with abstract paintings and lines some shelves with books, creating a luxurious space with paintings from a gallery in Chiatamone, she winds up—almost in spite of herself—enlivening the boutique's appeal and enriching its profitability like a charm (2:345).

LILA MAKES A LIVING

In a letter written by Ferrante in 1998, six years after the publication of *Troubling Love*, reprinted in *Frantumaglia*, the author explains to her editor, Sandra Ozzola, why she has not succeeded in delivering a promised novel revolving around the life of a working-class woman. Responding to Ozzola's proposed titles for the new book, Ferrante declares a preference for "Working Women" (*le lavoranti*) over the alternative of "Women Workers" (*le lavoratrici*) (F 72). She confesses to struggling with the beginning of every new project until her fragmentary efforts gather strength and coalesce. From this tipping point "a time of intense enjoyment" ensues in which the characters spring to life and the plot seems "inevitable, definitive" before she finishes her composition and faces the fear that "nothing is written as you had imagined it" (F 73–74).

This fright at the prospect of losing control over her creation is the state in which she finds herself reflecting on the manuscript of "Working Women." She asks Ozzola for help in finding examples of novels that depict women's mental and physical exertion as the object of an obsessive, frequently hostile male gaze: "Are there any? If you have any title in mind—it does not matter if it is a good book or junk—write to me. I doubt

that work ennobles man and I am absolutely certain that it does not ennoble woman. So the novel is centered on the hardship of working, on the
horror implicit in the necessity of earning a living, an expression in itself
abominable" (F 74). Ferrante strikes an ironic note here when she differen-
tiates between the supposedly exalting effects of labor on man and on
woman. The assertion "work ennobles man" in fact cites a proverb in Italian that evidently advances a claim of universality or gender neutrality for
the noun *man,* treating it as a synonym of terms such as *person* or *human
being.*[7] By reminding her reader that the toil of making ends meet means
different things to the two genders, the author exposes the presumption
and undermines any naive idealization of work.[8] That women suffer cru-
eler degradation than men in the economy of power regulating the work-
force is a point that she drives home in *The Story of a New Name* and *Those
Who Leave and Those Who Stay,* when Lila has to find a way to make a
living after fleeing with Enzo and Gennaro to San Giovanni a Teduccio.
For philosophically minded readers, Ferrante's argument may recall the
position of Hannah Arendt, who raises the question why society tells us
that "whatever we do, we are supposed to do for the sake of 'making a living,'" thus reducing "all serious activities" to the lowest common denomi-
nator of sheer survival.[9]

Ferrante's anxiety regarding the fate of "Working Women" suggests
that its subject matter is of particular interest to her, even if she cannot
bring herself to share with the public a story that her editor seems ready to
publish. To justify her failure to send Ozzola the manuscript, she wavers
between claiming to have detected some trace of "editorial disappointment" with the contents of the book and worrying that it is too long (F 72).
Nevertheless, the author declares that she has written the novel "because it
has to do with me," adding that she "was inside it for a long time" and, as
she made progress, "kept shortening the distance between the protagonist
and me" (F 72). Ferrante's avowed personal identification with the heroine
of "Working Women" offers a clue as to what is at stake in the Neapolitan
Quartet's most sustained exploration of the injustices that proletarian
women routinely face, namely the episode of Lila's employment at the Soccavo salami factory. This long segment is one of only a small handful of
incidents that the novelist had in mind when she first set out to chronicle
Lila and Elena's friendship: "I always knew the end of the story, and I knew
some central episodes very well—Lila's wedding, the adultery on Ischia,

the work in the factory, the lost daughter—but the rest was a surprising and demanding gift" (F 253). Why, we may ask, is the tale of Lila's factory job so important to the author's project? Unlike the other elements from which Ferrante began constructing the narrative, Lila's ordeal at the meat-processing plant on first glance may not look like an obvious symbolic or dramatic turning point in the storyline. Yet the account of her experience in the industrial workplace represents one of the central strands from which the novelist weaves the fabric of events and characters that comprises the larger tetralogy.

When Lila starts working at the plant, her responsibilities degenerate from the artisanal and entrepreneurial pursuits of the shop in Piazza dei Martiri to the menial and hazardous tasks of meat production, imposing on her a slavelike subalternity in exchange for a way to keep herself and her family alive.[10] The facility represents a kind of industrialized, modern reinterpretation of Dante's Inferno replete with divisions that make up its own distinct circles of hell: the sausage-stuffing department (*insaccatura;* 2:460 EN, 2:459 IT), the mixing department (*impastatoio;* 2:461 EN, 2:459 IT), the storerooms (*celle;* 2:461 EN, 2:459 IT), the seasoning room (*stagionatura;* 3:111 EN, 3:96 IT), the drying room (*essiccataio;* 3:112 EN, 3:97 IT), the vat room (*piscine;* 3:112 EN, 3: 98 IT), the refrigerated rooms (*celle frigorifere;* 3:121 EN, 3:106 IT), and the gutting section (*spolpatoio;* 3:124 EN, 3:109 IT). Like Naples' Palazzo dei Granili, which, according to Anna Maria Ortese in her essay "The Involuntary City," gave homeless families during World War II a bombed-out ruin in which to squat, the Soccavo salami factory embodies for its occupants the involuntary reduction of life to little more than animal subsistence.[11] The brutal conditions that the site inflicts on employees are even worse for women, as they become objects of sexual harassment and abuse on its premises. With decisive bluntness, Lila articulates the rule that determines the operation of the factory and behavior of its workers: "The union has never gone in and the workers are nothing but poor victims of blackmail, dependent on the law of the owner, that is: I pay you and so I possess you and I possess your life, your family, and everything that surrounds you, and if you don't do as I say I'll ruin you" (3:122).

When Elena travels across town to reach Lila in San Giovanni a Teduccio, she discovers that the very commute itself amounts to an infernal assault and, as the noise, chaos, and aggravation on her bus ride persist, finds herself regressing to "the most violent dialect of the neighborhood"

with her fellow passengers (2:456). Shortly after reaching the grim building
where Lila lives with Enzo, she notices that Lila's young son Gennaro similarly drops "a nasty insult in dialect" when talking to a playmate (2:459).
As readers, we may infer from Elena's observation that Lila, who pictured
herself, when Gennaro was little, running a day school not only for him
but also for the other children of the rione, has lost the imaginative energy
that animated her maternal interest in his education. If motherhood may
be regarded in some sense as a job, Lila sadly fails the test of its ongoing
demands, losing enthusiasm for the care of her son over time as she does
with other occupations.

Elena's journey on foot from the building where Lila lives with Enzo to
the Soccavo factory is even more nightmarish than the bus ride to their
district, taking her through a sordid landscape of garbage piles, the repugnant odor of animal fat, and open bonfires. It takes her a while to track
down Lila, whom the management constantly orders from one post to
another in an attempt to wear down her resolve. When she at last finds her
friend working in the refrigerator rooms, Elena notes with distress how
many traces of violence the drudgeries of the plant have left on Lila's body:
"I was struck by the swelling of the hands and the wounds, cuts old and
new, a fresh one on the thumb of her left hand whose edges were inflamed,
and I could imagine that under the bandage on her right hand she had an
even worse injury" (2:463). This observation may be said to mark the point
of greatest divergence in the story between the two friends' respective fortunes. After having completed her college degree at the Scuola Normale in
Pisa, Elena has gotten engaged to Pietro, entered into his family's revered
and influential circle, and received the news that her first novel has been
accepted for publication. By contrast, Lila has been abandoned by her lover
Nino, fled in turn from her husband Stefano, and resigned herself to the
punishing afflictions of her job at the factory. When the two friends come
face-to-face, Elena does not dare to embrace Lila for fear that her body will
"crumble" (2:462). Instead, Lila hugs Elena "for long minutes" and, when
she blurts out the news of her book, takes her hand and kisses it on the
back and palm in a singular gesture of affection that Elena barely registers
due to her shock at the sight of the scars on Lila's own hands (2:462–63).

After telling her friend of the start of her literary career, Elena restores
to Lila her schoolgirl manuscript, "The Blue Fairy," which Elena has recovered from their teacher Maestra Oliviero, confessing that the novel she is

about to publish was inspired by the "book" that Lila wrote when they were ten years old (2:463–64). Lila replies with typical bluntness that if this is true, then her publisher is crazy. On the face of it, Elena's claim indeed sounds somewhat naive. As readers, we may find it hard to imagine how the two works are linked to each other insofar as we have no clue as to the plot of Lila's fairy tale, while we do know that Elena's fiction is based on what happened during her encounters with Donato Sorratore on Ischia (2:433). Yet Elena asserts that "Lila's childish pages were the secret heart of my book" (2:455) and unequivocally tells her friend that "the story is still beautiful today . . . I read it again and discovered that, without realizing it, I've always had it in my mind" (2:464). Elena's stress on the unconscious nature of her attachment to "The Blue Fairy" makes clear that she regards their friendship as an instinctively structuring, productive bond, which for her possesses the thickness of a family relationship rather than the hollowness of a voluntary arrangement. Lila by contrast betrays no emotion when Elena gives her back her girlish composition. The two friends' reunion, as Elena admits, is deprived of the luxury of "tears . . . confidences and reconciliation" that she had imagined for them (2:464). She does not have time to tell Lila about either her sexual assault by Donato Sorratore or her engagement to Pietro. Yet in spite of the dismal circumstances, such as the stink of fat and constant pestering by managers, Lila entices Elena into giddily playful discussion of their "foolish adventures": "Time simply slipped away without any meaning and it was good just . . . to hear the mad sound of the brain of one echo in the mad sound of the brain of the other" (2:467). When Elena and Lila finally part, we witness their most open avowal of reciprocal attachment in the saga, as each declares she does not want to lose the other. While walking away in "great agitation," Elena turns back to wave at Lila, whose factory smock transforms her into a shapeless figure, and sees her leafing through the pages of "The Blue Fairy" before tossing them into a nearby bonfire (2:467).

That Lila shows little interest in the romantic dreams of her childhood ought to come as no surprise, given the reality of her harassment by Bruno Soccavo and the other men at the plant and, to borrow her own term, the "dissolving boundaries" of her self-confidence under their attacks. Soccavo demeans her from the first moment of their accidental reunion on the street in San Giovanni a Teduccio, asking repeatedly if she "really" has separated from Stefano and, when she makes clear that she needs a job, scribbling a note on a napkin in a café rather than arranging for a letter of employment (2:446–47). Soon after she starts to work at the facility, he summons her to the seasoning room and, while babbling about how the smell of drying salamis reminds him of the odor of sex, grabs hold of her and tries to force himself on her "in an exploration without pleasure, a pure intrusive desire" (3:112). Braving his unwanted attentions, Lila is reminded of Stefano's fits of violence against her and "for several seconds . . . felt annihilated" until she starts hitting Soccavo in the face and between the legs and compels him to retreat (3:112). Although he does not further assault her, he authorizes the factory supervisors to retaliate by perpetually moving her between stations, goading her to the point of exhaustion, and bullying her with verbal obscenities (3:113). Despite the harassment, Lila continues to work "extremely hard" (3:124) and musters her "usual efficiency" in fulfilling all her duties (3:135).

While working at the factory, Lila falls in again with her old schoolmate Pasquale Peluso, who has become active in the efforts of the Italian Communist Party (Partito Comunista Italiano or PCI) to unionize workers. He retains much of his childhood admiration for her dynamic personality: "There is no woman like you, you throw yourself into life with a force that, if we all had it, the world would have changed a long time ago" (3:115). She in turn becomes interested despite herself in his brand of "angry activism" (3:116). When she joins the union, she does so grudgingly and with no greater aim than to affront Soccavo, yet while her initial motivations may be muddled, her ultimate political views and actions are not. Accompanying Pasquale and Enzo one night to a PCI committee meeting on Via dei Tribunali, she gives a speech castigating the participants' ignorance of how real people live and work yet winds up winning over her audience, which mostly consists of students, through sheer eloquence. One of her admirers turns out to be Professor Galiani's daughter, Nadia, who strikes her as the sort of poseur that means well in abstract but "in the concrete couldn't understand a thing" (3:123).

Lila's entanglement in the alliance between young, petit bourgeois radicals and the working women and men with whom they have nothing in common mimics the historical tension between participants in the student-led protest movement that swept through Italy in 1968. On March 1, this hostility led to a violent clash at Rome University between protesters and the police, which moved Pier Paolo Pasolini in his poem

"The PCI to the Young!" ("Il PCI ai giovani!") to proclaim greater sympathy for policemen who were the "sons of the poor" (*figli di poveri*) than for students whom he derided as "daddy's boys" (*figli di papà*).[12] Confronting the other meeting attendees, Lila may be said to adopt a view reminiscent of Pasolini's when she declares that she knows nothing of the working class, only something of her fellow factory workers (3:121). To accentuate her distrust of the students, Ferrante italicizes a rare interjection of Lila's thoughts in the first person: "*I know*—it stayed in her head without becoming sound—*I know what a comfortable life full of good intentions means, you can't even imagine what real misery is*" (3:123). Lila thus occupies a position of mediation between two camps. On the one hand, she becomes both a skeptic and a member of the union. On the other, she is both a spokeswoman and a scapegoat for her coworkers, who hate her because she acts "as if the need to work didn't go hand-in-hand with the need to be humiliated" (3:126).

Without her consent, the committee publishes a pamphlet that reproduces her speech verbatim. Trouble soon develops at the plant, as the union organizers encounter fascist hoodlums that Soccavo brings in to protect his business. Under the stress of constant threats, insults, and pay deductions, Lila suffers an extended bout of dissolving boundaries (smarginatura) during which she hallucinates scenes of her humiliation by supervisors, feels her heart pounding violently, and is soaked in cold sweat (3:128–29). She recalls with shame her attempt to placate Soccavo when he accuses her of causing problems: "She felt on her face the pretty little expression she had made when she said to Bruno: *Trust me, I have a small child, I did not do this thing*, a charming affectation, perhaps seductive" (3:129–30). After berating Nadia, her brother Armando, and Pasquale in Professor Galiani's elegant apartment on Corso Vittorio Emanuele for circulating her speech without telling her, Lila decides to document all the factory workers' complaints including the injuries they have sustained to hands, bones, and lungs (3:152). She turns this report into a list of demands for better job conditions, which she delivers to Soccavo and Michele Solara, the latter of whom eventually reveals himself as the true owner of the operation. When the three of them meet in Soccavo's office, Michele pays Lila a compliment, while speaking to Soccavo, that disquietingly blends praise and threat:

You think you hired a worker? It is not true. This woman is much, much more. If you let her, she'll change shit into gold for you, she's capable of reorganizing this whole enterprise, taking it to levels you can't even imagine. Why? Because she has the type of mind that normally no woman has but also that not even we men have. . . . But she has a crazy streak, she thinks she can always do what she wants.

(3:168)

It is telling that Michele delivers these remarks in the grammatical second person to Soccavo. His rhetoric relegates Lila to a marginal position in the third person, outside the circuit of direct discourse between speaker and addressee. While in one sense acknowledging Lila's brilliance, his ambiguous encomium highlights the problem that her genius poses for Italy's misogynist culture. Perceptive as ever, Michele understands that Lila is too intellectually vital to be kept among the ranks of manual laborers. Yet precisely because she has the sort of mind that "not even we men have," she violates the norm of women's presumed mental inferiority in Neapolitan society. Consequently, she must be reminded that her wish to live according to her own judgment represents a punishable "crazy streak" in the eyes of those around her.

The episode recounting Lila's tribulations at the Soccavo factory clearly calls to mind Ferrante's plan for a novel about working women (le lavoranti) as opposed to women workers (le lavoratrici). The distinction that she draws in the letter to Ozzola implies a split between the politics of gender (working *women*) and that of class (women *workers*), ultimately privileging the question of sexuality. Although Lila's allegiance belongs to Pasquale and the union organizers of the PCI rather than to Michele and the fascist mob, her story does not follow what the reader might surmise to be its ideologically expected or conventional trajectory. The Italian gerund *le lavoranti* places emphasis on the femininity of its plural referent while invoking the act of working as a qualifying attribute. The term avoids the specific identification of workers with members of the proletarian class that the noun *le lavoratrici* may connote. If, as she claimed in her letter to Ozzola, Ferrante's purpose in "Working Women" was to "tell a story of women's work obsessively observed by an idle, malicious, sometimes fierce gaze" (F 74), it is fair to say that the episode surrounding Lila's employment at the factory more than fulfills this project. In the environs of the plant, men's mistreatment of women, Lila among them, is constant and pervasive. When Elena asks a man who is repairing a pipe where she can find her friend, he flashes a "malicious smile" and proclaims Lila to be "a pain in the ass" (2:461). Little solidarity exists between workers, and male guards ritually grope "the shy girls" as they leave the facility on the pretense of conducting a bodily search to deter theft called "the partial" (3:127).

The bullying goes hand in hand with an atmosphere of heightened sexuality at the factory, which results from the repetitive, hazardous, and exhausting nature of the work. In such a setting, men "propositioned you if they merely passed by" (3:109). Women at the plant "fell in love," we are told, because love offers them distraction from "the labor and the boredom" (3:110). Both the misogynistic aggression of the men and the overheated amorousness of the women are symptomatic of the displacement or denial of workers' frustrations with the dehumanizing brutality of their jobs: "In the factory—she (Lila) had immediately understood—overwork drove people to want to have sex not with their wife or husband in their own house, where they returned exhausted and empty of desire, but there, at work, morning and afternoon" (3:109). Making things even more sordid, the very goods being produced manifest in abjectly literal terms the laborers' relegation to an animal state of being. Soccavo drives home this point when, before assailing her in the seasoning room, he tells Lila that, despite being sickened by the factory since childhood, he enjoys what he describes as the salamis' "compact, hard" feel and sexually suggestive odor (3:112).

Lila faces a struggle at the plant that contrasts starkly with the idyllic period of her love affair with Nino in Ischia, when she first met a different, seemingly genteel Bruno Soccavo. The indignity of her position differs as well from Elena's newfound respectability as Pietro's fiancée and the soon-to-be author of an acclaimed first novel. Whereas in the guise of shoe designer and store manager Lila exerted her creative powers with magical results, she finds that in the role of factory hireling her genius only gets her in trouble. She has to fight merely to keep her job. Because talking about work is too painful, she even has to keep silent about her "everyday harassments" with Enzo, prompting him when he learns the truth to ask why she never says anything (3:113, 124). It is only thanks to Lila's spontaneous outburst at the PCI meeting that Enzo and Pasquale in fact learn of her mistreatment. Repulsed by the "pedantic phrases" of the students and their brandishing of "ideas that were almost too obvious about capital" (3:120), she speaks with a frankness and urgency that immediately set her apart from everyone else:

> Can you imagine, she asked, what it means to spend eight hours a day standing up to your waist in the mortadella cooking water? Can you imagine what it means to have your fingers covered with cuts from slicing the meat off animal bones? Can you imagine what it means to go in and out of refrigerated rooms at twenty degrees below zero, and get ten lire more an hour—ten lire—for cold compensation? If you imagine this, what do you think you can learn from people who are forced to live like that? The women have to let their asses be groped by supervisors and colleagues without saying a word.
>
> (3:121–22)

Lila's recounting of her misery on the job makes her an instant sensation with the students. She, by contrast, cannot stomach their efforts to publicize her exploitation among workers who already know it firsthand, men and women who speak in "unrepeatable sounds that no one would ever say, write, or read and that nevertheless held as potential the real causes of their inferiority" (*subalternità*; 3:131). For Lila, the worst offenders are armchair radicals such as the Galianis, who treat the risks run by others like a game in which they have nothing to lose. The two children, Nadia and Armando, in particular exemplify the condescension of privileged Italian leftists toward people of the laboring class. Confronting them in their family's home, Lila replies to Armando and Nadia's glib assurances that everyone on "the front lines" of defying oppression runs equal risk with a scathing question: "So, if I should lose my job, I'll come and live here, you'll feed me, you'll assume responsibility for my life?" (3:142). While granting how pressing are the absolute physical necessities of housing and food, she places final stress on the mental anxiety of a responsibility that weighs unequally on people of different circumstances. As she asks herself while reflecting on her dissatisfaction with her lot in life, "So why don't you resign yourself? Blame the mind that can't settle down, that is constantly seeking a way to function. . . . The mind, ah yes, the evil is there, it's the mind's discontent that causes the body to get sick" (3:163).

The pessimism with which Lila views the effects of material need on mind and body calls to mind the critique of industrialization set forth by Simone Weil in the journal entries recounting her work in French factories in the mid 1930s. Weil in fact went on sabbatical from teaching in order to acquire experience as a manual laborer at the Alsthom electrical plant, the Forges de Basse-Indre, and the Renault automobile factory from December 1934 to August 1935. Lila's dismay with her fellow workers for acquiescing to their own debasement and for their lack of solidarity harmonizes with Weil's loathing of the slavelike restrictions on thought and movement she encountered on the assembly lines. In her journal, Weil argued that the "rationalization" of tasks brought about by the so-called scientific management practices known as Taylorism condemned workers to perform round the clock at levels of stupefying intensity. The impossibility of stopping to rest and think and the continual surveillance and regimentation emptied action of any meaning except mechanical efficiency.[13]

Although Soccavo's salami-making operation may not explicitly reflect the doctrines of Taylorism, Lila mounts an attack on the factory's methods that Weil would have applauded when she condemns in a formal complaint "the organization of the work, the pace, the general conditions of the factory, the quality of the product, the permanent risk of being injured or sick, the wretched compensations, wage increases" (3:154). Despite the cogent criticism, however, she seems skeptical of achieving lasting change for the better. Like Weil before her, Lila shows little faith that the voices who call for a "march of the proletariat of the whole world" will improve the plight of the plebeian multitudes in any meaningful sense: "No way. March to become what? Now and forever workers? Workers who slave from morning to night but are empowered? Nonsense. Hot air to sweeten the pill of toil. You know that it is a terrible condition, it should not be improved but eliminated" (3:163). Both Lila and Weil seem to reach the conclusion that there is nothing redeeming about work or being a worker, no magic formula to ameliorate the harshness of mass production. At the same time, we may find it easy to envision Lila scoffing at the mere thought of comparing herself to Simone Weil. What, she might have asked sarcastically, could a poor, uneducated Neapolitan woman have in common with a university-trained French philosopher who temporarily retreated from teaching to try on the job of a machinist? Surely Lila would have despised the class condescension and dilettantism implicit in Weil's project, yet the former winds up embracing much of the latter's critical agenda. If Lila's instinctive political radicalism has a guiding principle, it consists in her refusal to reason in the abstract and determination to act on the basis of what she knows and experiences firsthand. In this sense, we may view her ironically as very much following in Weil's footsteps.

Although the analogy between Weil and Lila may seem improbable at first glance in several respects, the likeness becomes harder to deny if we compare their views on the state and its supposed protection of the social contract by means of the law. On this score, Weil's distrust of the law's claim to rationality most fully comes into focus as a source of inspiration for the school of Italian feminism known as "the thinking of difference" (*il pensiero della differenza*), which followed the French philosopher in rejecting the notion of emancipation through rights. The foundational manifesto of this movement is a "genealogy" of feminist practices by the Milan Women's Bookstore Collective that bears the eloquent title *Do Not Think You Have Any Rights: The Engendering of Female Freedom in the Thought and Vicissitudes of a Women's Group* (*Non credere di avere dei diritti: la generazione della libertà femminile nell'idea e nelle vicende di un gruppo di donne*, 1987). The initial assertion of the designation exactly translates the first sentence of a crucial passage from the second volume of Weil's *Notebooks*, a passage that in fact supplies the Milan collective with the epigraph for their feminist treatise:

> Do not think you have any rights. That is, don't obscure or deform justice, but don't think that one can legitimately expect that things happen in a way that conforms with justice; especially since ourselves are far from being just.
>
> *Vertical superimposition.*
>
> There is a bad way of believing we have rights, and a bad way of believing we do not have any.[14]

Italian feminism, about which I will say more in the next chapter, advances a theory of sexual difference that is premised not on the ideal of equality for all under the law but rather on the ideal of freedom for women through social practices of entrustment. In this sense, the Milan Women's Bookstore Collective is right to acknowledge our debt to Weil for teaching us not to "expect that things happen in a way that conforms with justice." Given the importance of this debt, we may find ourselves puzzled by the fact that the anglophone edition of the Milan collective's treatise, which is translated by Patricia Cicogna and Teresa de Lauretis, replaces the original Italian title with a much clunkier and less evocative label: *Sexual Difference: A Theory of Socio-Symbolic Practice.*

When it comes to Lila's faith in the possibility of justice, Elena aptly sums up her friend's Weil-like indifference toward the state's promises of equal rights following the news of Bruno Soccavo's murder, which leaves the narrator worrying that her friend somehow may have been involved in the bloodshed: "Lila . . . takes no account of police, the law, the state, but believes there are problems that can only be resolved with a shoemaker's knife . . . Lila who has connected, is connecting our personal knowledge of poverty and abuse to the armed struggle against the fascists, against the owners, against capital" (3:312). In Lila's disbelief at the idea that the institutions of "police, the law, the state" may help to redress the most primally human disputes, we encounter a decisive refusal to conform with the bad faith notion of "justice," a refusal that Simone Weil voiced in her journals as a personal credo. Elena's observation that Lila connects her "personal knowledge" to a collective "struggle" that has no legal means of enactment captures Weil's revolutionary spirit with precision as well.

THE VANISHING PROGRAMMER

During the same period in which Lila works at the Soccavo factory, Elena receives the contract for her first book, a fictionalized memoir of her experiences in Ischia. As we know, she believes that the source of inspiration for her novel is Lila's childhood story, "The Blue Fairy." When Elena tries to help Lila recover wages that Soccavo has withheld out of malice, she turns Lila's list of complaints about the factory's conditions into an article for *l'Unità* that launches her own career as a journalist. Elena's dependence on her friend for courage and creative motivation, in other words, represents a leitmotif of the series. This reliance manifests itself again when Elena, who is living at the time in Florence, gets the idea for what will be her third book from a long-distance phone call with Lila. As the two friends converse, Lila retells the story of Don Achille's murder and its place in the long-lasting enmity between fascists and Communists that convulsed the rione, while Elena "followed her step by step, adding my voice excitedly to hers" (3:264). Only with her second book, which criticizes the myth of man's creation of woman, does Elena assert a measure of intellectual independence from Lila.

In *Relating Narratives: Storytelling and Selfhood* (2000), Adriana Cavarero argues that the act of narration "reveals the finite in its fragile uniqueness" and thus offers a more satisfying response than philosophy to the fundamental question "Who am I?"[15] Focusing on the interdependence of women's narratives in the chapter "On the Outskirts of Milan," Cavarero reexamines the case of two friends, Amalia and Emilia, who enrolled in the state-funded 150 Hours School program for workers in Milan and whose experience originally was reported in the Milan Women's Bookstore Collective's *Do Not Think You Have Any Rights*.[16] The more gifted writer of the two women, Amalia, assumes the responsibility of transforming the anecdotal reminiscences of the less gifted Emilia, who dies prematurely at the age of fifty-three, into a coherent narrative. When Amalia initially writes down her friend's life story after having learned it by heart, Emilia takes to carrying the manuscript with her in her bag and reading it "again and again, overcome by emotion."[17] As an author who cites the theory of entrustment set forth in *Do Not Think You Have Any Rights* and who keenly admires Cavarero's thought, Ferrante may be surmised to have had in mind the relationship between Amalia and Emilia as a model for the friendship of Elena and Lila in the Neapolitan Quartet. Yet in the end the two pairs of women friends can be said to share a faint resemblance at best. Amalia and Emilia achieve a kind of mutually productive equanimity through their friendship. By contrast, Lila proves to be an unwilling and defiant subject of Elena's narration, whereas Elena finally appears to need her less educated friend more than Lila needs her.

In the Neapolitan Quartet, no job escapes the corrosive influences of time and self-blindness. To be a writer like Elena, a scholar like Pietro, or a man of affairs like Nino does not endow one with a special sense of purpose. At the age of fifty-eight, Elena is seized by a gnawing conviction of the "scant value" of her own books (4:458). Despite his bona fides as a serious academic and a sober Communist, Pietro meets with the scorn of his students and worldlier peers. Although as a classicist he specializes in the potentially sensational topic of Bacchic rites, Pietro's research amusingly results in a monograph on the anodyne topic of the ritual relationship between wine, honey, and milk (3:32). Even in his high school years, Nino exhibits a mania for statistics that compels him to publish an essay with the prosaic title "The Numbers of Poverty" (1:128). He thus embraces the technocratic jargon of the social sciences in the 1960s, which even books such as Lorenzo Milani's landmark critique of the schooling of lower-class Italian students entitled *Letter to a Teacher* (*Lettera a una professoressa*, 1967) could not elude. Perhaps unsurprisingly, Nino in adulthood winds up as a professor in the arid field of economic or urban geography (3:33, 356). Ironically, it falls to Elena to rewrite his essays, making them a "little less dry" for a collection that she arranges to bring out through her own publisher (4:113). Over time, he even lapses from his youthful admiration for nonviolent activists such as Bertrand Russell and Martin Luther King Jr. into the cynical opportunism of a deputy of the Italian Socialist Party, which imploded following the revelations of its criminal dealings during the anticorruption investigations of the 1990s. His jailing and comically easy political resuscitation represent the logical conclusion of his all-too-logical career of self-promotion, which he only briefly interrupts as a teenager when he falls in love with Lila.

What is most important, however, is how Ferrante depicts her two protagonists at work, because they embody women's unique understanding of "the horror implicit in the necessity of earning a living," to borrow a turn of phrase from her letter to Ozzola (F 74). Elena represents the woman in search not of a job but rather a métier. Her vocation turns out to be the alluring horizon of writing, an endlessly deferred destination whose elusiveness becomes increasingly discouraging in old age. Unlike her author, she accepts as the price of literary fame the onus of self-promotion: the repetitive book tours, pompous critics, and mindless small talk and posturing. Through Elena's experiences, we thus may grasp Ferrante's own aversion to the competition for cultural prestige. Adele's talent for publicity and negotiation, which at first lends her an air of pragmatic craftiness, is cast in a totally different light when Elena tires of her marriage with Pietro and discovers her mother-in-law's hypocrisy and malice. Even the more sympathetic Mariarosa, who professes enthusiasm for the "unstoppable flow of events" (3:62–63), reveals herself to stand for little more than the platitudes of "flower power," despite her cachet as a professor of art history and bohemian radical. Following the suicide of Franco Mari, she abandons her work in academe, renounces her involvement in worldly causes, and evidently surrenders to a bitter feeling of defeat.

In Lila's case, we encounter a far more original notion of work, which results in a career of shifting circumstances and changes of fortune. Throughout these vicissitudes, she shows no particular loyalty to any of her jobs whether as shoe designer, grocery store clerk, luxury boutique manager in Piazza dei Martiri, or even owner of a successful software development company. In an interview collected in *Frantumaglia*, Ferrante divulges that Lila's character was inspired by a real-life acquaintance who as a student impressed the author with both her intellectual gifts and indifference to new job opportunities. At first jealous of her dazzlingly talented friend, the novelist confesses that in the end she found something irresistibly seductive about her insouciant attitude. We may feel nevertheless that Lila's nonchalance with respect to work threatens the prevailing narratives of mainstream feminism. That she never seems to associate her identity or potentiality with her job makes her an unusual and even unsettling heroine. For example, Elena depicts Lila's achievements in computer programming neither as victories of neoliberalism nor as signs of modern progress. Her success contrasts sharply with the ersatz claims of empowerment generally associated with prominent women executives in technology, such as Sheryl Sandberg or Meg Whitman. When Lila starts to learn programming languages, her interest develops almost randomly as a result of Enzo's desire to study computers and her determination to help him (3:27). As he advances as a consultant for IBM, he gets Lila hired as his assistant and, according to Elena's report of their long-distance conversations, "her enthusiasm grew with every phone call" (3:262). In fact, it is Lila who gains a reputation inside IBM as "the best in the business," with expertise that lands her an offer making four hundred thousand lire a month as head of technology (*capocentro*) for the Solaras in Acerra (3:302, 316). Before long, she and Enzo manage to strike out on their own by founding a profitable software start-up, which they drily name Basic Sight. Her ascent in particular is meteoric, yet she rarely seems to enjoy her work. Indeed, she appears to find owning her own venture to be useful mainly insofar as it enables her to support Ada, Rino, Alfonso, and other relatives and friends in need (4:131).

Lila exploits her brief stint with the Solaras to steal all the records of their criminal activities and appreciates the money that she gains from Basic Sight, but we know that her heart is not in the business. To Elena,

Lila's occupation looks exciting because it is "very new" and allows her to act with "absolute freedom," leading Elena to conclude that "hers was a life in motion, mine was stopped" (3:346).[18] Yet Lila, to the contrary, declares that "it's a boring job . . . you waste a lot of time" and intimates that her only real ambition is to assuage her "dissatisfied mind" by one day erasing every trace of herself save for a few "diagrams" that may be recorded on a "perforated tape" (3:345). That her own talent for writing code makes a reality of Michele Solara's long-standing desire to buy Lila's ingenuity "the way you buy pearls" underscores how easily the new technology can be assimilated to the most ancient and corrupt practices (3:334). Clearly, Ferrante does little in the Neapolitan Quartet to encourage a romantic view of commerce. Lila invests less passion in her own work than in an ill-fated collaboration with Elena to "change the neighborhood" (4:267). When Elena, under Lila's sway, authors a blistering exposé of the Solaras's crimes but gets cold feet before publishing it, Lila goes behind her back and submits the article to the newspaper *L'Espresso* (4:315). As it gradually becomes clear that the Solaras will emerge unhurt by the controversy surrounding the report, Lila suffers an emotional blow that in effect brings about "the end of her childhood" (4:318). According to Elena, the experience leaves Lila feeling "humiliated at having always ascribed a power to things that in the current hierarchies were insignificant: the alphabet, writing, books" (4:318).

We indeed may ask whether the publication of the story in *L'Espresso* does not end the childhood of Lila and Enzo's daughter Tina in a horrifyingly literal sense. After Tina abruptly vanishes toward the end of *The Story of the Lost Child*, it becomes clear from the reactions of Antonio, Enzo, Pasquale, and to some degree Elena that everyone in the neighborhood ascribes this event to the Solaras's taking their revenge on Lila. If Lila also were to accept that the Solaras murdered Tina, she would have to face the grievous conclusion that she herself bears some responsibility for her daughter's death. After all, shortly before Tina's disappearance, Michele Solara threatens to take away everything Lila has, causing her to worry naively about Enzo and Gennaro (4:307). As the question of what happened to Tina never receives a clear answer, the traumatic costs for Lila multiply with the passage of time.[19] As the years pass, she begins to claim that she "never liked" her livelihood and only feigned curiosity for Enzo's sake (4:361). When Elena learns that Lila plans to sell Basic Sight altogether and asks in surprise what she intends to do, she gives a simple answer: "Does a person necessarily have to do something? . . . I want to waste time" (4:379).

THE SCHOLAR

Lila's genius, Elena observes late in the two friends' saga, inheres in its "gratuitiousness," in her refusal to place her ingenuity at the service of purely pragmatic or utilitarian ends (4:403). This characterization, which recurs in variations throughout the series, hints at her affinity for one type of work above all: specifically, the pursuit of knowledge for its own sake associated with scholarly study. Her extraordinary aptitude for learning becomes evident in childhood, and she gains her first experience of anguish when her parents refuse to support her high school education. Not only does she place first as a young girl in the neighborhood library's book reading contest, but after obtaining library cards for her brother, mother, and father she wins the remaining prizes in their names too. As an adolescent, she teaches Elena how to translate classical Latin texts into Italian and inspires in Nino an uncharacteristic willingness to grapple with such famously difficult, modernist authors as Beckett and Joyce. During the fleeting interval of their affair, she demands that Nino "stimulate her mind" as much as her desire and constantly stays beside him "when he studied or wrote" (2:341, 358). She more easily achieves equilibrium by helping Enzo with his studies, exclaiming to Elena that "together it's great, one of us says one thing, one another" (2:465).

As we note earlier, she saves her highest admiration for the earnestly professorial Pietro, whom she drolly praises to Elena for sounding "like you, but more natural" (4:266). She confesses that when Gennaro was a small child she wanted him to grow up to be just like Pietro. Years after Tina disappears, Elena is startled to learn that Pietro wrote Lila a letter of consolation for her loss, which she remembers with "genuine gratitude" (4:392). Pietro and Lila exhibit surprising mutual sympathy as well when she devotes herself in middle age to the study of Naples' historical ghosts, the forgotten stories of its colorful persons and collective spaces, as if following his lead. Her dedication to recovering these remnants evokes the erudite impression that Pietro gives when he visits Elena's family for the first time and surprises everyone by showing that he knows all about "the history of Naples, the literature, fables, legends, anecdotes, the visible monuments and those hidden" (3:96). In this sense, Lila may be said to share Pietro's zeal for the city's arcane secrets, although Elena ultimately attributes to her friend rather than to her ex-husband the ability to transform these riddles into "a single work of great significance . . . [that] would be read and reread for hundreds of years" (4:461–62).

That Lila chooses to tell Pietro rather than Elena about her research in the Biblioteca Nazionale is especially fitting. Renouncing the compromises of *vita activa,* Lila becomes free to enter the vita contemplativa of a scholar. As Elena's reaction makes clear when she learns of Lila's new calling, this course of life suggests a circular, albeit ironic, symmetry: "Lila again in a library, not the neighborhood library of the fifties but the prestigious, inefficient Biblioteca Nazionale? That's what she was doing when she disappeared from the neighborhood?" (4:395). Accordingly, Elena can never be a genuine role model for Lila, because, for all her university training, Elena invests her energy in the production of cultural commodities that by her own admission "used the language of every day to indicate things of every day" and gradually "passed out of fashion and sounded foolish" (4:458). Lila does not like Elena's books and forbids her to write about the neighborhood, because she feels that Elena is capable neither of capturing the "teeming chaos" of history nor of weaving the imaginative "thread" of fiction (4:464). It is in fact when Elena publishes her final book, *A Friendship,* which under a thin veneer of fiction retells the story of the two friends and Tina's vanishing, that Lila cuts off all contact with her, forcing her "to acknowledge that our friendship was over" (4:464).

In spite of her long-standing aspiration to an intellectual's life, Elena herself grows increasingly dubious of the value of her literary contributions as she ages. In one conversation with Lila, she insists that there are too few real intellectuals, only a mass of critics who parrot other people's ideas and divert themselves with sadistic attacks on rivals (4:268). When her publishing house takes out advertisements in *La Repubblica* for her third book, which recounts the murder of Don Achille and the rise of the Solaras, the company luridly hypes the narrative's "bloodred" violence (4:270). Worse still, Elena's torment at the novel's circulation after encountering the furious Michele and Marcello Solara is aggravated by Lila's disapproval of the book on the grounds that it represents neither history nor fiction but something in between (4:285). Elena's self-doubt gives way to feelings of depression after her books stop selling, her ill-advised attempt at a daytime TV show on classical literature bombs, and a younger editor forces her out of her post as the head of a small publishing house in Turin (4:337–38).

When she realizes that Lila has returned to her first love of "the books," Elena admits to envying her friend's limitless capacity to study for "pleasure," especially in contrast to her own need to read and write for "work" (4:444). Becoming more and more convinced of the vanity of her own labors, she imagines on the evidence of Lila's spellbinding remarks on the people, places, and moods of Naples that her friend already has completed "a vast text" about the city's history, next to which her own life and career starts to look like "a petty battle to change my social class" (4:448, 459). Responding to Elena's observation of how she enjoys scholarly toil, Lila demurs that "I'm not studying" (4:444). Nevertheless, she warms to the topic of the city as if Naples "had revealed only to her a secret sparkle," leaving Elena to marvel that "she, who learned with effortless speed, now seemed able to give to every monument, every stone, a density of meaning, a fantastic importance such that I would have happily stopped the nonsense that I was busy with to start studying in turn" (4:445). Her friend furthermore notices that Lila studies not in the plodding, methodical manner of a student at school but rather "in her usual extemporaneous way," according to the rhythm of her enthusiasm (4:445). More important, it is possible that her scholarly project may represent a coming to terms with Tina's loss, as Elena suddenly surmises when she is about to leave Naples for good in 1995 (4:452).

In *Idea of Prose*, the philosopher Giorgio Agamben reminds us that the etymological root of the word *studium* connotes a "crash" in the sense of the "shock of an impact": "Studying and stupefying are in this sense akin: those who study are in the situation of people who have received a shock and are stupefied by what has struck them, unable to grasp it and at the same time powerless to leave hold."[20] Lila's study of Naples certainly betrays a vulnerability to shock in Agamben's sense or, as Elena puts it, to "unexpected interests that later weakened and vanished" (4:445). Indeed, it is this susceptibility to the unexpected that causes her to alternate ambivalently between the bitter "aesthetic project" of eliminating her own traces from view and "the pleasure of inventing images" that sustains her writing (4:455).[21] Her equivocation between impulses of self-delight and self-eradication thus implies a condition similar to the pathological form of mourning that Freud called melancholia, which he associated with ambivalence so strong that it led the mourner to blame herself for the loved one's loss.[22]

Perhaps the earliest stirring of this melancholic inclination explains why Lila develops a fascination in particular with the dead languages of Greek and Latin as a girl. Although she is gifted in other subjects such as mathematics, she pursues her youthful rivalry with Elena most starkly in the arena of serious scholarship par excellence, namely classical literature. It is true that both Lila and Elena in their childhood hope to follow in Louisa May Alcott's footsteps and make their fortune through writing novels as Alcott did with *Little Women*, but Lila soon becomes so engrossed in the most impractical of subjects that she boastfully promises to teach Elena how to write "gramophone" in the ancient Greek alphabet (1:141). The fact that in interviews Ferrante has emphasized her own education in classical studies only adds to the intrigue surrounding the role and meaning of antiquity in the Neapolitan Quartet (F 252, 347). While knowledge of Greek and Latin may be a signifier of class standing in Italy, Lila's eagerness to master the classical languages appears to spring not from class resentment but rather from a true longing to recover a historically distant and obscure past.

If humanistic study is the only field in which Lila feels at home, it is all the more apt that Naples provides her area of specialization. Elena learns of Lila's fixation with the city from Pietro and Imma, the latter of whom Lila brings along on her wanderings through the streets. The news of Lila's consuming passion reaches Elena, we might say, as a distant echo in an imaginative space of transference. Naples becomes identical for Lila with her memories of Tina and so represents in her mind the site where her shock can be displaced. For her, the city is the right subject of study precisely because of its ongoing history of violence, which has engulfed innumerable victims like Tina since its founding. It is true that, unlike Elena, Lila in old age succeeds in finding a redemptive vitality in Naples' capacity to gain new life from an endless succession of changes including arriving waves of immigrants: "Seeing Africans, Asians in every corner of the neighborhood, smelling the odors of unknown cuisines, she became excited, she said: I haven't traveled around the world like you, but, look, the world has come to me" (4:460). At the same time, Lila's claim that by forsaking the worldly life she has acquired a richer relationship to her world seems at some level to imply a melancholic admission of irreparable self-sacrifice. Although Elena is haunted by the idea that Lila has authored a labyrinthine compendium of her "wandering and readings" that stands in contrast to Elena's own, "linear" last novel, *A Friendship* (4:448, 465), we should remember that there is no proof in the narrative that Lila actually writes anything. As a true scholar, she perpetually keeps studying, leaving the potentiality of her knowledge intact. When Lila declares that she is not writing because she does not wish to be survived by any work of her own making, she in fact may be telling Elena the truth: "If I could eliminate myself now, while we are speaking, I'd be more than happy. Imagine if I am going to start writing. . . . I want to leave nothing, my favorite key is the one that deletes" (4:454–55). It is hardly coincidental that the failure of the article Lila coauthors with Elena for *L'Espresso* represents so crushing a disappointment for Lila that it in effect ends her childhood. From this episode it becomes apparent that for Lila to be a writer is not the same thing as to be a scholar.

What Elena defines as Lila's "aesthetic project" of removing herself from others' view, of making herself invisible, may be thought to coincide with the life of the scholar who always remains immersed in her books with no other ambition than that of learning. After Lila indeed disappears without a trace, Elena fantasizes her friend at last leaving Naples behind and setting out to travel around the world while living off the money that she made by selling her company. However, this image only calls to mind the ending of a bad movie in which, following the dramatic denouement, the camera captures the hero on a sunny beach sipping a piña colada. Elena knows that it is not in Lila's character to accept such a fate. The mystery of Lila's withdrawal into obscurity, which symbolically recapitulates Tina's disappearance, is never solved. We may imagine that, if Lila can be found anywhere after vanishing from Elena's sight, it would be inside the Biblioteca Nazionale, poring over her beloved books and exploring the secrets of the shadowy metropolis where the specters of history, just as much as the emissaries of the worldly present, ultimately can come to her.

If the Neapolitan Quartet belongs to one literary genre above all, the likeliest candidate would have to be the Bildungsroman or perhaps its closely related offshoot, the *Künstlerroman*. The Bildungsroman reached its heyday by the end of the eighteenth century with Goethe's *Wilhelm*

Meisters Lehrjahre (1795–1796) and its sequel *Wilhelm Meisters Wander-jahre* (1821–1829). Of course, Ferrante's exploration of the emotional and intellectual dialectic between Elena and Lila, two Neapolitan women of the lower classes whose lives she follows from childhood into maturity, may well be said to revitalize and transform the educational novel of self-cultivation that reached its zenith in Goethe's treatment of it.[23] The self-consciousness shared by the two friends, which Ferrante often depicts through the women's relation to the very act of writing, affirms the Bil-dungsroman's commitment as a form to dramatizing the process of self-critique and introspection. Of the two friends, Elena at first may appear to be the likelier protagonist of the implicit Bildungsroman narrative that runs through the Neapolitan Quartet, inasmuch as she claims to act on the basis of rational judgment, unlike the supposedly more impulsive Lila. Ele-na's social ascent in this light seems steadier and more deliberate than Lila's almost accidental success as a computer programmer and businesswoman.

The form of Bildung that is at stake in the two friends' story, however, is not limited to the domains of professional advancement and worldly acclaim in which the bourgeois tradition of the genre has flourished. Elena's disen-chantment with her own books as we near the end of the tale and anguish at the thought that she has been nothing more than a literary poseur preclude attempts to read her life as a positive example of creative and intellectual "becoming," to invoke the name that she gives to women's Bildung.[24] Her anxiety plainly corresponds to the fear of dilettantism that Goethe empha-sizes at the end of Wilhelm Meister's chronicle and that Thomas Mann dra-matizes in several variations on the theme of the troubled artist's ending of life from *Death in Venice* to *Doctor Faustus*.[25] Wilhelm's potential vanity as a poet and actor foreshadows Elena's vanity as a writer and intellectual, which Armando Galiani reassures her "is a resource" while also acknowl-edging it as a vice that Lila does not share (4:344).

Although Lila does not move forward in her education along an orderly course of progress, she spontaneously accomplishes the most important goal of Goethean Bildung, which is to attain pure vitality of mind as opposed to money, power, or even pleasure. She understands more clearly than Elena does that in order to practice the art of living with care what matters is not to finish every task. Perhaps this insight explains why Lila does not need to write the book on Naples that she appears to be research-ing, which Elena imagines as "a manuscript, a notebook, a *zibaldone*"

(4:452).[26] Despite her years of apprenticeship and travel, Elena is not able to perfect the craft of self-creation as Lila does through the cultivation of her potentiality rather than the exercise of her will. Her genius is beguiling precisely because of its anarchic character. She does not capitalize on her gifts and therefore cannot be tamed: "She possessed intelligence and did not put it to use but, rather, wasted it, like a great lady for whom all the riches of the world are merely signs of vulgarity. . . . She stood out among so many because she did not submit to any training, any use, or to any purpose" (4:403). Her incorruptible "gratuitousness" of intellect enables Lila to reorder the fortunes and power structure of her community, albeit in an impermanent way, as no one else in the neighborhood can do: "All of us had submitted and that submission had—through trials, failures, successes—reduced us. Only Lila, nothing and no one seemed to reduce her" (4:403).

It is noteworthy in what a striking manner Elena's description of Lila's attitude inverts her class. The comparison to a "great lady" of course pays homage to her exquisite discernment but also suggests the degree to which she is perceived as a magical or miraculous being in light of her indifference to worldly concerns. By transforming Lila, the shoemaker's daughter, into a fairy-tale embodiment of privilege, wealth, and urbanity, Elena confirms Walter Benjamin's dictum that "the idea of happiness is indissolubly bound up with the idea of redemption" (OCH 389).[27] Over the course of their friendship, Lila becomes unforgettable for Elena and for the reader because of her heroic rejection of subalternity as an oppressed and stigmatized state of being. Embodying so perfectly the gifts of the mind, Lila ends up subverting the ultimate claims of Bildung as a process. Fittingly, she leaves us with what Elena sarcastically calls Lila's "usual speech about the annihilation of hierarchies," which also may be defined as the most brilliant aphorism in the narrative about the proper place of genius in the world: "So much fuss about the greatness of this one and that one, but what virtue is there in being born with certain qualities, it's like admiring the bingo basket when you shake it and good numbers come out" (4:455).

Chapter Three

POLITICAL COSMOLOGIES

LOST IN TRANSLATION

At the heart of both the philosophical genealogy of Italian feminism and the language of the Neapolitan Quartet resides the problem of subalternity. Ferrante is not an overtly political writer, inasmuch as she appears to possess no clear ideological agenda. Where she most effectively approaches political topics is in the space of what we might call the intimate public sphere in which the personal is political, as the saying goes, and we may find ways to act through relationships of intimacy. Indeed, it is in Elena and Lila's friendship first of all that we confront the question of the subaltern. Can the subalternity of women be made politically effective as a basis for their mutual entrustment? This line of inquiry follows the Italian school of feminism that originates with the aforementioned "thinking of difference" (*il pensiero della differenza*), which is less interested in securing legal rights than in finding forms of creative freedom through social practices.

Ferrante finds indications of the route to an answer in the writings of the East German author Christa Wolf. The historical "depth of field" that Wolf achieves in novels such as *Cassandra* (1983) and *Medea* (1996), which allegorically diagnose women's modern political situations by revisiting the narratives of classical heroines, provides a crucial source of inspiration that Ferrante acknowledges with a rare textual signal of her possible identity as Anita Raja. In *My Brilliant Friend*, Lila and Elena become fascinated with the figure of Dido, whom they read not simply as the victim of her thwarted passion for Aeneas but, more important, in her role of queen as the essential spirit of her *polis*, because her death leaves Carthage bereft and imperiled as an example of a city without love. Not only does the two friends' zeal for Dido's story resemble Wolf's concern in *Cassandra* with a woman's effort to find her place in her own culture but their description of Carthage's deprivation following Dido's suicide echoes Raja's characterization of Troy in her introductory essay to the Italian edition of Wolf's novel. Both Elena and Lila struggle in different ways throughout the Neapolitan novels with the difficulty of arriving at a meaningful form of life in Naples. Whereas Elena pursues the more recognizable path of becoming a writer and intellectual, Lila ends up like Cassandra in a distressingly prophetic role, which her recurring visions of smarginatura, dissolving margins, make evident. Regarding her earlier novels, we should notice that Ferrante's characters in *The Days of Abandonment* and *The Lost Daughter* veer uncomfortably close to Medea-like states of mind inasmuch as they threaten verbal and even physical violence against children.

Can the subaltern speak? Gayatri Chakravorty Spivak poses this question to readers in the title of a landmark essay criticizing Western representations of the Other.[1] It is a question that Ferrante, too, seems determined to raise in the Neapolitan Quartet. Although Spivak answers her own demand with a resounding no, Ferrante offers a more ambivalent response that at least grants otherness some affirmative potential, however qualified. Indeed, this hope is one of the quartet's most compelling qualities. Whereas Ferrante's earlier novels focus on middle-class women intellectuals, *My Brilliant Friend* marks a political shift toward imagining her characters' lives in terms not only of gender but also of class. It is telling in this regard that the novelist repeatedly deploys the Italian word *subalterno* and its variants throughout all four volumes of the series. Unlike her earlier works, the Neapolitan novels may be read as a feminist reinvention of the national-popular project espoused by the great Marxist thinker Antonio Gramsci, who in fact defined the term *subaltern* in light of the class conflict in Italy and thus gave rise to an enduring domain of political theory.

In her English translation, however, Ann Goldstein erases the word, replacing it in every instance with more ordinary-sounding synonyms such as *subordinate, subservient,* and so forth.[2] On stylistic grounds, one perhaps could claim that she has good reason for this decision. To an English speaker's ear, the term sounds oddly abstruse, as it has little currency today beyond the academic debates of postcolonial studies. Yet to adopt this position is to ignore the example of Ferrante's original. For the same reasoning holds true in Italian, where *subalterno* rarely occurs in casual conversation and, for contemporary readers who are philosophically minded, unmistakably evokes Gramsci's idea of the dynamic potential of lower-class social factions. Gramsci reappropriated the notion of the subaltern, which arose in Italian long before his use of the term, and gave it a specific emphasis on the ability of poor and excluded groups to intervene in the hegemonic social order, eschewing typical conceptions of the underclass that deny this capacity. Unlike traditional categories of the oppressed or exploited, the subaltern is a marginalized figure who does not consent to the established organization of power and fights to create her own space of cultural authority.

Without reciting chapter and verse of Gramsci's theory of the dialectical relation between structure and superstructure, we may observe that, by disseminating the lexicon of subalternity throughout the quartet, Ferrante spotlights a philosophical trace left by the Sardinian thinker on the ordinary language of her protagonists. At the center of the Neapolitan Quartet looms what Spivak aptly defines as "the immense problem of the consciousness of the woman as subaltern."[3] On this score, it is noteworthy that Ferrante so methodically refracts readers' understanding of the power relationships into which women enter through the lens of class. Gramsci's notion of subalternity from this perspective may be seen to represent the political unconscious of the novels and their characters. In different, complementary ways, Lila and Elena both resist at no small price the mute destiny that their society dictates for them. Understood in proper context, their intertwined stories come to represent no less than an epic of defiance and personal courage.

Before considering the most salient episodes of this epic, however, we must return to the question of the author's pseudonymous identity. Far from mattering not at all, as some readers insist, Ferrante's class and gender are important lenses through which to understand the Neapolitan novels in particular. Cultural appropriation is a fraught historical problem, which we struggle with today in implications both evident and subtle.

In her essay, Spivak warns readers of the dangers of appropriating the Other by assimilation, decrying a logic that inevitably flattens the heterogeneity of the subaltern. Efforts to give voice to subaltern groups are indeed notoriously treacherous. If we can no longer deny knowing that Elena Ferrante is the pseudonym of Anita Raja, as I have argued throughout this book, then we must acknowledge that the novelist grew up in an upper middle-class family with an esteemed judge as her father and a language textbook author as her mother and went on to a career as Italy's preeminent translator of German writers such as Christa Wolf, Ingeborg Bachmann, and Georg Büchner. To be an established literary professional who also happens to be married to Domenico Starnone, another distinguished Neapolitan writer, means to inhabit a very different social milieu from the one she portrays in the quartet.

In her book of essays, *Frantumaglia*, Ferrante drops possibly false hints for readers about her identity, suggesting that she possesses a degree in classics, has a professorial job outside of Italy, and, most importantly, comes from a humble family (F 252, 347, 356). If she is in fact Raja, these red herrings add up to a not wholly innocent fantasy. Gramsci certainly viewed the representation of subaltern groups in Italian literature as problematic, famously assailing the nineteenth-century writer Alessandro Manzoni for his condescendingly "democratic" attitude toward the poor in his novel *The Betrothed* (1827). In Gramsci's eyes, Manzoni depicts the subaltern as having no history and therefore as being incapable of class conflict.[4] This accusation, of course, does not apply to Ferrante. Rather, one may argue that her very recurrence to the language of subalternity in the Neapolitan novels bespeaks at some level an impulse to acknowledge and problematize her own authorial privilege. At the same time, the doubts surrounding her professed identity deny readers the consolation of taking the tetralogy as autobiographical fiction, leaving us on slippery terrain when it comes to judging her writing's ethical and political claims.

SUBALTERN CHARACTERS

Lila and Elena's friendship thrives on Elena's acceptance of the subaltern role in their relationship. Only occasionally does she manage to exert her independence. Lila is her muse and creative genius, but one who takes the form of a furious, argumentative demon. When Elena publishes her first book, the initially mysterious source of inspiration turns out to be Lila's schoolgirl fable, "The Blue Fairy." As if enacting the perfect Gramscian narrative, Elena gains the upper hand—or "hegemony"—for momentary stretches, thanks to her education and incursions into the world of intellectuals, but her struggle remains endless. Other characters, however, are not so resilient. They resign themselves to permanently subaltern positions that define their place in the world. In such cases, their lives turn hopelessly static, devoid of social aspiration or any other purpose.

This is surely the situation of Lila and Elena's fathers in the narrative. Somewhat derisively, the people of the neighborhood refer to Lila's father Fernando Cerullo as a *scarparo* (e.g., 1:61 EN, 1:100 IT), using a crass word in dialect for his job of shoemaker rather than the polite name in Italian, which is *calzolaio*. From Elena's narration, we learn that, after flirting in his youth with a factory job, Fernando returned to his roots as a lone craftsman who distrusts talk of change, especially when it comes to letting Lila design new shoes. He relents on this score only out of deference to the wishes first of Marcello Solara and then Stefano Carracci. However, when Stefano asks Lila in front of her family to marry him, Fernando "gasped slightly, then murmured, with the same subservience that in times gone by he had manifested toward Don Achille: 'We're offending not only Marcello but all the Solaras'" (1:251). In the Italian edition, Ferrante describes Fernando's fearful manner, which Goldstein labels "subservience," as *subalternità* (1:247 IT). Elena's father never even enjoys the privilege of being identified by his proper name in the novels, answering simply to the epithet of "the porter," which is his job at City Hall. He seems practically invisible in the story, appearing only as an embodiment of the family's disempowered state, as for example when Elena returns to Naples and confronts her parents over her sister Elisa's engagement to Marcello Solara: "My father's voice was hoarse with emotion, he seemed thinner, even more subservient" (3:319–20). Here again, the English translation weakens the force of Ferrante's final adjective in the original sentence, which is *subalterno* (3:291 IT). The difference is by no means minor. Ferrante's insistence on the terminology that Gramsci uses in his critique of the underclass makes clear in these episodes that the despair of Lila and Elena's fathers is not only psychological but also cultural and political in nature.

In other words, the Solaras can maintain their reign of terror and violence over families such as the Cerullos and Grecos because they know precisely how to exploit the subalternity of the rione. The people of Ferrante's Naples stand at a distance from the vital figures who populate, for instance, Pier Paolo Pasolini's narrative tours de force of the same period such as his first novel, *Ragazzi di Vita* (1955), or even his brilliantly elegiac debut as a film director, *Accattone* (1961).[5] As the years advance in Ferrante's quartet from the 1950s to the 1960s and beyond, many of Elena and Lila's contemporaries from the neighborhood—for example, Antonio, Rino, Stefano, Ada, and Carmela—become trapped in irredeemably subaltern roles. Elena grows painfully conscious of Antonio's subalternity, especially when comparing him to Nino: "I was dazzled instead by the way Nino talked to me: without any subservience" ("Ero abbagliata invece da come mi parlava Nino: senza alcuna subalternità"; 1:325, 1:322 IT). After working for a while as a mechanic at a gas station, Antonio resigns himself to performing menial tasks for the Solaras, as he can find no alternative that would enable him to refuse their patronage.

Notwithstanding the initial successes of his family's grocery and the shoe store that he establishes with Rino in Piazza dei Martiri, Stefano, the son of Don Achille, gradually has to surrender all his properties to the Solaras. Yet, thanks to Lila, Stefano for a time succeeds spectacularly in overcoming his circumstances. As a couple, Stefano and Lila fleetingly enjoy all the comforts of consumerism during the years of the Italian economic boom that Pasolini denounced as symptoms of cultural homogenization or "homologation" (*omologazione*). Young, attractive, well-dressed, equipped with a new car, the couple strike Elena as being as glamorous as "John and Jacqueline Kennedy visiting a neighborhood of indigents" (1:273). It is in particular their short-lived calm—their ability to rise above neighbors' petty slights and the neighborhood's oppressed conditions "as if none of the old rules were valid for them"—that characterizes Stefano's golden age. Already at their wedding, however, Stefano's weakness becomes evident to Lila when she notices that he gave Marcello Solara the shoes she made herself as a prototype for her family's business. A few hours later, when they reach the hotel on the Amalfi Coast where they have driven for their honeymoon, Lila discerns in Stefano an unmistakably "subservient attitude" (1:34).[6] The downfall of Lila's brother Rino is even more precipitous, as his greed and helpless self-delusion doom him to constant begging for money and an eventually squalid death, presumably from a drug overdose, in an abandoned railway car (3:115, 4: 357).

Ferrante thus chronicles the transformation of some characters from the psychological well-roundedness of youth to the affective flatness of an adulthood experienced as subalternity without resistance, which the more educated characters identify with the classical notion of the plebs. Elena and Lila's elementary school teacher Maestra Oliviero, for instance, concludes that the fate of Lila's family is to remain trapped in a brutish life— because they belong to the plebs. In ancient Rome, the plebs were the common people who, unlike the patricians, did not rule over any of the city's political or social institutions. Not only were the plebs excluded from positions of power, such as magistracies, but they often were ignorant of even the laws by which they were governed. When Lila's parents refuse to continue her schooling, the maestra turns bitter and angry, knowing that the subaltern cannot escape her misfortune without an education. On being asked by Elena if she has read Lila's precocious short story, "The Blue Fairy," Oliviero retorts by asking in turn: "Do you know what the plebs are, Greco?" (1:71). Young Elena naively answers that "the tribunes of the plebs are the Gracchi," naming the brothers who famously championed the needs of Rome's poor through legal reforms until being assassinated by their enemies. Oliviero acidly replies: "The plebs are quite a nasty thing . . . and if one wishes to remain a plebeian, he, his children, the children of his children deserve nothing. Forget Cerullo and think of yourself" (1:71–72). On the night of Lila's wedding celebration, the teenaged Elena looks around at the pageant of crassness and anguish unfolding around her and suddenly comprehends what her teacher meant by the plebs:

> The plebs were us. The plebs were the fight for food and wine, that quarrel over who should be served first and better, that dirty floor on which waiters clattered back and forth, those increasingly vulgar toasts. The plebs were my mother, who had drunk wine and now was leaning against my father's shoulder, while he, serious, laughed, his mouth gaping, at the sexual allusions of the metal dealer. They were all laughing, even Lila, with the expression of one who has a role and will play it to the utmost. (1:329)

Repudiating plebeian forms of life, their coarse sensibility and lack of worldliness, proves to be the adult Elena's lifelong mission. In *The Story of the Lost Child*, Elena succumbs to the sarcastic prompting of her ex-lover

Franco Mari and tells her daughter Dede to recite the "silly fable" of Menenius Agrippa. Agrippa famously likens the labor of ancient Rome's plebeians in sustaining the city's patricians to the activity of the body politic's limbs in serving the needs of the "stomach" (4:104). Dede recognizes this tale as an allegory of the very ideology of subalternity, making sure that Oliviero's malediction regarding the "children of his children" is proven wrong.

The risk of returning to the subaltern, however, does not arise only in the form of being reabsorbed by the plebs. In particular, the narrative arc of Nino Sarratore's life and career makes clear that relentless social climbing leads to an ethical and political subalternity that may be more devastating than any menial subsistence. We have noted already that one reason why Nino becomes an object of adoration for Elena from an early age is his dazzling way of carrying himself *senza alcuna subalternità* (1:322 IT) or, in the English, "without any subservience," which makes him "almost" Lila's equal (1:325). When Elena watches the home movie of Lila's wedding, she is struck by Nino's indifference to the all-powerful Solaras, who otherwise are ensconced in their menacing smugness: "Looking at him, I was seduced. He seemed to me an ascetic prince who could intimidate Michele and Marcello merely by means of a gaze that did not see them" (2:61). Over time, however, Nino's own decisions and actions gradually complicate Elena's first impression of him. By becoming a senator in the Italian Socialist Party, which was plagued by corruption scandals in the early 1990s, he reveals a political opportunism and servility that belie the air of independence he possessed as a young man. In his private life, his perpetual indiscretions eventually bring to light, even in Elena's eyes, the increasing resemblance of Nino to his father Donato, the neighborhood lothario, railway conductor, and ersatz author. However pedestrian they may be, Donato's journalistic and poetic efforts at first hint at some ambition to overcome the disadvantages of his class, but eventually reveal themselves as no more than a ruse for his pursuit of young women. The pseudo-lyricist of mellifluous sentiments turns out to be a detestable creep who molests the fifteen-year-old Elena when she and the Sarratores are boarding in the same house in Ischia.

To overcome the role of the subaltern, or to discover within it a genuinely productive alternative to the hegemonic order, in other words, requires more than mere attitude. The drama of Elena's Bildung indeed consists in whether she has the strength to resist subalternity in all its forms. This struggle pervades even her relationship to language. First in Naples and then in Pisa, she is determined to renounce her native Neapolitan dialect and to speak in the educated discourse of Italian. In fact, her most bitter humiliations at the Scuola Normale Superiore in Pisa have to do with her accent. Before her relationship with Pietro Airota confers on her his family's patronage, Elena is mocked for her "inflection" of certain words by a girl from Rome and derogatively called "Naples" by a rejected admirer (2:332, 406). Notwithstanding her education, eventual career as a writer, and marriage to Pietro, Elena finds that to redefine her standing in the given distribution of power is neither easy nor certain.

From her physical appearance to her sexuality, intellect, and talent as a writer, she continually perceives herself to be subaltern to Lila. On the night of Lila and Stefano's wedding, Elena fixates on the idea that, by losing her virginity, Lila will enter a domain of experience that she cannot share, and so imitates her friend by having sex with Antonio in the marshland bordering Naples. When, after her marriage, Lila elopes with Nino in Ischia for one night, Elena again apes her friend's imagined passion by having sex with Donato on the beach, despite her disgust at his past assault on her. That night becomes a kind of narrative blind spot between the two friends, as Elena does not tell Lila about it, and Lila asks her no questions, even after reading the thinly veiled fictionalization of the episode in Elena's first book.

Readers of the Neapolitan Quartet may well conclude that, if subalterns cannot speak, they sometimes can still turn to writing. In Elena's literary debut, her night on the beach with Donato provides the scandalously "risqué" core of her novel. At first, the publication of her story feels to Elena less like an assertion of authority over the event and more like admission of a shameful secret. She meekly assents to the view that her book is marred by "dirty pages" and only after a conversation with the literary professor Tarratano does she accept her artistic ownership of the work itself:

> And he explained to me that . . . my novel wasn't simply the episode on the beach, there were more interesting and finer passages. . . . Obscenity, he said, is not alien to good literature, and the true art of the story, even if it goes beyond the bounds of decency, is never risqué. . . . I was submitting to

the public's myopia, its superficiality. I said to myself: Enough, I have to be less subservient (*subalterna*). And I decided that at the first opportunity I would be more severe with anyone who wanted to talk about those pages. (3:65–66 EN, 3:54 IT)

Even this modest gain in awareness comes at a price, as, following their conversation over dinner, Tarratano tries to kiss Elena in an elevator, as if to imitate Donato's predatory advances. Elena takes pains to resist being victimized by this associate and peer of Pietro's family, but in a larger sense she is not entirely successful at protecting herself against bullying. After her marriage to Pietro, she often catches herself speaking to him and his family in tones of "resentment and inferiority" ("risentimento e subalternità") (3:243 EN, 3:219 IT). Her success as a bourgeois intellectual, which is due in no small part to having married into the Airota family, brings her both new freedoms and oppressions. Her mother-in-law Adele on the one hand helps her to publish her first book, but on the other repeatedly uses her power in the family and in society to control Elena.

It is always in relationship to Lila, however, that Elena fears remaining trapped in a subaltern position. After the publication of her debut novel and the completion of her degree from the Scuola Normale, Elena returns to Naples to find Lila sick and depressed, living in the suburb of San Giovanni a Teduccio with their childhood friend Enzo and Lila's son Gennaro. Lila has abandoned her demeaning and physically dangerous job at the Soccavo salami factory after having defied the manager Bruno Soccavo as well as Michele Solara, who turns out to be the real owner of the business. After attending a few meetings of the Italian Communist Party with Pasquale Peluso, another friend from childhood, Lila writes an exposé of workers' conditions in the factory and transforms it into a list of demands that she delivers to Bruno. Her health, however, rapidly deteriorates. Not only have her hands been lacerated and left scarred by the butchery, but her body is wracked by a chronic cough because of the damp and cold. When Elena finds her, she is running a high fever and has grown frightened of the escalating violence between the Communists who protest outside the factory in the name of the workers and the fascist thugs hired by the Solaras to protect their business.

The doctors to whom Elena brings Lila for help initially fear that she may have a heart murmur, then a neurological disorder, but, in the end, determine that she is simply consumed by fatigue and needs to rest. Thanks to Adele's limitless network of contacts, Elena manages not only to set up all of the doctors' appointments for Lila but forces Soccavo to pay Lila the missing wages he owes her. At her mother-in-law's urging, Elena, moreover, writes an editorial in the newspaper *l'Unità* regarding the abuse and exploitation of the workers at the Soccavo salami factory. For the first time, Elena feels confident in a social status that allows her to help Lila. Whereas Lila used her money to buy Elena the textbooks that she needed in high school, now Elena is able to lend money to Lila, to hire the lawyers who recover her salary, and to find the doctors who help restore her health.

Elena soon finds, however, that all her efforts are in vain and her subalternity is as manifest as ever. On a visit to Professor Galiani, whose daughter Nadia has taken up with Pasquale, the couple ridicules Elena for the futility of her attempt to teach Soccavo a lesson (3:220). Unimpressed by her intervention on behalf of Lila, they remind her that the class struggle is something else entirely, and Elena feels particularly stung when, siding with the pair, Lila tells her, "That's enough, Lenù, they are right" (3:222). Things do not improve with the arrival of Professor Galiani, who greets with indifference Elena's gift of a copy of her novel and pays no attention to the article in *l'Unità*. To make matters worse, Galiani spends the time praising Lila for her write-up of the workers' demands, a copy of which the professor has obtained through Nadia. At the end of the visit, before Lila and Elena go their separate ways for what winds up being an interval of several years, Elena feels oppressed by an inescapable sense of Lila's superiority. Because its exact wording is important, I will cite here Elena's declaration of her emotions in its entirety both in English and then in Italian: "Certainly she was false, and she was ungrateful, and I, in spite of all that had changed for me, continued to feel inferior. I felt that I would never free myself from that inferiority, and that seemed to me intolerable" ("Di certo era falsa, ed era ingrata, ed io, malgrado tutti i miei cambamenti, seguitavo ad essere subalterna. Di quella subalternità seniti che non sarei mai riuscita a liberarmi e questo mi sembro insopportabile"; 3:226 EN, 3:204 IT). Elena's transformation of the adjective *subalterna* into the noun *subalternità* marks the transition from a personal feeling of being subaltern to the publicly acknowledged—and indeed stigmatized—condition of subalternity, thus registering how deeply intertwined for the narrator are the personal and the political. (The avoidance of the English cognate in the translation of these sentences seems particularly unfortunate.) In her anger, she concedes that Lila once again has preceded her in learning a crucial lesson: namely, that the incessant struggle they both face cannot be solved by the Airotas, that to revolt against subalternity meaningfully requires honesty, bravery, and even a certain radicalism. The question is not only psychological, and the answer is not simply for her to "get over" her inferiority complex. Like her genial friend, Elena occupies a specific place in an immense web of power relationships that cannot be changed in any lasting way without coming to terms with the necessity of a real and difficult sacrifice.

FEMINISM AGAINST SUBALTERNITY:
THE THINKING OF DIFFERENCE

In an interview with American writer Elissa Shappell, Ferrante explains how the encounter with feminist ideas upended her view of the world: "I grew up with the idea that if I did not let myself be absorbed as much as possible into the world of capable men, if I did not learn from their cultural excellence, if I did not pass brilliantly all the exams that world required of me, it would be tantamount to not existing at all. Then I read books that exalted the female difference and my thinking was turned upside down. I realized that I had to do exactly the opposite: I had to start with myself and with my relationship to other women—this is another essential formula—if I really wanted to give myself a shape" (F 332). The Neapolitan novels in this light may be regarded as a complex, self-questioning investigation of "female difference." If the quartet represents an autobiographical project, it is in the specific sense of enabling Ferrante to "give myself a shape" through the lens of "my relationship to other women."

When Elena marries Pietro and becomes a mother in *Those Who Leave and Those Who Stay*, her life begins to unravel. Bored and dissatisfied, she is introduced by her mother-in-law Adele, who is an editor and translator, to "the new radical feminist tracts" then in circulation among Milanese women intellectuals (3:245). Without invoking them by name, Ferrante clearly alludes here to first-generation Italian feminists of the 1970s, especially the thinkers and activists who founded the Milan Women's Bookstore Collective in 1975 and gave rise to the thinking of difference.[7] For the Milan collective, sexual difference is not a matter of securing particular legal and economic rights but rather a problem of social relations. What is at stake is not a mirage of equality under the law, but rather a search for freedom of mind and collaboration with authoritative female interlocutors: "The politics of claiming one's rights, no matter how just or deeply felt it is, is a subordinate kind of politics" (SD 32; NC 19). Ferrante's tetralogy thus gives readers a chance to rediscover the importance of the thinking of difference, which American feminists at times dismiss for supposed essentialism. At a moment when feminism risks surrendering to the chirpy capitalist obligation to "lean in," the Milan collective's insistence on women's intellectual and practical nonconformism represents a crucial political corrective.[8]

After faltering beneath a string of personal and professional disappointments and the stress of motherhood, Elena's enthusiasm for reading and writing revives when she first encounters the thinking of difference. An eager learner from elementary school through high school, she first feels the weight of institutional misogyny at the Scuola Normale Superiore of Pisa, where only men of a certain social class like Pietro are taken seriously. This burden exerts a wearing effect on her. At university, she often appears to be stuck recapitulating lessons from her youth, such as the interest of Dido's role in the fourth book of the *Aeneid,* rather than developing new passions. From a professor's very different treatment of her and Pietro, she realizes that she is perceived as capable only of passing a civil-service exam to teach secondary school, not of joining the ranks of university faculty (2:431–32). Elena eventually reaches the conclusion that students who succeed at the Scuola Normale are indoctrinated from an early age in a rarefied subculture: "They were youths—almost all male, as were the outstanding professors and the illustrious names who had passed through that institution—who excelled because they knew without effort the present and the future use of the labor of studying" (2:403). When her sister-in-law Mariarosa arrives in Florence to give a talk on a friend's book about the Madonna del Parto, presumably meaning Piero della Francesca's celebrated version of the theme completed in 1457, Elena is struck by Mariarosa's emphasis on the importance of studying "as women and not as men" (3:279).[9] It is telling that in this episode free-spirited Mariarosa does not present her own scholarship, but rather a book written by one of her female colleagues. She thus affirms the practice of cultural "entrustment" (*affidamento*) most fundamental to the thinking of difference, which is to say the sharing of knowledge and building of community between women.

Elena soon receives an invitation to join a small feminist group in Florence that meets for weekly discussion and begins poring over the treatises given to her by Adele. The essay with which she starts, due to its provocative title, is Carla Lonzi's celebrated polemic *Let's Spit on Hegel* (1970):

> Every sentence struck me, every word, and above all the bold freedom of thought. . . . Spit on Hegel. Spit on the culture of men, spit on Marx, on Engels, on Lenin. . . . The author of those pages was called Carla Lonzi. How is it possible, I wondered, that a woman knows how to think like that. I worked so hard on books, but I endured them, I never actually used them, I never turned them against themselves. This is thinking. This is thinking against. I—after so much exertion—do not know how to think. . . . Lila, on the other hand, knows. It's her nature. If she had studied, she would know how to think like this.
>
> (3:280–81)

Of course, Elena immediately thinks of Lila as her intellectual exemplar or, to use the Milan collective's term, her *authoritative interlocutor,* which is the figure needed by the female subject "to articulate one's life according to the project of freedom" (SD 31, NC 18). It is precisely this shared project of freedom that specific acts of entrustment affirm, thus giving Italian feminism its positive, nonsubaltern potential, its meaning independent of any demand for vindication or reparation. Linda Zerilli, in her seminal reading of the collective's theory of sexual difference, argues that the methodology of Italian feminism consists not in essentialism, as hostile critics have charged, but rather in a "creative and collective practice of world-building."[10] Rather than belabor the debate between a feminism of rights-based claims to equality and one of immutable gender categories, she proposes that we think of the Italian feminist ideal as the pursuit of new social practices under "the banner of freedom."[11] If we accept this premise, we no longer need to regard the thinking of difference as revolving around ontological or metaphysical distinctions between man and woman. Instead, we may view Italian feminism as aiming at the discovery of critical, social, and political strategies through which women can affirm their freedom from misogyny and the patriarchal organization of power. For Zerilli, this freedom coincides with the creation of new forms of political life and symbolic practices rather than with redress of past grievances or acting out fantasies of sovereignty.[12]

The search by Italian women activists for creative forms of freedom that reject a subaltern politics of victimhood evidently strikes a chord with Elena. The productive effect of her feminism is all the more apparent as she emerges otherwise unmoved by the radical unrest of the times. Unlike the student-led revolt that swept through Italy and France beginning in 1968, the thinking of difference helps Elena realize that she needs to become her own woman, even in relation to Lila. Reflecting on how Lila has lived with "absolute freedom" from conventional expectations of a woman's role as wife and mother, Elena concludes that she has not yet found the sense of purpose that will enable her to become her proper self:

> *Become.* It was a verb that had always obsessed me, but I realized it for the first time only in that situation. *I wanted to become,* even though I had never known what. And I had become, that was certain, but without an object, without a real passion, without a determined ambition. I had wanted to become something—here was the point—only because I was afraid that Lila would become someone and I would stay behind. *My becoming was a becoming in her wake.* I had to start again to *become,* but for myself, as an adult, outside of her.[13]
>
> (3:346-47)

A few months after this revelation, she hits on the idea for her second book in conversation with Mariarosa and begins "to study almost in secret the invention of women by men, mixing the ancient and the modern worlds" (3:347). Yet Ferrante carefully avoids making Elena's story into a schematic allegory of entrustment. Although at first she enjoys her sister-in-law's support and encouragement, Elena's exploration of the patriarchal myth of men's authorship of women, which extends from the biblical accounts of creation to Marcel Duchamp's female alter ego Rose Sélavy, ironically finds its most direct motivation in her reunion with

Nino in 1976: "I concentrated on the texts I was studying, but I did it as if Nino had commissioned that work and on his return would expect first-rate results" (3:363).

LITERARY ENTRUSTMENTS

Uncannily, Elena's encounter with Italian feminism provokes the same ambivalence that she feels toward Lila. All of Elena's reading entails "the same admiration, the same sense of inferiority [subalternità] that I felt toward her (Lila)" (3:281 EN, 3:255 IT). Above all, the bluntness with which members of the feminist group "confronted each other—explicit to the point of being disagreeable" exemplifies an "urge for authenticity" that inexorably brings Lila to mind, forcing Elena to confess that "I felt that I should do something like that with Lila . . . we should tell each other fully what we had been silent about" (3:281–82). Lila, who stayed in Naples while Elena settled into family life with Pietro and their two daughters in Florence, thus becomes for her friend an imaginary ideal of critical engagement—in a sense, the very spirit of the thinking of difference.

When Elena feels compelled to share her enthusiasm for the new feminist writings with Lila over the phone, the latter is unimpressed and grows vulgarly scornful on learning the title of Lonzi's essay, "The Clitoral Woman and the Vaginal Woman."[14] Ironically, her crass response in the Neapolitan dialect may be said to fulfill Elena's wish for authenticity, although Elena, who characterizes their exchange as a "fiasco," is too dismayed to notice: "What the fuck are you talking about, Lenù, pleasure, pussy, we've got plenty of problems here already, you're crazy. . . . Work, do the nice things you have to do, don't waste time" (3:282). The episode poses a subtle paradox. Notwithstanding Lila's contempt for her friend's new fascination, she encourages or, in the Milan collective's sense, authorizes Elena's fundamental quest for "nice things," acting in all respects as the symbolic mediator needed to perform the feminist practice of entrustment: "In its most crystallized form, the person to whom one entrusts oneself is the woman (or women) who supports one's desire for freedom, who says, Go on" (SD 33–34).

Indeed, Elena does go on to write her own seventy-page treatise on the problem of "men who fabricate women," beginning with the two biblical accounts of creation in Genesis 1:1–2:3 and Genesis 2:4–2:24 (3:361). The project reflects a dawning awareness of how her education, as she puts it, "had shaped my mind, my voice" and conditioned her to strive "to give myself male capacities," leading her eventually to ask "what must I unlearn" (3:282). When she sets out on a series of talks in France to promote the new book, she starts every appearance with the same avowal: "I felt that I had been invented by men, colonized by their imagination" (4:56). Yet it is to Lila that Elena in her imagination ascribes ultimate authorship of her own life's story. When Elena publishes her first novel, she realizes in hindsight that Lila's childhood story, "The Blue Fairy," was her source of inspiration. This is perhaps the reason why in her role as narrator Elena never specifies what the title of her novel is, as if through its anonymity to acknowledge her debt to Lila. In a sense, Lila personifies for Elena the same sort of authority that Virgil represents for Dante in the first canto of *The Divine Comedy*. As the practice of women's attribution of authority to other women has an inaugural meaning for feminist poetics, if we agree with the implications of the Milan collective's thinking, the comparison with Dante is less farfetched than it may seem. The very notion of authorship has to be established and socially recognized among women in critical and political opposition to the patriarchal literary genealogy initiated by Dante.

For the thinking of difference, women's literature plays an important role in the effort to find a "female symbolic" and establish a theory of social-symbolic practice (SD 108–13). Convinced that victimhood is no basis of a successful politics, the members of the Milan collective set out to redefine the limits of their freedom through experiments in critical thought that focused on women authors. Their purpose was not to distill a new feminist doctrine from whatever shared ideology could be ascribed to these authors, as many of the writers resisted gendered readings of their work, but rather to compile a "yellow catalogue" of mediating figures who might be recognized as "the mothers of us all" (SD 109).[15] Among these figures, we find Jane Austen, Charlotte Brontë, Virginia Woolf, and Elsa Morante, whose first novel, *House of Liars* (*Menzogna e sortilegio*), is a crucial touchstone for Ferrante. Women's literature in this light represents an exercise in world building and free judgment: a signifier of feminism and not merely a signified.

Ferrante thus exposes readers of the Neapolitan novels to a vertiginous sense of the possibility of women's lives through critique of, and

engagement with, literature. Elena demands no recognition for her grievances. Instead, she entrusts herself to a passionate and at times stormy
attachment to Lila. What is fascinating about the bond between the quartet's protagonists is that it has little to do with their mutual resemblance or
sympathy. The friendship thrives on their disparity, rather than their similarity: "Entrusting oneself is not looking to another woman in a mirror to
find in her a confirmation of what one actually is. . . . In the relation of
entrustment, a woman offers to another woman the measure of what she
can do and what in her wants to come into existence" (SD 149). Indeed, as
we note in the introduction, Elena and Lila's story represents no less than a
feminist rewriting of the drama of Faust and Mephistopheles. Before reaching the table of contents, the reader of *My Brilliant Friend* encounters an
epigraph taken from the prologue of Goethe's *Faust* in which the Lord
avows that he does not hate Mephistopheles, because "of all the bold, denying Spirits / The waggish knave least trouble doth create" (1:7). Elena implicitly confirms that the two friends recapitulate the story of the learned doctor's bargain with the "waggish knave" when she tells Maestra Oliviero's
cousin Nella that "Lila never made a good impression the first time. Since
she was little she had seemed like a devil, and she really was, but in a good
way" (2:286). The narrative of the quartet, we might say, exerts the impudent appeal of a woman's pact with the devil, which emancipates her creative intelligence from the burden of politically correct resentment, hence
from the need to define herself in relation to man. What is most controversial about the practice of entrustment espoused by the Milan collective is its
underlying premise that the relation between women is always asymmetrical. Rather than advance the cause of sameness, the thinking of difference
insists, in a way that may seem scandalous to some, that the sharing of
knowledge and power between women is always unequal.

Elena and Adele's relationship exemplifies all the promises and risks of
entrustment in this sense. Married to the renowned scholar Guido Airota,
Adele leads a charmed life in an apartment in Genoa full of light and books.
She is accomplished, well-connected, and so influential in literary circles
that she immediately places Elena's first book with a major Milanese publishing house. Even the family's name, Airota, underscores the distance
between Adele and Elena insofar as its pronunciation, due to the initial
combination of vowels, strikes a note of hauteur to an Italian ear, especially
when compared to names such as Greco, Cerullo, etc. Not surprisingly,

Elena considers herself fortunate when Adele takes her under her wing and helps launch her professional career. From Adele, Elena in time learns how to style her hair, dress fashionably, and visit the dentist. Adele's preternatural command over every social situation becomes most evident when Elena needs help caring for Lila, after she collapses from the exhaustion of her job at the Soccavo salami factory. Elena describes Adele as possessing the self-assurance of a woman who "knew how to ask in such a way that saying no was impossible. And she crossed ideological borders confidently, she respected no hierarchies, she tracked down cleaning women, bureaucrats, industrialists, intellectuals, ministers, and she addressed all with cordial detachment, as if the favor she was about to ask she was already doing for them" (3:182). From this passage, it is clear that Elena's admiration for her mother-in-law is equivocal. She implies not only that Adele's genius for seeming to be the giver rather than the recipient of favors is a form of hypocrisy but also that her demands are all the more presumptuous for falsely equating the cost of effort incurred by accomplices ranging from cleaning women to ministers. Yet there is no denying Adele's effectiveness in this episode on behalf of Lila and Elena. Not only does she line up appointments for Lila with the best medical specialists, but she gives Elena a timely piece of advice. She encourages her to write about the exploitation of workers at the Soccavo factory and gives her the name of the editor at *l'Unità*: "Do not be timid. You are a writer; use your role, test it, make something of it. . . . And begin with the scum in your area, put their backs to the wall" (3:183).

Adele also helps Elena and Pietro to find and furnish their apartment in Florence. The couple name their first daughter Adele in her honor, and Elena gladly entrusts herself to her mother-in-law's authority. Over time, however, their relationship undergoes a metamorphosis. When Elena abandons Pietro for Nino, Adele becomes a vengeful tyrant. Not only does she promise to withdraw her support from Elena's literary efforts, but actively undermines her reputation, spreading false rumors with her Milanese publisher. The break becomes decisive when Elena observes that Adele preaches morality while having had her own extramarital affairs. Class tensions consume the relationship, casting doubt on the idea of entrustment at the heart of the thinking of difference. In the wake of this rupture, Elena's mother Immacolata at last assumes her proper symbolic role when Elena names her youngest daughter after her mother.

Finally, Elena and Lila provide the only example of successful entrustment in the quartet. The vitality of their rapport stems from the fact that their differences have less to do with money or privilege than with their talents and forms of courage. Consequently, they can exchange symbolic positions without damaging their relationship. For example, when Lila falls sick in San Giovanni a Teduccio, she entrusts herself and her son Gennaro to Elena, who neglects the planning of her own wedding in order to devote herself to organizing their care (3:178–79). That the bond of entrustment (affidamento) between Lila and Elena is reciprocal becomes clearest with respect to their children. In Italian, the word *affidamento* refers chiefly to an adult guardian's act of assuming legal custody of a child. It thus is telling that the two friends take turns throughout the Neapolitan novels entrusting their children to each other. As noted, Lila does so during her sickness, asking Elena to care for Gennaro if something happens to her. At a later moment, when their friendship appears to be ebbing, Lila nevertheless sends Gennaro to Elena for a long stay in Tuscany. For her part, Elena happily entrusts Dede and Elsa to Lila when she is pregnant with Imma and on her way to the United States with Nino. Lila not only accepts without hesitation but helps Elena's daughters come to terms with their mother's separation from their father. After Elena gives birth to Imma and moves back to Naples and into Lila's building in their old neighborhood, Imma seems to spend most of her time as a young girl with Lila's daughter Tina. Elena's account of Tina's mysterious disappearance from home in fact leaves open the possibility that Lila loses sight of her daughter because she is engrossed in trying to interest Nino, who has been a reluctant father, in Imma's upbringing. In the epilogue to *The Story of the Lost Child*, Lila performs a final act of entrustment when she leaves on Elena's doorstep the dolls that as children the two friends supposedly lost in Don Achille's basement, symbolically marking the end of their adventures and friendship.

If Ferrante's Neapolitan Quartet holds any promise of a corrective to the problem of subalternity, in other words, it consists in Elena and Lila's mutual entrustment. Their reciprocal acts of friendship may be viewed as feminist practices that do not aim at capitalist gains of wealth, legal vindications of rights, or metaphysical proofs of knowledge. Elena and Lila instead exemplify a more radical hope for emancipation. In the course of their story, neither of Ferrante's protagonists is able to fully achieve this ideal and neither pursues it without lasting personal cost. Yet the aspiration itself remains their lifelong common bond. What the two friends share, in the end, is a desire for nothing less than new social roles and creative means, new ways of living and being. They spur each other on, giving each other the strength to search for what Teresa de Lauretis, in an essay on the thinking of difference, succinctly describes as "a freedom that demands . . . only a full, political and personal, accountability to women" (SD 12).

THE POLITICS OF HISTORY

Seven years after Tina vanishes, Elena surmises from Imma's daily anecdotes that Lila may be composing a history of "Naples in its entirety," which the narrator ruefully describes as "an enormous project that she had never talked to me about" (4:437–38). As years pass and Elena comes to fear that her brilliant friend's history of Naples will eclipse the reputation of her own books, however, Lila displaces the notion of her authorial ambition during one of their conversations with "the idea of eliminating herself," as Elena reports, explaining that "eliminating herself was a sort of aesthetic project" (4:454–55). Ironically, it is when Elena publishes her account of the two friends' story in her last book, *A Friendship*, that Lila puts her aesthetic project into practice by "refusing in every possible way" any further contact with Elena and vacating the neighborhood without a trace (4:464, 471).

Why does Lila end their friendship with such finality? Why does she abandon the place and people that make up her life? Ferrante gives an unexpected answer to Elissa Shappell's question about the meaning of Lila's disappearance:

Every day we find ourselves faced with the intolerable, and no promise of utopia—whether it be political, religious or scientific—is capable of calming us. Each generation is obliged to verify this horror anew for itself, and to discover that it is impotent. So either you take a step forward or you take one back. I am not talking about suicide. I am talking about refusing to engage, about removing oneself from the picture. The sentence, "No, I will not," when it comes from the depths of the intolerable, seems to me very weighty, full of meaning, with everything to recount.

(F 339)

Far from justifying Lila's choice on the ground of her unbearable grief after losing Tina, Ferrante implies that her erasure of herself "from the picture" of the neighborhood provides an image of political resistance. Lila's withdrawal may represent "a step forward" in the effort to address the inadequacies of our received "promise of utopia." Ferrante's reading of the act of "refusing to engage" revitalizes a familiar line of criticism regarding the operations of capitalist modernity. Whereas Melville's Bartleby rebuffs his employer's requests, and indeed all appeals to social interaction, with the politely conditional refrain, "I would prefer not to," Ferrante calls for a more forceful disengagement from the "intolerable" rhythm of daily life with the declarative assertion, "No, I will not."[16] Ferrante's readers may well suspect that her explanation of Lila's act of self-erasure on the grounds of "horror" at the cultural and social inequities of the rione to some degree reflects the author's own determination to escape the pressures of literary commodification by vanishing into pseudonymous obscurity.

Ferrante may not strike the reader of her early writings as a politically committed writer. Of course, in one way or another, all her works raise feminist concerns, yet her initial efforts tend to be less overt in confronting questions of class, ideology, and justice. Nevertheless, even in one of her first novels, *The Days of Abandonment*, she portrays Olga as bluntly critical when it comes to the avarice of the "happy little families" who live in her building: "I did not give a shit about them. Happy little families, good money from professions, comfort constructed by selling at a high price services that should be free" (TDA 95). Although her tone of rage may seem more directly inspired by her husband's abandonment of her than by any definite ideological position, her observation of her neighbors' hypocrisy in enjoying goods "that should be free" nevertheless lands a convincing blow. When it comes to politics, Ferrante is a provocative and at times unsettling writer, precisely because she eschews gestures of party allegiance or doctrinal conviction. In her writing, the political encompasses a number of disparate operations. At certain points, it appears to signify practical methods of control over wealth, power, or ideas. At others, it suggests an ethical form of life that resists the prevailing institutional order while avoiding the cul-de-sac of resentment. Ferrante in this sense aligns herself with Walter Benjamin's ringing exhortation in the sixth thesis of his celebrated essay, "On the Concept of History": "Every age must strive anew to wrest tradition away from the conformism that is working to overpower it" (OCH 391). Benjamin's essay, as we shall see, indeed provides Ferrante's tetralogy with several of its crucial premises regarding the idea of history and its relationship to the characters of the novels.

Shunning the modernist paradigm that Proust established in his own serial masterpiece, *In Search of Lost Time*, Ferrante refuses to grant the Neapolitan Quartet a decisive sense of order in its last volume. In fact, quite the contrary. By framing the two friends' story in the prologue of *My Brilliant Friend* in terms of Lila's disappearance, Ferrante undermines any expectation of rational order or progress that readers may bring to the series. She builds narrative momentum up to the apocalyptic final events of Tina and Lila's disappearances with stoic, almost Beckettian sangfroid. And like the blind Hamm in Beckett's *Endgame*, Lila plays a quasi-prophetic role in Ferrante's quartet. At the time of her affair with Nino in Ischia, as we note earlier, Lila admits in her diary to feeling as if she is about to be hit by a truck in the stradone and "dragged away" (2:295). Long before living with Enzo and giving birth to Tina, in other words, Lila experiences what can only be described as a premonition of her daughter's disappearance from the neighborhood and, in all likelihood, death. It is also telling that, while at Ischia, Lila happens to read Beckett's last play, *All That Fall* (1957). The drama's protagonist, Maddy Rooney, is an old, ailing woman who is tormented by the loss of her daughter, Minnie. Her blind husband, Dan Rooney, may or may not be responsible for the death of a child, who either has fallen or been pushed from the train on which Dan was returning home. By linking Lila explicitly to Beckett's repertory of characters, Ferrante does not so much resolve the conflict between the microcosm of her protagonists' inner lives and the macrocosm of their historical situations as she highlights their anarchic and absurdist impulses in the face of the conflict. Politics, in all its discursive and ideological aspects, may be a persistent object of satire in the Neapolitan novels, yet Ferrante allows her dramatis personae to inhabit the entire spectrum of political attitudes and convictions.

The novels chronicle a stretch of roughly six decades starting with the post–World War II boom period known as the Economic Miracle, which generally is regarded as spanning from the early 1950s to the mid-to-late 1960s. The series continues through the student-led unrest of 1968 to the years of Silvio Berlusconi's prime ministry, although he is never directly mentioned by name. However, explicit references to the tragic terrorist attacks of Bologna and Brescia, the kidnapping of ill-fated prime minister Aldo Moro, the vicissitudes of the Italian Communist Party, and the volatile influence of the militant left do provide us with specific historical coordinates. Yet Ferrante tends to cite or allude to these events in passing rather than to engage in their sustained imaginative reconstruction. This approach leaves readers with the impression that for her, as for Elsa Morante, history represents a perpetual scandal from which in truth nothing can be expected.

If the Neapolitan Quartet reflects a particular historical outlook, it would have to be the withering critique of the "homogeneous empty time" of modernity that Benjamin advances in "On the Concept of History" rather than the cyclical view of history espoused by the Neapolitan philosopher Giambattista Vico, which has little to do with the understanding of the past that the novels advance. Benjamin's reflections on the possibility of messianism and redemption in the essay evince his constant effort to maintain a critical relationship to the past, which he defines as "the concern of history" (OCH 390). His thinking regarding the dynamic relationship between past, present, and future in fact supplies a pattern that Ferrante's characters elaborate in arresting ways. When Elena at the age of fifty-one in 1995 reflects on the transformation of her native city, for example, she describes Naples as "the great European metropolis" whose fate demonstrates beyond a doubt that "the dream of unlimited progress is in reality a nightmare of savagery and death" (4:337). Her historical pessimism in middle age recalls what she once amusingly described as Lila's "quite unbearable" conviction, with which she harangued Elena for a whole summer when they were girls, that "there are no gestures, words, or sighs that do not contain the sum of all crimes that human beings have committed and commit" (1:154). It is hard not to hear in both Lila's childhood assertion and Elena's middle-aged pronouncement echoes of the famous dictum from Benjamin's seventh thesis that "there is no document of culture which is not at the same time a document of barbarism" (OCH 392). For Elena and Lila, who both witness and endure their neighborhood's violence, the scars of history run deep, and cannot quickly or easily be healed, yet may help survivors of past bloodshed recognize their present need for action. In the sixth thesis of his essay, Benjamin eloquently articulates this point of view when he identifies a paradoxical "hope in the past" that arises as a critical consequence of the knowledge that *"even the dead* will not be safe from the enemy if he is victorious" (OCH 391).

The storyline revolving around the Peluso family certainly affirms this declaration. At a pivotal moment late in the series, Elena and Lila's childhood friend Carmela Peluso reveals how her father Alfredo, who was an antifascist hero in the Resistenza, remained tormented after the end of the Second World War by the violence that the fascists under Don Achille inflicted on their enemies. When Don Achille is murdered by an unknown assailant, Alfredo is charged with the crime and dies in jail. After his death, Alfredo's wife Giuseppina eventually kills herself. Their son, Pasquale, joins a leftist revolutionary group, embraces armed violence, and, after years of living on the run, is arrested by the police. Yet despite threatening to repeat his father's fate, "Pasquale carried on his war even in prison" like someone whose hope in the past sustains his belief in the present (4:425). Of course, the most famous image of Benjamin's essay on history occurs in the ninth thesis when he describes the "angel of history" depicted in Paul Klee's painting *Angelus Novus* (1920), whose "face is turned toward the past" in order to see the growing chain of events and wreckage of human progress (OCH 392). Like Benjamin's angel, Pasquale wishes to make the dead and the defeated whole again, convincing his friends that only by acknowledging the truth of the past can we approach the future. Notwithstanding his ideological extremism, Pasquale functions in the narrative as a sort of embodiment of Benjaminian materialist consciousness.

We may find it unsurprising that, of all the characters in the novels, only radical Pasquale and brilliant Lila heed Alfredo's warning and examine with a critical eye their historical circumstances. Their mutual fascination with the vanished stories of the oppressed originates in their childhood friendship, when they would talk about "the things that happened before us" and how their parents "thought that what had happened before was past . . . and so, without knowing it, they continued it" (1:162–63). The need to recover these lost histories culminates poignantly in the middle-aged Lila telling Elena's daughter Imma a series of fantastic tales about Naples's neglected past, in which "palaces with paradisiacal gardens fell into ruin," the "spirits of dead children" possess the deserted buildings and neighborhoods, and the shades of the forgotten invade "the head when it thinks, because words are full of ghosts but so are images" (4:440–41). What Lila passes on to Imma with this "permanent stream of splendors and miseries"

(4:440) is the importance of listening to the voices from the past whom the powerful and complacent have tried to silence, of recovering the narratives of the disappeared, and of making an effort, in Benjamin's words, "to brush history against the grain" (OCH 392).

Even as twelve-year-old girls, it should be noted, Lila and Elena wonder who in truth is Don Achille's killer. In the "unbearable" surroundings of the neighborhood, they begin to question the official account of the crime and consider alternative explanations. By contrast, Maestra Oliviero warns Elena against Pasquale, because in the teacher's eyes he is a "construction worker" from a bad family, whose father is a Communist and murderer (1:124). Pasquale, however, is interested in Lila, not in Elena. It is from Pasquale, in fact, that Lila receives her first declaration of a suitor's love (1:183–84). Although she gently refuses his youthful proposal, they nurture a friendship that increasingly takes root in their shared political ideals, as Pasquale takes pains to answer Lila's questions about "the things of before" (1:163). She interrogates him about how these manifestations of the before have shaped postwar Italy, starting with the fascists, monarchists, and black market (1:153) and eventually progressing to include "the Resistance . . . the republic . . . the neo-fascists, Christian Democracy, Communism" (1:184). Soon, however, she surpasses Pasquale's knowledge and reads books on her own until she can connect the facts "in a chain that tightened around you on all sides" (1:155).

Coming to terms with the past for Lila and Pasquale is no academic exercise. On this score, we may imagine them sympathizing with a point that Benjamin makes in his fourteenth thesis. Specifically, the German critic contends here that history is "charged with now-time" (*Jetztzeit*), which is to say it is "shot through with splinters of Messianic time" (OCH 395, 397). Now-time or messianic time in Benjamin's eyes is discontinuous with the homogeneous, empty time of the ruling class and, not being intelligible in terms of the victors' narrative of history, offers the potential of a "dialectical leap" into a revolutionary future (OCH 395).[17] Alive to this very possibility, both Pasquale and Lila may be said to respond to the claims of the past and its casualties by trying to engage what Benjamin, in a supplement to "On the Concept of History," called "the emergency brake" on the "locomotive of world history."[18]

After Lila endures in middle age the loss of Tina, she enlarges the scope of her investigation of the before until it reflects a more generous, all-encompassing view of the world of "the befores, the afters, the thens" (4:439). In Imma's enthralled company, she visits some famous and some lesser-known Neapolitan sites, retracing the origins of Piazza dei Martiri, Vasto, and Fosso Carbonario. One crucial ghost for Lila is that of Masaniello, whom she pronounces "a funny and terrible spirit, he makes the poor laugh and the rich tremble" (4:441). Her recounting of the life of the legendary Neapolitan fisherman who in 1647 led a revolt against the feudal nobility and their sovereigns in Habsburg Spain emphasizes his most impertinent feats of derring-do rather than, say, his successful demands for citizens' rights or reduced taxes. She thus regales Imma with tales of how Masaniello decapitated the portraits of the noblemen who opposed him and how he dressed up in jewelry and silk like a prince to mock the ruling class. From her delight in her protagonist's audacity, we may surmise that she regards him as something of a kindred spirit, as I will argue at greater length in chapter 4, *"Genius Loci."* The similarity of their attitudes encourages us to regard Lila as a sort of modern incarnation of the Masaniellan spirit. Her skepticism toward the workings of the law and the state, her irreverence and panache, and her loyalty to the subjugated are all traits that point back to the Neapolitan popular hero as an archetypal model.

POLITICAL COSMOLOGIES

If Lila's genius is revolutionary because it is gratuitous, why is politics so important in the Neapolitan novels? What insights do we gain into the characters' psychologies, if we grasp their political affiliations? With these questions in mind, we may find it helpful to consider how Ferrante portrays the Italian party denominations in the narrative. The two figures of greatest importance when it comes to grasping the novelist's undertaking on this score are Nino and Lila. In the Neapolitan Quartet, we encounter a systematic contrast between politics as reflexive tribalism, which is exemplified by Nino and a few other, mostly male characters who behave like allegorical avatars of the major political parties, and politics as creative resistance, which is embodied mainly by Lila and perhaps in a few more minor respects by Elena. As Ferrante makes clear in an interview, Nino represents the type of personality that has become all too recognizable in contemporary Italy:

Nino's traits are more widespread today. Wanting to please those who exercise any sort of power is a characteristic of the subordinate who wants to emerge from his subordinate position. But it's also a feature of the permanent spectacle in which we are immersed, which by its nature goes hand in hand with superficiality. Superficiality is a synonym not for stupidity but for the display of one's own body, pleasure in appearances, imperviousness in the face of the spoilsport par excellence, the suffering of others.
(F 242–43)

Nino suggests something of the unprincipled opportunism of the last secretary of the Italian Socialist Party, Bettino Craxi, as well as Craxi's most eminent protégé, Silvio Berlusconi. Craxi's notorious betrayal of the ideals of the socialist tradition, which I consider at greater length later in this chapter, helped to bring about the implosion of Italy's government during the corruption trials of the 1990s and the coarsening of Italian culture that came with the privatization of mass media under Berlusconi's influence.

Lila instead offers the only example of meaningful resistance in Ferrante's saga to the violent and oppressive forces that control the social order in Italy. (Although Elena may be said to mount outspoken critiques of Italy's sexist social conventions in her writings, she herself comes to feel that her books have no lasting relevance as she grows older.) Notwithstanding her humble background, Lila courageously defies not only the Camorrist power of the Solaras but also all the ruses and diversions of contemporary false consciousness. In the same interview in which she aligns Nino's mentality with the cultural spectacle that thrives on the superficiality of the ruling class, Ferrante adds this succinct description of Lila's temperament: "Lila's traits instead seem to me the only possible pathway for those who want to be an active part of this world without submitting to it" (F 243). The delight that Lila takes in the "gratuitousness" or extravagance of creative intelligence, in other words, stems from a refusal to allow her ideas to be put to subaltern uses, from an instinctive contempt for hierarchy that enables her to reimagine the conditions of her own thoughts, words, and actions with the freedom of an iconoclast.

Very few characters identify themselves outright as members of Christian Democracy (Democrazia Cristiana), the conservative party that, from 1946 until its dissolution in 1994 due to corruption scandals, generally represented the largest bloc of votes in the Italian Parliament. Only Tarratano, the professor of Italian literature who meets Elena in Milan and makes an unseemly pass at her in Turin, declares that he is a Christian Democrat (2:37). As Elena observes, the Solaras are fascists who act like monarchists or Christian Democrats when it is convenient for them (3:132–33), while maintaining connections to members of the neofascist Italian Social Movement (Movimento Sociale Italiano or MSI; 3:59). Ferrante tends to avoid mentioning famous political names and events, but makes two notable exceptions in the series. The first is for Enrico Berlinguer's proposal in 1973 to form a governing coalition between the Italian Communist Party and the Christian Democrats (3:296). The second is for the tragically ill-conceived kidnapping of Aldo Moro in 1978, before he could sign the resulting Historic Compromise into law (4:86–87). Moro's abduction and botched ransoming led to his murder by the Red Brigades when the authorities refused to negotiate.

Pietro Airota, the father of Elena's two older daughters, is a member of the Italian Communist Party (Partito Comunista Italiano or PCI). The PCI was famous for garnering the largest electoral consensus of any communist party in Western Europe, before disintegrating in the 1990s after the fall of the Berlin Wall.[19] During the years of its heyday, the PCI was led by Berlinguer in the role of secretary general (1972–1984) and as a party had a reputation for honesty and integrity but also for a certain rigidity of thinking.[20] One of Berlinguer's last crusades in the 1980s was to rally the PCI around the "moral question," prophetically calling for a public fight against corruption and organized crime, which he deemed crucial to Italy's future. In his opinions and actions, Pietro is quite typical of his political party, demonstrating admirable moral decency, a certain resistance to new ideas, and perhaps a hint of self-righteousness. He continually gets into disputes with his students, especially when they flirt with political extremism, and becomes enraged with Elena at the thought that, because of her old ties to Pasquale and Nadia, he briefly may have sheltered two terrorists in his own home (3:380–83). Unlike the more pliable Italian Socialist Party (Partito Socialista Italiano or PSI), the PCI famously supported the state in refusing to bargain with the Red Brigades for Moro's release.

At the same time, Pietro is capable of genuine warmth and kindness. In his successive visits to Naples, he grows close not only to members of Elena's family but also to Lila, who develops real admiration for him. At one point after he and Elena divorce, Lila tells her friend that, although she is very smart, Pietro has a superior gift when it comes to speaking with unforced eloquence (4:266). Even before meeting Pietro, Lila adds, she hoped Gennaro would grow up to be an intellectual who, like Elena's ex-husband, might possess a natural touch. Whereas Pietro is an exemplary Communist, his parents Guido and Adele are Socialists, albeit of the self-consciously leftist variety. Led by Riccardo Lombardi, who was a founding member in 1942 of the Action Party (Partito d'Azione) that played a central part in the Resistenza, the leftist Socialists claimed to be the most authentic branch of the PSI on account of their direct connection to the party's historical roots in the struggle against fascism. As a leftist Socialist who happens to be a professor of classical literature, Guido certainly possesses expert knowledge of the past, but we soon learn that he is also far more modern and cosmopolitan than his son. For example, Guido can banter with Mariarosa in playful "skirmishes" over contemporary issues and talk about a wide range of topics as Pietro cannot do (2:409). Adele's industriousness as a social maneuverer appears to reinforce the notion that Socialists are canny types who feel at ease in the fray of current events. The PSI, which never embraced Communist principles, clearly profited in the 1980s from waning enthusiasm for Marxism and opportunistically styled itself as more savvy than other leftist groups in Italy.

Over the years, the political differences between the two largest parties of the left became more marked. Unlike the PCI, the PSI occasionally entered into governing coalitions with Christian Democracy. After Craxi became the PSI's leader in 1976, the party underwent a process of pseudo-modernization that, in the end, amounted to nothing more than an embrace of bribery and empty political spectacle. The annual congress of the PSI became an elaborately staged event on which millions of *lire* were spent. Not coincidentally, Craxi helped to foster the financial and political ascent of Berlusconi in Milan. The Socialists prided themselves on being far worldlier than the Communists, adopting a posture neatly exemplified in the quartet by Nino Saratorre. At first, Nino plays a role similar to what the Marxist philosopher Antonio Gramsci would have called an "organic intellectual," meaning a member of the intelligentsia whose expertise derives directly from society's economic processes and who gives his or her class its awareness of its own function, in Nino's case by using data to buttress his political claims. As time goes by, however, he winds up as an elected official of the PSI who goes to jail for corruption in the early 1990s, but, after serving his sentence, manages to regain public office thanks to the cynicism of the electorate.

The parable of Nino's public career offers an emblematic glimpse of the larger descent of Italy into political chaos during this period. The *Mani Pulite* or Clean Hands scandal of the 1990s destroyed several political parties including both the PSI and Christian Democracy. Prominent party members were caught taking bribes and kickbacks, and investigations into the criminal purchasing of favors eventually uncovered evidence of the involvement of a number of corporations, including Berlusconi's Fininvest. In the more or less two decades leading up to the turmoil of Clean Hands, numerous grassroots organizations flourished on the extreme left of the ideological spectrum, including the newspaper *Il Manifesto*, which a dissenting faction of Communists founded in 1969, the radical collective Continuous Struggle (Lotta Continua), the far-left party Proletarian Democracy (Democrazia Proletaria), and the terrorist Red Brigades (Brigate Rosse). Professor Galiani's son Armando belongs to Proletarian Democracy, which ostensibly devoted itself to keeping workers at the front and center of political debate. In time, he gives up his work as a doctor caring for the poor, makes a failed bid for Parliament in the early 1980s, and subsequently becomes a muckraking reporter for a private television channel. He provokes Lila's wrath by telling her that, while investigating construction sites for a segment on the aftermath of the 1983 earthquake, he heard rumors of a truck that was scrapped in haste for sinister reasons, implying that it had something to do with Tina's disappearance (4:343).

When Berlinguer, in the wake of Allende's overthrow in Chile, began to champion an alliance between the political right and left, many intellectuals broke with the PCI. For these dissidents, the Historic Compromise was a bureaucratic ruse worthy only of their contempt. Berlinguer's plan drew opposition in particular from the left's more radical wing. In the quartet, Professor Galiani expresses bitter disappointment with the PCI when Elena and Lila pay her a visit, after Elena publishes an exposé of the Soccavo salami factory in *l'Unità*. Elena painfully realizes during their reunion that her teacher wishes to make a show of preferring Lila over her, because as a worker Lila confronted the factory's management (3:224). Perhaps moved by envy of Elena's literary successes, as Lila insinuates, and evidently swayed by a fetishistic reverence for the proletariat, Galiani dismisses with a sniff *l'Unità*, which was the official organ of the PCI, as "a newspaper of bureaucrats" (3:224). Yet we may recall that Galiani gave the very same paper to the adolescent Elena as a means of rousing her intellectual ambitions in the lyceum (*liceo*) or high school (2:133). Galiani's daughter Nadia pursues a decidedly senseless political fate, following Pasquale into an unnamed militant group before falsely testifying against him once she is arrested (4:401). The product of a privileged upbringing, Nadia, in marked contrast to Pasquale, represents the hypocrisy of some of the student radicals during the social upheaval of the late 1960s and 1970s who were capable of committing acts of criminal brutality while sanctimoniously invoking the cause of Italy's workers. Even a brief glance at the life of Renato Curcio, an exemplary figure of this period of unrest, helps bring into focus the darker and bloodier consequences of the alliance between the Italian left's workerist and academic wings. After struggling through a rough working-class upbringing, Curcio became a zealous proponent of Maoist and Marxist theories at the University of Trento before dropping out and founding the terrorist group known as the Red Brigades. Whereas Nadia "repents" to the state by naming her former comrades-in-arms in exchange for a lesser prison sentence, thus taking part in the historical movement of *pentitismo* in Italy, Pasquale demonstrates to the end a steadfast adherence to his principles by refusing to incriminate those who have helped him.

For her part, Elena never makes explicit exactly where her own allegiance resides. On the evening when Pietro tells Elena about Lila's research in the Biblioteca Nazionale, he teases her about what she calls "my halfway feminism, my halfway Marxism, my halfway Freudianism, my halfway Foucault-ism, my halfway subversiveness" (4:394). Indeed, the fact that Elena was never a true believer in the gospel of the PCI and at times criticized Pietro, while taking "political positions no different from those of the students who made things so hard for him," persistently caused friction between them (3:250). Yet her revulsion over time at Nino's growing acceptance of right-wing views reaches a boiling point when he starts making claims that governing is more important than justice and that "we should learn to talk" to fascists (3:228). His "craving to be politically surprising" strikes her as unpleasant and leads her to repeat the judgment of a friend who accuses Nino of cynicism (3:227, 229). As a result, she grows increasingly bored and impatient with what she calls his "provocative yet opaque way" of issuing political pronouncements as if only he understands what she calls "the daily moves and counter-moves of a system that to me, to his own friends, seemed rotten to the core" (4:229). When he overhears Elena assure Dede that the people always have a possibility of "turning everything upside down," Nino tries to refocus the girl's priorities by smugly faulting Elena because "she doesn't know much about how the world we live in functions" (4:229). In response, Elena falls silent, perhaps in disgust at the crassness with which Nino now conforms to the pragmatist imperatives of those in power.

In the epilogue to *The Story of the Lost Child*, Elena's narration sets up an unfavorable comparison between the aging Nino and Pasquale, the latter of whom she visits in the prison to which he has been sentenced for terrorist acts. The last impression that Nino gives Elena is of the "useless labor" of "wasted time," which she damningly notes fits with his "bloated" physique and habit of "constantly celebrating himself" (4:470). We should note the cutting irony of Elena's pronouncement that Nino, who in his youth always strove to demonstrate intellectual concern for the conditions of workers, in his advanced maturity epitomizes useless labor. By contrast, Pasquale "is much better preserved than Nino," devotes all his time in prison to study, and consequently has earned a higher degree in astronomical geography. His serenity and joyful intelligence, even while undergoing punishment for his crimes, moves Elena to observe with admiration that Pasquale "hasn't moved a hairsbreadth out of the space of generous ideas" in which his Communist father immersed him as a child (4:470). The very subject in which Pasquale has completed his degree, astronomical geography, neatly signifies this generosity of spirit. Free to dedicate himself to whatever challenge most interests him, he focuses on questions of literally cosmic significance in a difficult field that advances knowledge for its own sake rather than for any ulterior motive. Unlike Nino, who as a university student specialized in the socially and politically instrumental field of economic or urban geography (3:33, 356), Pasquale late in life returns to the sort of innocent idealism that stirred him as a child. The parable of his reawakening in prison implicitly reminds us that Italy's educational system may have failed boys such as Enzo and Pasquale strictly because of their class and provincial ties. Perhaps due to awareness of the difficulties that confronted their friends since youth, neither Elena nor Lila ever waver in regarding Pasquale as *"our* Pasquale . . . whatever he had done or was doing" (4:91).

In contrast to Nadia, Pasquale does not seek to lessen his own sentence by testifying against his comrades in arms. Historically, many terrorists in Italy did bargain with the state for lighter punishments by giving up the alleged names of their coconspirators, leading at times to confrontations rife with reciprocal threats and false accusations. Following her detention by the police, Nadia not only inflates her confession by "telling a pack of lies" about Pasquale but even gets Enzo arrested when she details his friendship as a young man with Pasquale and possibly claims his involvement in some of the terrorist group's actions (4:401, 424). Although Nino, Nadia, and Pasquale form the corners of an ironic romantic triangle, their very different fates make clear how, despite facing common historical predicaments, their ethical horizons remain monadic in disposition. At the end of the saga, the only sign of hope that our disparate viewpoints someday may join in a shared vision of the future is Lila and Elena's undimmed affection for Pasquale. In Elena's appreciation of Pasquale's fidelity to "generous ideas" and his delight at the thought of Lila "doing intelligent and imaginative things," the characters' wish for a radicalism of mind that is free of ideological enmity achieves its simplest expression (4:470).

ANARCHIC SPIRITS

Bored by politics but at times enamored with the power of "subversive words" (4:85), Elena delivers a harsh judgment on Western, neoliberal societies as the story of her friendship with Lila draws to its close: "In the wealthier countries a mediocrity that hides the horrors of the rest of the world has prevailed" (4:457). In honest, direct language that shuns theoretical buzzwords, Elena unsparingly denounces the culture resulting from global capitalism. Other passages throughout the series confirm Elena's radical sympathies, even if she never announces her ideological loyalty. A telling example occurs when she compares the type of wealth amassed by Eleonora's family of lawyers and bankers to that acquired by the Camorra: "Her father was a lawyer, also her grandfather, her mother was from a banking family. I wondered what difference there was between their bourgeois wealth and that of the Solaras" (3:373).

Less in love with subversive words than Elena, Lila knows from grim experience in the salami factory that certain kinds of work should not be reformed but rather eliminated (3:163). It is true that, in tightly compressed language, she authors a manifesto listing all the abuses of workers taking place at the factory and the workers' demands for rights, and that this call to arms scores a hit in the community of radical leftist students. Yet Lila does not only author polemics. She also solicits votes for the Communist Party in the neighborhood, defying the wishes of the Solaras. The PCI is good enough for her, unlike a snob such as Professor Galiani. At the same time, Lila is far more distrustful than Elena of the law as a means of achieving justice: "The law is fine when you are dealing with people who pay attention if you merely say the word 'law.' But you know how it is here" (3:273). After the police arrest Nadia in the municipality of Chiasso, Elena suggests that it would be better for Pasquale's safety to surrender to the officials. Lila grows furious at the idea of relying on the state and vents her anger at her friend: "She made a concise list of thefts and criminal collaborations old and new by ministers, simple parliamentarians, policemen, judges, secret services from 1945 until then, showing herself as usual more informed than I could have imagined. And she yelled: '*That* is the state, why the fuck do you want to give it Pasquale?'" (4:383).

Once Pasquale is finally caught and sent to jail, Elena ironically recapitulates Lila's line of reasoning, validating her conclusions. She becomes convinced that "laws and guarantees count for nothing" and fears that Pasquale will be killed in prison (4:398). Ultimately, she seems to arrive at a view resembling those leftists who, during the controversy over Moro's kidnapping and its aftermath, adopted the slogan "neither with the state nor with the Red Brigades." In conversation with Lila and Carmen, Elena voices repugnance at the brutality that she and her friends have witnessed in Naples since childhood, yet in the next breath rationalizes "a modest amount" of violence to repel the "fierce world" that confronts them (4:398). Unlike Pietro, who, as a good Communist, censures both Pasquale and Nadia as "murderers," Elena refuses to apply the label to Pasquale, who stands accused of killing several hated antagonists, from Bruno Soccavo to Manuela, Marcello, and Michele Solara (4:397). Pietro and Elena's divergence of opinion is revealing, as the Communists took a hard line against extremism at the height of the Years of Lead that ran from 1968 through the end of the 1970s, a period that saw Italy engulfed in both right- and left-wing violence. Not only did the PCI, in contrast to the Socialists, refuse to negotiate with the Red Brigades for Moro's liberation, but Communist Party members became targets of assassination. The Communist union leader Guido Rossa, for example, was shot by the Red Brigades in 1979. We thus would be mistaken to take Pietro's dig at Elena's "halfway subversiveness" as evidence that she is a political moderate. Although she provokes Lila's ire by showing naive credulity in the benevolence of the state, she never over the years rejects Pasquale, regardless of "whatever terrible acts" he may have committed (4:127), and finally espouses a pessimism regarding the benefits of contemporary consumer society in Italy that harmonizes with Lila and Pasquale's radical views.

Unlike the spoiled and capricious Nadia, Lila and Elena cannot be dismissed as leftist poseurs. Elena confesses to having stopped voting in the late 1980s and in the early 1990s recognizes that a cultural shift has occurred in the reception of what was once called historical materialism: "The old skills resulting from long study and knowledge of the correct political line suddenly seemed senseless" (4:386, 424). Against this background, Pasquale's refusal to collaborate with "the servants of the state" in order to excuse himself or incriminate others (4:425), and his reaffirmation of love of his father's teachings shine at the end of the series as examples of ethical responsibility, even if he also betrays a glimmer of "inextinguishable rancor" that alarms Elena when he speaks with satisfaction of the deaths of the "two shits," i.e., Michele and Marcello Solara (4:471). If there is a political hero in the Neapolitan Quartet, however, we might well conclude that in fact it is Pasquale's father, Alfredo, the intrepid Communist. For Alfredo, as his daughter Carmen reminds us, is the one figure in the neighborhood who when forced to kiss Mussolini's photo "had spit on it," survived torture by the fascists to defeat them in the Resistenza, and taught his children why "there is no history of those whom the fascists killed and then 'disappeared'" (4:127).

CHRISTA WOLF'S CITY WITHOUT LOVE

A recurring question of this book is whether Ferrante's novels ought to be read differently following the allegation that "Elena Ferrante" is in truth Anita Raja. If we give some credence to this suggestion, we may find it useful to invoke Raja not as the key that decrypts all of Ferrante's mysteries but rather as one among several frames of reference that help to deepen the resonances of her narratives. When it comes to the politics of Ferrante's writing, which gives rise to her acid critique of Italy's capitalist and patriarchal norms, Raja's lifelong dedication to the translation of German literature offers a vantage point from which to consider the novelist's skepticism toward the supposed benefits of contemporary Italian life. Her experiences in particular as the translator and friend of the East German writer Christa Wolf provide a palimpsest through which the fabric of the Neapolitan Quartet reveals added layers of meaning. What is at stake is not the question of direct influence, although in certain respects the characters and plot of Wolf's *The Quest for Christa T.* (1968) may be said to anticipate those of the Neapolitan Quartet. Rather, at issue is the matter of the two authors' similar pessimism regarding the fate of the Eastern and Western European nations, the material and immaterial conditions of modernity in such societies, and the gender roles that these cultures reflexively foist on women.

If Ferrante shares with Wolf a very particular sense of feminism's historicity, which is to say a feeling that the plight of women in the contemporary Western political order hearkens back to the classical origins of patriarchy, Raja supplies the critical link connecting them. In both the Neapolitan novels and *Frantumaglia*, we find telling examples of Ferrante's genealogical reading of the feminist tradition. Not only does Elena's critique of the misogynist notion of "the invention of woman by men" in her second book proceed by "mixing the ancient and modern worlds" (3:353), but Ferrante likens Olga, the heroine of her own novel *The Days of Abandonment*, to Madame Bovary and Anna Karenina insofar as they all "are, in some ways, the descendants of Medea and Dido" (F 187). Ferrante's bleak view of the tragic fates that the rules of patriarchy compel Medea and Dido to suffer once they have been abandoned evokes Wolf's depictions of Cassandra and Medea as allegorical exemplars of modern women's disempowerment. We see in both cases the author's effort to resist canonization of patriarchal representations of women by insisting on a feminist hermeneutics.

Wolf's specific style of feminism, we should notice, cannot be disentangled from her lifelong commitment to socialist politics. It is hard to imagine her sympathizing with those feminists who espouse an individualism of rights and rewards that does little to dispute capitalism's dehumanizing principles. Some of Wolf's more collectivist impulses as a feminist are echoed by Ferrante, for example in her conviction that the vital relationship between a city's historical fate and its inhabitants' communal spirit reveals itself most fully in the story of a woman. On this score, Anita Raja again provides a clarifying point of reference. In the essay, "City Without Hope" ("La città senza speranza"), which forms the preface to *Che cosa resta* (1991), her translation of Christa Wolf's *What Remains* (*Was Bleibt,* 1990), Raja elaborates precisely this notion of the woman as embodiment of her city's common fortunes in language which foreshadows Lila and Elena's adolescent musings on the same theme in *My Brilliant Friend.* When Elena goes off to high school and Lila instead goes to work in her father's shoe repair shop, Lila learns Latin, Greek, and English and reads the *Aeneid* before Elena begins to study these topics, growing fascinated with the character of Virgil's Dido, whom Elena ruefully admits "I knew nothing about" (1:160). After rehearsing Dido's narrative at length, Lila impresses Elena with a strikingly original articulation of the moral of the tale: "When there is no love, not only the life of the people becomes sterile but the life of cities" (1:160). For a school assignment, Elena subsequently equates Dido's significance in the *Aeneid* with her symbolic role in showing that Carthage is doomed because it is "a city without love" (1:188). Her composition's eloquence makes her a star pupil, but privately Elena has to recognize that she took the idea from Lila. The irony is that Lila and Elena's notion of the city without love barely reformulates the title of Raja's preface to *Che cosa resta*: "City Without Hope." In the end, this clue perhaps offers readers of her oeuvre the most enticing textual evidence of Elena Ferrante's presumptive identity as Anita Raja.

Of course, it would not be entirely correct to claim that Wolf's novel inspires Ferrante's account of Lila and Elena's thinking in *My Brilliant Friend.* In fact, the problem of the city comes from Raja's original reading of *What Remains* in her own prefatory essay. That some traces of Wolf's motifs and tropes are evident in Ferrante's writing, however, is beyond doubt. Wolf indeed proposes that a woman best exemplifies the influence of love on the life of a city in *Cassandra,* whose eponymous heroine's story in the author's hands becomes inextricable from that of Troy itself. It is almost as if Ferrante's portrayal of Lila and Elena's enthusiasm for the figure of woman as emblem of her city reflects not only the novelist's own beguilement by Dido, which she claims to have experienced only while writing the story of Olga in *The Days of Abandonment* when she realized that Virgil's queen transforms Carthage into "a polis of love" (F 149–50), but also what we can only surmise was Raja's excitement on reading and translating *Cassandra*. Like Wolf's depictions of Berlin in *What Remains* and Troy in *Cassandra*, Ferrante's Naples is a city of mythic importance to her story's protagonists, a metropolis whose vicissitudes are entwined thoroughly with Lila and Elena's destinies. Raja indeed was a friend of the Wolfs for many years and, like the East German author, regards the respective pathologies of patriarchy and of contemporary capitalism as not in the end utterly unrelated to each other. Wolf had no real faith in suggestions of political progress after the reunification of Germany, a stance that often led to her being mischaracterized and vilified. Ferrante evokes a similar attitude of defiance regarding the prevailing currents of history when Elena reports in the early 1990s that Pasquale remains admired in their old neighborhood for being "an upright man who, even after the fall of the Berlin Wall, didn't shed the uniform of a Communist his father sewed on him, who took on the sins of others and will never surrender" (4:426–27). Maintaining the "upright" bearing that he was taught as a child even after "the fall of the Berlin Wall," Pasquale personifies the shared refusal of his community to accept subalternity in the face of the supposed historical triumph of global capitalism. We may find it telling in the case of this episode that Ferrante associates her characters' hostility toward the course of events at the end of the twentieth century not with any of Italy's own political convulsions but rather with the failure of the hopes of the former East Germany.

Raja has written two major essays on Wolf. The first, which dates back to 1990, supplies the postface to her translation of Wolf's *Cassandra* while the second is the aforementioned "City Without Hope," which makes its appearance in 1991. Both essays precede the invention of Elena Ferrante, as her debut novel, *Troubled Love* (*L'amore molesto*), initially appeared in 1996. That Raja has continued to translate Wolf's often voluminous works of fiction and nonfiction throughout her career is noteworthy. An essay of hers on Wolf entitled "Words Against the Ruin of the World: Reflections on the Language of Christa Wolf" came out this past summer in the journal *Asymptote*.[21] Wolf indeed has been a constant presence as both a role model and a friend in Raja's life, hence in Ferrante's development. When it comes to Raja's own emergence as a translator, it is significant that the two texts by Wolf on which she first chooses to comment are *Cassandra*, the German novelist's defining feminist statement, and *What Remains*, one of her most politically controversial works. In the latter, Wolf depicts a day in the life of a woman who suffers under the oppression of surveillance by the Stasi. As she wrote the story in 1979 but did not publish it until after the opening of the Berlin Wall ten years later, hostile critics in the German press loudly accused her of cowardice. The revelation in 1992 of her comparatively brief and equivocal collaboration with the Stasi from 1959 to 1962 further contributed to an air of scandal around Wolf, who, however, was defended by the likes of Günter Grass and a group of seventy-four American academics who avowed their support in *Die Zeit*.[22]

That Wolf's global reputation was not irreparably damaged is due in no small part to her feminist bona fides as a critic of the ways in which Western society subjects women to coercion. She elaborates this analysis through the character studies that populate all her novels including those of *Cassandra* and *What Remains*. As Raja stresses in "City Without Hope," both texts explore the plight of a woman who no longer recognizes her city or her world, who places her faith in people that have become strangers. Cassandra comes to stop trusting Priam and the people of Troy, and the anonymous narrator of *What Remains*, who happens to be a writer, learns a similar lesson in Berlin. Both women are led by their insight and imagination to become critics rather than evangelists of power. In the postface to *Cassandra*, Raja contends that the myth of Cassandra is the story of a woman whose determination to have an intellectual role in her culture conflicts with the will of gods and men.[23] Wolf thus may be said to provide her feminism with what Raja describes as a genealogical "depth of field" that ultimately allows us to discern in Ancient Greece its original primal scene.

We have remarked earlier that the feminism of Ferrante's Neapolitan Quartet reveals a similar depth of perspective when it comes to Lila and Elena's fascination with Dido and the very broad historical scope of Elena's critique of patriarchal culture in her second book. Lila even bears a certain resemblance to Cassandra insofar as each woman is cursed with foresight, which leads her to a pessimism at odds with the prevailing order of power in her culture. Both Cassandra and Lila's status as outsiders makes them exemplary of the well-known feminist principle that Ferrante in an interview has called "an essential concept," namely the idea that "the personal is political" (F 332). On this score, it is telling that Lila utters arguably her most wrenching prophecy while pregnant with her daughter Tina when she tells Elena that "nothing lasts, Lenù, even here in my belly, you think the creature will endure but it won't" (4:178). That this intuition becomes possible for Lila only through its communication to Elena is made clear a moment later when Lila confesses that "I don't even know how to keep friendship alive. You're kind, Lenù, you've always been patient. But tonight I finally understood it: there is always a solvent that . . . undoes everything" (4:178). For Wolf and Ferrante, in other words, what motivates the search for what we are calling depth of perception with respect to one's genealogy is women's need to create new models of affinity or community in order to survive.

On this score, it is fitting that Ferrante and Wolf have enjoyed comparable reception from readers, especially when it comes to the enthusiasm with which their idiosyncratic forms of feminism have been welcomed in the anglophone world. In 2018, we might observe, the *New York Times* included Ferrante on a list of writers that the paper labelled the "New Vanguard" for Women's History Month, where she joined the company of Rachel Cusk, Rachel Kushner, Zadie Smith, Chimamanda Ngozi Adichie, etc.[24] Such accolades cannot be called typical of Ferrante's reception in Italy, where her achievements as an author often are dismissed with a mixture of suspicion and condescension. For example, the scholar Stefano Jossa goes so far as to suggest with more than a whiff of hysteria that Ferrante should not be studied at university.[25] Filippo La Porta bizarrely accuses the pseudonymous Ferrante of "literary narcissism" (*narcisismo letterario*), Massimo Onofri huffs in pompous tones that *My Brilliant Friend* is "an epigonal, retro book" (*libro epigonale, retro*), and Paolo di Paolo has the chutzpah to sniff that the Neapolitan Quartet represents "a stylistically very slim feuilletton" (*un feuilletton stilisticamente molto esile*).[26] The mansplaining of Ferrante's purported shortcomings by her detractors suggests the resentment of a clique of blowhards who cannot forgive the novelist for attaining worldwide fame while writing in a realist mode that avoids high modernist clichés.[27]

Ferrante follows Wolf as well as the Austrian poet and writer Ingeborg Bachmann in examining the misery and self-destructiveness of women who are forced constantly to revolt against their societies' misogynist customs and institutions. Whereas Elena struggles to keep sane under the

burdens of a joyless marriage, motherhood, and a literary career that provides inadequate means of support, her brilliant friend Lila, after suffering
the loss of Tina, mysteriously vanishes without a trace like the protagonist
of Bachmann's novel, *Malina*, who magically disappears through a wall.
Wolf in fact lionized *Malina* in one of a series of lectures on *Cassandra*
that she delivered at the University of Frankfurt in 1982; the series was
published in German as *Voraussetzungen einer Erzählung, Kassandra*
(1983) and in Italian as *Premesse a Cassandra* (1984). In her reading of
Bachmann's novel, Wolf sets out to articulate a theory of moral imagination that refuses to simplify problems of sexual and historical difference,
reminding us that Flaubert is not Madame Bovary while maintaining that
Bachmann indeed is the woman without a name in *Malina*.[28]

THE QUEST FOR CHRISTA T.

With respect to the overall organization of its narrative, the most relevant
of Wolf's novels for Ferrante as a potential source of inspiration is most
likely *The Quest for Christa T.* (1968). Wolf confronts us in this work with a
character who, in a gesture that anticipates one of Ferrante's recurring
strategies, bears the author's first name. The anonymous narrator recounts
the story of her friendship with her genial, unconventional friend,
Christa T., from childhood during the Second World War through the
events of the 1960s. The tale culminates in the narrator's grief over Christa's early death at the age of thirty-five. As in Ferrante's tetralogy, the narrator of *The Quest for Christa T.* assumes the vain task of resisting her
friend's vanishing from life and memory. "I feel that she is disappearing,"
the narrator unhappily confesses, "she is disappearing."[29] Unlike Lila at
the end of *The Story of the Lost Child*, Christa T. is dead and buried in the
village cemetery. Yet the narrator of Wolf's novel and Elena in the Neapolitan Quartet face the same obligation to fight the caustic influence of
time, thus protecting the absent friend from oblivion. Although this predicament may not be an idea unique to Wolf and Ferrante, the two authors
stake out an original project by rewriting in feminist terms the genre of
novelistic elegy, which is to say the bearing witness of a narrator to a
friend's life.[30]

Ferrante's *My Brilliant Friend* and Wolf's *The Quest for Christa T.* also
share a similar framing device. In both cases, the tale begins with a

contemporary prologue before backtracking in time to depict the start of the protagonists' friendship in childhood. Lila even resembles Christa in several respects, the most basic of which is the trait of "long limbs" that Wolf's narrator ascribes to her friend (QCT 6). Christa makes an initial impression on the narrator strikingly like the image of Lila that beguiles Elena throughout the Neapolitan Quartet: "She was not aware of the effect she had; I know. I have seen her later, walking through other towns, with the same stride, the same amazed look in her eyes" (QCT 13). The fact that Lila "had slender, agile legs, and was always moving them" is fundamental to Elena's fascination with her (1:46), as if the friend's limitless potentiality can be captured only while in motion.

Like Christa, Lila shows literary talent at an early age, authoring diaries, letters, and a short story in childhood that Elena compulsively reads and rereads. Like Lila, Christa is "averse to anything formless" and suffers a nervous breakdown while working at a factory job where she cuts uniforms (QCT 29). Wolf's narrator's practice of calling Christa by her private name, Krischan, may be said to foreshadow Elena's habit of addressing her friend not as Lina but rather as Lila. Even Christa's marriage to her dependable but unexciting companion, Justus, after more heated attachments fizzle out, appears to presage Lila's decision to live with Enzo Scanno following the end of her love affair with Nino Sarratore. Finally, perhaps the most important trait that Christa and Lila have in common is their perpetual willingness to try something new, to take up an activity only to drop it for a different interest. Lacking what Wolf's narrator calls "the wisdom of self-restraint," Christa and Lila are women who never waste their potential on satisfying conventional expectations, who always keep in reserve "latent possibilities" (QCT 48).[31] We indeed can say of Lila, as the narrator says of Christa, that "she lived strenuously even when she seemed lackadaisical" (QCT 55).

A PAST THAT DOES NOT PASS

Although she has translated many other German writers, it is with Wolf that Raja has sustained the longest relationship. As we learn from one of Wolf's most personal works, the memoir *One Day a Year: 1960–2000* (*Ein Tag im Jahr*, 2003), Raja became a personal friend of Christa and Gerhard Wolf and visited them often in their apartment in East Berlin. The book, which Raja has translated as *Un giorno all'anno* (2006), represents a diary of Wolf's reflections on the twenty-seventh of every September during the years stretching from 1960 to 2000.[32] Over the course of four decades, Wolf rehearses her thoughts, feelings, and actions on the same day each year, chronicling first her life and progress as a writer in East Germany and then her uncertain place in the cultural order of Germany after reunification.

While in Cologne in 1985, she reports a meeting with Raja, who gives her a draft of an unpublished book entitled "A Past That Does Not Pass" (in German "Eine Vergangenheit, die nicht vergeht" or in Italian "Un passato che non passa"). Wolf tells us that inside the manuscript she discovered a note from Raja that read as follows: "Dear Christa, when I read your *Ricordi di Christa T.* (*Nachdenken über Christa T.*), I was halfway through the manuscript of this book. I hope you will understand why the one and the other (*Cassandra!*) have been so important. Yours, Raja."[33] Thinking of her return to East Berlin, Wolf voices the fear that the border police may find the manuscript authored or translated by Raja along with that of a book by Lev Kopelev, a Russian Germanist who fled to West Germany for political asylum in 1980. From Wolf's entry, we learn that Raja is throwing a party that night for dissident writers formerly from the German Democratic Republic (GDR) who now live in West Germany. Wolf notes that she is too sick to attend but drily adds that defectors from the GDR always suffer from nostalgia, which they can freely admit only to East Germans.[34] The entry is helpful in revealing not only the importance of Wolf's work for Raja but also the depth of Raja's involvement with intellectuals and dissidents from East Germany.

At several points in the Neapolitan novels, Ferrante uses indirect discourse in a manner that can only be defined as stream of consciousness to mimic the inane garrulity of political opinionizing, in the process sidestepping established associations of the mode with representation of feminine subjectivity. She adopts this technique to frequently satirical effect, but the mimicry also demonstrates her remarkable sensitivity to the language of political debate. As Wolf's diary entry of 1985 makes clear, Raja's interest in politics seems to have stemmed largely from her literary activities, and through her own writing she engages with the political illusions and debates that have preoccupied not only Italy but Western Europe as a whole in recent decades. Wolf's *One Day a Year* offers yet another clue as to a potential source of Raja's personal, intellectual, and political sympathies. Among the list of historical personae mentioned in the book, there is a brief entry for Raja that she herself must have either supplied or approved: "Anita Raja, 1953. Librarian in Rome; her mother a German Jew, migrated (*emigrata*) to Italy. Translator in Italian of C.W.'s books, a close friend of the Wolfs."[35] In this biographical synopsis, Raja clearly feels obliged to allow open reference to her mother and the fact that she was a German Jew. Even more telling is the choice of the word *migrated* to describe her mother's move to Italy rather than the phrase *sought refuge* or *sought asylum,* as if this relocation were the result of a carefree choice.

In a blog post entitled "The Story Behind a Name," which he published in the *New York Review Daily* on October 2, 2016, Claudio Gatti condemns Raja for not leaving any clues when she writes in the guise of Ferrante regarding the hardships and horrific losses endured by her mother Golda Frieda Petzenbaum or her family during the Nazi persecution of Jews in the 1930s. As we know, Raja admits only that her mother "emigrated" to Italy with her family in 1937, without disclosing their hope for refuge in Milan from the violence in Germany. Yet Italy, too, was becoming a dangerous place, thanks to Mussolini's racist declaration of martial law. Starting in June 1940, the government ordered all foreign Jews to be arrested and sent to camps in central and southern Italy. Petzenbaum was sent to Spezzano della Sila, a remote town in Calabria, but not the site of a camp, and eventually was able to flee to Switzerland. Not everyone in her family was so lucky. Her parents were interned in the prison camp of Ferramonti in 1943, although they eventually were freed by the Allies and reunited with her, while many of her relatives were killed either in Auschwitz or under uncertain circumstances. In the end, however, Raja's mother and her parents survived. Perhaps this privilege has made Raja reticent about her mother's fate, given the weight of responsibility to the millions of Jews murdered in the Holocaust. Ferrante has declared in no uncertain terms that she is interested only in stories that are hard for her to tell (F 243). Golda Frieda Petzenbaum's story may be too easy or too obvious to recount, as apparently even Gatti can do it in a blog post.

One cannot help but wonder as well whether Gatti would raise such objections to Raja's wish for privacy if she were a man. With almost ghoulish presumption, he seems to expect her as a woman to shoulder some undeclared obligation to rehearse publicly what the journalist himself calls "the tragedies" endured by her family.[36] Absurdly, he even insinuates that we should question Raja for admiring the ability of Christa Wolf's Cassandra to rebuild "an independent female self . . . to move away from the life rhythms of an era of horrible butchers," when the example of Raja's mother in Gatti's eyes invites autobiographical confession. His criticism of Raja through Wolf may come as no great surprise, given that Wolf grappled with the troubling ghosts of Nazi Germany throughout her life. One of her more celebrated novels, *Kindheitsmuster* (1976), which is rendered in Raja's Italian as *Trama d'infanzia* and in English as *Patterns of Childhood*, relates the story of the narrator Nelly Jordan, whose embrace of Nazism as a girl in the Hitler Youth, westward flight in 1945 from the advance of the Russian army, and struggle in the 1970s to come to terms with her memories of childhood become emblematic of the rise and fall of National Socialism itself. The past that does not pass, the hopes and disappointments of socialism, and the illusory claims of progress under Western capitalism were some of the recurring concerns that animated Wolf's fiction.

A member of the East German writers' union, Wolf's interpretation of socialism in the GDR changed over time, and although she was not a catalyst for dissident protest in the same way as a popular figure like the songwriter Wolf Biermann, she explicitly distanced herself from the Ministerium für Kultur and the country's political forces. After the Berlin Wall came down in 1989, Wolf met with heated recriminations when the fact was revealed that she had been for a time an informant of the Stasi. She also faced accusations that, by publishing her vivid chronicle of the torments of East Germany's culture of surveillance in *What Remains* at an all-too-convenient moment in 1990 despite having completed the novella in 1979, she dodged any risk of angering the authorities. Without reciting chapter and verse of Wolf's political decisions, however, we can observe that as a writer she neither was intellectually subaltern to the GDR nor to Western capitalism.[37] Wolf in fact began taking critical flak in the 1990s less on account of her ambivalence toward the GDR than for her refusal to embrace the new world order of economic globalization. As she wrote in 1994: "A scary, increasingly speedy process of the revaluation of all values is under way, in whose course those members of the intelligentsia are or were bound to be run over who are looking for ideological alternatives to capitalism's process of estrangement."[38]

If we seek a likely source of inspiration for Ferrante's quiet resistance to contemporary capitalism, we may be hard pressed to do better than Wolf. There are moments in *The Story of the Lost Child* when Lila or Elena openly rebels against the historical destiny that seems to have befallen Naples and the world at large. As the twentieth century draws to its conclusion, Elena expresses suspicion of the capitalist mania threatening to displace socialist hope in a bitter, world-weary tone that sounds more than a little reminiscent of the East German novelist:

> They were complicated years. The order of the world in which we had grown up was dissolving. . . . Anarchist, Marxist, Gramscian, Communist, Leninist, Trotskyite, Maoist, worker were quickly becoming obsolete labels or, worse, a mark of brutality. The exploitation of man by man and the logic of maximum profit, which before had been considered an abomination, had returned to become the linchpins of freedom and democracy everywhere.
>
> (4:424–25)

The long catalog of "obsolete labels" that Elena recites in recognition of the changing times conjures up the rapidly hastening extinction of entire ecosystems of political solidarity and collective action. From the 1950s through at least the mid 1970s, the left-wing parties of the Communists and Socialists not only thrived in Italy but arguably occupied the positions of greatest cultural and social centrality to the nation, especially during the renaissance of the 1960s when Communist Party membership was the largest in Western Europe.[39] Starting in the mid 1970s and culminating in the disastrous events of the early 1990s, however, the country underwent a mutation that out of all the Western European democracies perhaps most closely approximated the dispersion of political energies that occurred with the collapse of East Germany. In *Frantumaglia*, Ferrante stakes out a position similar to Elena's damning repudiation of "the logic of maximum profit" when she redefines the idea of "unlimited progress" in capitalist societies as "the great cruel squandering of the wealthy classes of the West" (F 242). Far from being a self-effacing belletrist whose only interest is the pure pleasure of storytelling, Ferrante in this light may well take on the air of a Cassandra-like prophetess of historical conflict. With ferocious indignation, Elena and Lila's epic of friendship exposes the false optimism of contemporary culture and denounces its savage waste of hope and potential.

A GRAMSCIAN EXPERIMENT

For modern Italian culture, the primacy of the ideas that Gramsci articulated in his *Prison Notebooks* cannot be overstated, although their luster has faded with the advance of time.[40] Few, if any, recent creative works can be said to exemplify Gramsci's beliefs as the Neapolitan Quartet does. The dearth of comparable projects by other writers makes it all the more startling to notice the contrast between Ferrante's earlier novels, which maintain an almost solipsistic focus on the struggles of women belonging to the contemporary bourgeoisie, and the story of the two friends, which confronts sweeping questions of sex, family, class, education, work, culture, politics, and history. It as if the author decided in the tetralogy to conduct a Gramscian experiment on an epic scale of imagination. With respect to its underlying concerns, Lila and Elena's saga shares more with Gramsci's philosophical critique of culture and society than it does with the fictive treatments of these topics in the novels of Italian authors such as Giovanni Verga, Elsa Morante, or Pier Paolo Pasolini.

As I observe at the start of this chapter, Ferrante insists throughout the Neapolitan novels on the importance of subalternity to her characters' understanding of the social energies of marginalized groups and their potential for political resistance. Without suggesting conscious knowledge of the meaning that Gramsci ascribed to the concept, Elena's narration of the two friends' story invites a Gramscian reading of their actions and situations while also expanding the category of the subaltern into the register of gender, thus taking up a distinct line of inquiry from that of the Sardinian thinker. This expansion indeed is the source of the pathos behind Elena's recognition, on reading Carla Lonzi's *Let's Spit on Hegel*, of an iconoclastic and militantly feminine form of reasoning that she herself never grows comfortable with and first encounters as a girl in her friend Lila's simultaneously inspiring and infuriating example: "Everything I read in that period ultimately drew Lila in, one way or another. I had come upon a female model of thinking that, given the obvious differences, provoked in me the same admiration, the same sense of inferiority (*la stessa subalternità*) that I felt toward her. Not only that: I read thinking of her, of fragments of her life, of the sentences she would agree with, of those she would have rejected" (3:281 EN, 3:255 IT). Notwithstanding the obviously feminist stakes of Elena's rueful admission, we should note at the same time that Ferrante never liquidates the problem of class as some recent theorists do in favor of a politics that revolves exclusively around the fortunes of particular identitarian constituencies.

Yet to identify Gramsci's influence on the narrative merely with Ferrante's use of the language of subalternity runs the risk of gross oversimplification. The Marxist philosopher aimed to redefine the value of culture generally and the potential role that literature specifically could play in bringing radical political transformation to Italy. On the one hand, then, we may find it useful to read the quartet in light of his reflections on not only subaltern communities but also national-popular literature, the question of language, the school system, civil society, and organic intellectuals.[41] On the other hand, while the novelist's revival of these themes makes apparent where her sympathy lies, we should bear in mind that the series specifically dramatizes how Gramsci's hope of redeeming Italian society by cultural means came to a bitterly disappointing end.[42] Certainly, the characters who at first glance seem most vividly to personify this hope, whether it be Lila and Elena themselves or secondary figures such as Nino or Pietro, eventually fall short of the ideal in some way and find themselves either directly or indirectly swept up in the political devastation ensuing from the *Mani Pulite* imbroglio, which Elena likens to a natural disaster: "A black wave, which had lain under the gaudy trappings of power . . . became increasingly visible and spread to every corner of Italy" (4:433). If over time Elena and Lila increasingly grow disenchanted with the apparatus of government, however, the two friends' fleeting successes in creating shared forms of life and creative expression still manage to suggest the horizon of a new social order that accords with Gramsci's own vision of a revolutionized civil society beyond the hegemonic reach of the state. Broadly speaking, we may conclude that Gramsci and Ferrante demonstrate real critical affinities on the evidence of their shared ideals such as the value of education, the dynamism of cultural practices, and the vitality of subaltern communities. In this context, Henry A. Giroux's attribution to Gramsci of the view that culture amounts to "a field of struggle . . . of competing interests in which dominant and subordinate groups live out and make sense of their given circumstances and conditions of life within incommensurate hierarchies of power and possibility" applies as much to Ferrante as it does to its originator.[43] Both Gramsci and Ferrante inhabit much the same liminal space between national and transnational readerships insofar as their writings represent bodies of ideas and dialectical propositions that arise in response to Italy's specific historical situation but gain prominence from their global reception.

Gramsci maintained in his *Prison Notebooks* that "a national-popular literature, narrative and other kinds, has always been lacking in Italy and still is" by which he meant that the problematic historical association of the Italian nation and language with reactionary influences such as the caste tradition and Catholicism had led to a deep cultural schism between the intellectual classes and the people (SCW 210). In his eyes, literature in Italy had never developed the ability to engage the masses and thus served no purpose in edifying them, as was not the case in nations such as Russia or France.

> Of course, in theory nothing prevents the possible existence of an artistic popular literature. The most obvious example is the "popular" success, even today, of the great Russian novelists. But in fact neither a popular artistic literature nor a local production of "popular" literature exists [in Italy] because "writers" and "people" do not have the same conception of the world. In other words the feelings of the people are not lived by the writers as their own, nor do the writers have a "national educative" function: they have not and do not set themselves the problem of elaborating popular feelings after having relived them and made them their own.
> (SCW 206–7)

Unlike their French or Russian counterparts, Italy's traditional intellectuals did not produce artistic works in which the common people were both the object and the subject of imagination. More than any other art, the linguistic nature of literature gave it immediate social and didactic value, which organic or revolutionary intellectuals could put to use for dialectical purposes in the creation of a new moral and political hegemony. Gramsci lamented that the lack of a popular literature in Italy as evinced by the absence of serial novels, detective stories, and other demotic forms had encouraged Italian readers to turn to fiction "translated from foreign languages, especially from French" in order to satisfy their appetite for storytelling that was both pleasurable and enlightening (SCW 201). As little girls, Elena and Lila strikingly exemplify this predicament in their preference for the exciting surprises of Louisa May Alcott's *Little Women* over the sentimental platitudes of Edmondo De Amicis's *Heart* (1:68).

Circumstances such as the fragmentation of the Italian language into multiple dialects and historically late adoption of a national standard following the political unification of the country in the nineteenth century, the painful strife that the Risorgimento or unification itself brought about with the imposition of Northern administrative controls on Southern constituencies, and the gulf between the cosmopolitan orientation of intellectuals and the national-popular interest of the people all contributed in Gramsci's eyes to Italy's cultural oppression. In his view, the cosmopolitan mentality of traditional intellectuals in Italy did not reflect a worldliness of intelligence that everyone might attain but rather "the creation of a ruling caste removed from the people" (SCW 169). Cosmopolitanism in this sense was the consequence of an ideological mystification, specifically the nostalgic pretension to a direct cultural inheritance from the ancient Roman Empire through medieval Catholicism and Renaissance humanism that misleadingly facilitated the conflation of cultural authority with social privilege. Unlike the French or Russian literatures of the nineteenth century, which were epitomized by the accomplishments of writers such as Balzac, Tolstoy, and Dostoevsky, modern Italian literature possessed no writers with direct, "organic" ties to the people and thus no vanguards in the effort to produce critically challenging popular works.

That we ought to interpret the global sensation of Ferrante's Neapolitan novels in terms of Gramsci's theory of the national-popular at first may seem like an odd claim to make, especially in light of the cool critical reception the series generally has received in Italy.[44] On closer inspection, however, we may note that the very qualities enabling the novels to achieve their phenomenal worldwide success represent for Gramsci *conditiones sine quibus non* of national-popular literature. He indeed identified the national-popular with the making of "universal human content" that could address a wider range of concerns than those of the upper classes on which literary treatises such as Giovanni della Casa's *Galateo* (1558) traditionally focused (SCW 267). The historical sweep of Elena and Lila's story from the years immediately following World War II, when Gramsci's

Prison Notebooks first were published in Italy, to the first decade of the 2000s may well give readers the impression of observing events that recognizably represent the life of the nation seen from the everyday viewpoint of women who have no central role in its political fortunes. We may look at the very serial structure of the tetralogy as something of an homage to an older, less esoteric literary culture that did not dissociate serious writing from the pleasure of reading for the plot. The author continues this gesture in the direction of popular storytelling through the revival of practices such as titling the subsections of each of the four novels and prefacing each volume with an "index of characters" that groups the dramatis personae according to their families. As we note at various points, she is equally capable of flirting with lowbrow genres such as fairy tales or folklore as she is with highbrow categories such as the Bildungsroman or feminist social realism. In light of Ferrante's eclectic tastes, it is useful to remember how zealous Gramsci was to explain the varieties of modern popular fiction from Victor Hugoesque revolutionary spectacles to detective stories, gothic novels, and scientific adventures (SCW 359–60). He insisted in particular that the serial novel was "a powerful factor in the formation of the mentality and morality of the people," even if it had been corrupted by commodification over time (SCW 34, 36).

What makes the Neapolitan Quartet national-popular in nature, however, is more than a matter of the novelist's technique. Ferrante avows a decided preference for literary substance over manner when she responds to a question from Liz Jobey about the distinction between "good" and "true" writing with this answer: "A page is well written when the labor and the pleasure of truthful narration supplant any other concern, including a concern with formal elegance" (F 352). On this score, she takes a position that the Marxist philosopher would have approved without reservation. Gramsci championed the merits of "contentists" (*contenutisti*) who gave passionate expression to morally and intellectually serious questions as opposed to those of "calligraphists" (*calligrafisti*) who, as he amusingly put it, "drivel on about pure form which is its own content, etc., etc." (SCW 109, 117). Enlarging on this theme, he defined the contentists' task as nothing less than the formation of the national-popular mentality itself: "'Beauty' is not enough. There must be a specific moral and intellectual content which is the elaborated and finished expression of the deepest aspiration of a given public, of a nation-people in a certain phase of its historical development"

(SCW 264). Although hardly indifferent to questions of style and language, Gramsci resolutely took the side of the contentists, as only their works gave rise to the new ideas that could bring revolutionary change to the larger culture: "Since no work of art can be without a content, can fail to be connected to a poetic world and this poetic world to a moral and intellectual world, it is evident that the 'contentists' are simply the bearers of a new culture, a new content, while the 'calligraphists' are the bearers of an old culture" (SCW 117).

If we keep this contrast in view, it is hard not to recognize Ferrante as a modern-day member of the contentist camp. Her decision in the Neapolitan novels to foreground the friendship between two lower-class women whose efforts to resist subaltern fates take very different forms is a crucial source of the series' appeal and indeed may strike readers as a radical expansion of the contemporary novel's range of narrative possibilities. Remarking that the concept of entrustment posited by the Milan Women's Bookstore Collective provides the nearest thing to a model for Lila and Elena's friendship, Dayna Tortorici captures the exhilaration of this imaginative expansion when she asserts that "the story this dynamic produces is all too rare: a fully embodied heterosexual bildungsroman for women, in which sex and love and intellect are given equal space, with no two-dimensional heroines, no religious redemption, no suicide."[45] Tortorici's use of the word *dynamic* to describe a friendship that encompasses "sex and love and intellect" while resisting the conventional resolutions that global culture has imposed on women's stories aptly conveys the propulsive intellectual energy that animates the two friends' saga. Ferrante, in other words, invests both Lila and Elena with a force of mind that actively contests our expectations of what working-class women's lives can look like, giving her protagonists voices that seem utterly new and distinctive in their resistance to condescending or patronizing exploitation.[46] Her proletarian heroines are not, as Gramsci observed of Manzoni's characters, willing and humble collaborators with a conservative Catholic paternalism that regards them as deserving only "of indulgent benevolence, not shared humanity" (SCW 292).

The Marxist philosopher made this argument in particular with respect to Manzoni's celebrated novel *The Betrothed* (*I promessi sposi*). As Gramsci put it, the Milanese author's view of the poor prevented him from imagining the inner lives of lower-class characters and resembled nothing so much as the generosity of an animal protection society toward the animals, adding for good measure: "Manzoni reminds one of the epigram about Paul Bourget: for Bourget a woman must have an income of 100,000 francs before she can have an inner life" (SCW 292). In this light, Manzoni exemplified "the traditional attitude of Italian intellectuals" who treated "the humble" in the manner of an adult toward a child or, more damningly, of a self-proclaimed "superior" race toward the racial other (SCW 293). It is true that Gramsci's acid critique of Manzoni may, in certain respects, anticipate more recent denunciations of the practices of cultural appropriation. We should remember, however, that Gramsci cared less about an intellectual's actual class origin than her critical disposition and capacity to verbalize the dream of national-popular advancement.

On this point, his judgment is relevant to our reading of Ferrante in a specific sense. Whatever we surmise about the influence of Anita Raja's upbringing as an upper-middle-class Italian woman on Ferrante's works, we must recognize that she endows her plebeian protagonists in the Neapolitan Quartet with genius, complicated subjectivities, and a vibrant capacity for resistance to subalternity.[47] That she succeeds in enthralling the reader with her portrayals of Lila and Elena does not mean that she romanticizes the poor, however, as the proletarian characters of the four novels can be violent, duplicitous, servile, self-destructive, etc., but never seem to be psychologically unrecognizable as is the case in Manzoni's writing. If any figures have a more distant or opaque air about them, they tend to be members of the bourgeoisie such as the Galianis or the Airotas, whose generally less vivid representation reinforces the feeling that for Elena, Lila, and their neighbors the privilege of belonging to the hegemonic strata of society always remains unattainable. Comparing Ferrante to other Italian novelists only drives home the singularity of the tetralogy's heroines. Her decidedly urban characters are different in kind from the eponymous protagonists of Verga's unfinished five-volume series, the Cycle of the Vanquished (Il ciclo dei vinti), who are defeated by the absolute lack of vitality of the agrarian South.[48] Denying any similarity between the Neapolitan Quartet and Vasco Pratolini's representations of the working class in his choral novels, Paolo Mauri instead proposes a resemblance between Ferrante's account of the two friends' girlhood in *My Brilliant Friend* and Pier Paolo Pasolini's recurring representations of boyhood in *The Street Kids* (*Ragazzi di vita*, 1955) and other works.[49] Mauri's claim seems far-fetched, however, as Ferrante does not share Pasolini's penchant for idolizing subaltern youth in erotic and religious terms.

Elena and Lila's views about language in the Neapolitan novels revive many of the concerns that Gramsci embraced in response to what he called the "question of language." Ferrante frames the two friends' conversations as an antithetical struggle between the Neapolitan dialect and Italian, which the official national language wins in Elena's retrospective written account. As the *Prison Notebooks* make clear, Gramsci was fascinated by the historical vicissitudes of Italian, a language that was "Florentine in its vocabulary and phonetically but...Latin in its syntax" and did not achieve normative status until after the Risorgimento (SCW 169). He reminds us that, with the fall of the Medici and the demise of Florence's cultural hegemony at the end of the fifteenth century, Italian indeed "became the language of a restricted caste which had no live contact with an historical speech" (SCW 172).[50] In his opinion, only the living discourse of the people could guarantee their sense of "national linguistic unity," so Italy was doomed to represent something of a problem when it came to cultural identity (SCW 269). Of course, Gramsci's training in linguistics at the University of Turin played a considerable part in the development of his political theories, especially with respect to the concept of hegemony.[51] What is at stake in the question of language for both Gramsci and Ferrante, then, is not simply the philological outcome of a competition between dialects but more specifically the possibility for subaltern groups to adapt Italian to living usages, thus making it their own. It is revealing on this score to note that Ferrante pictures the two friends as laboring in their later years to resolve the "linguistic question" of how to communicate with each other when, as Elena puts it, Lila's "Italian was translated from dialect, my dialect was increasingly translated from Italian, and we both spoke a false language" (4:362). By dramatizing her heroines' growing estrangement from each other's habits of speech, the novelist evokes Gramsci's assessment of Italian as a language that remains "somewhat fossilized and pompous" in relation to regional dialects, even while enforcing an expectation that "the subaltern classes try to speak like the dominant classes and the intellectuals" (SCW 172, 181).

Ferrante takes pains throughout the saga to detail her characters' linguistic battles for hegemony. For example, Lila renders a harsh verdict on Elena's studious Italian when she confesses to preferring Pietro's way of speaking because "he puts the writing into his voice, but he doesn't speak like a printed book" (4:266). Lila's exacting judgment brings to mind Gramsci's condemnation of Italian for being "a cosmopolitan language, a sort of 'Esperanto,'" that often sounded in literary writing and especially in the dialogue of theatrical plays "like a recollection of words read in books or in newspapers or looked up in the dictionary—a bit like someone who has learnt French from books without a teacher listening to a play being performed in French" (SCW 269). We might conclude that for two girls from the rione Italian can only be a dead language they first learn in school rather than at home. Although Elena's aptitude in middle school for Latin crystallizes her subsequent academic path, her proclivity for the subject obliquely foreshadows her later separation from the native dialect that in the context of her verbal exchanges with Lila she movingly calls "our language of candor" (4:362). Her facility with both Latin and Italian, which for Elena equally represent languages of acculturation, at first seems to offer a way of escaping her subalternity that in the end leads only to frustration. If her genius takes her to the academically rarefied atmosphere of the Scuola Normale in Pisa for college, she discovers that for a woman from the Neapolitan lower class there are no further prospects in such a milieu, where only the Airotas can triumph. An important index of the shortcomings of HBO's television adaptation of the Neapolitan Quartet is its failure to do justice to the searching cultural critique that Ferrante achieves through sustained problematization of her characters' language in the novels. While the difficulty of their task is obvious, the screenwriters' decision to adopt Neapolitan as the primary regime of dialogue in the initial seasons of the drama replaces Ferrante's complex investigation of linguistic and cultural conflict with little more than an exercise in rhetorical set dressing.

INORGANIC INTELLECTUALS

According to Gramsci, lack of a national-popular literature was both a cultural and political problem for Italy. The lower classes had to learn to assert moral and intellectual leadership—to create their own forms of hegemony—if they were to succeed. Without disputing the importance of structure, he abandoned the formulaic thinking of Marxist dogmatists and instead devoted his attention to the decisive role of superstructure.

Consequently, he redefined the role of the intellectual class to include anyone who fulfilled an educational or leadership function in society. He took
interest in questions of pedagogy and education that are pivotal to the two
friends' story as well, reflecting in particular on the task of forming intellectuals from subaltern constituencies in order to release new cultural
energies that could transform the social order.[52] As Benedetto Fontana
puts it, Gramsci saw the relationship between teacher and student as the
model through which one could understand "the entire complex of social
and cultural relationships."[53] To Gramsci it was critically important to
highlight the relationship between hegemony, which he defined in terms
of moral and intellectual leadership, and education.

My Brilliant Friend elaborates the issue of education at length. Lila and
Elena thrill to every opportunity of developing their intellectual abilities.
In her depictions of teachers and professors, however, Ferrante makes a
systematic effort to show their detachment from the people. Gramsci
argued that the intellectual class had a particularly strong presence in
Southern Italy, which he attributed at least in part to the region's scarcity
of economic opportunities. Yet the intellectual class of the South in his
eyes was unable to engage the lower classes from which it originated.[54]
Advancing through the educational system from elementary- and middle-
school *maestri* to university professors, the detachment of intellectuals
from the lower classes only grew more pronounced. While Maestra Oliviero in elementary school clearly takes a personal interest in her pupils, her
curt dismissal of the Cerullos as "plebs" when they refuse to allow their
daughter's further education seals Lila's fate as a member of the proletariat. The school as an institution fails not only Lila but also Pasquale and
Enzo, whose respective gifts for history and mathematics go unrecog-
nized. In high school, Professor Galiani, who belongs to a very privileged
family but affects a chicly radical politics, encourages Elena's ideas, praises
her papers, and selects newspapers and books for her to read. Once Elena
makes it to university at the Scuola Normale, however, Galiani turns cold
toward her and instead takes a shine to Lila whom she encounters as a
result of efforts to unionize the Soccavo factory and believes she can patron-
ize. Taken as a whole, the subplot of the Galiani family may be said to
emblematize the failure of Italy's bourgeois, leftist intelligentsia to live up to
Gramsci's critical legacy. Instead of helping to bring about a new cultural
hegemony, Professor Galiani in her beautiful home full of books and art

eventually reveals herself to be an embodiment of "how tawdry everything had become over the years" (4:403), Galiani's daughter Nadia joins a terrorist group only to betray her comrades when the police arrest her, and the professor's son Armando becomes an earnest member of a minuscule and ineffective party of the extreme left, namely Proletarian Democracy. Reflecting on the relationship of university to popular and civil society in the tetralogy, we may discern a stark measure of the distance between the faculty of the Scuola Normale and a Southern Italian woman such as Elena in the sheer absence of her professors' names from the narrative.

Gramsci believed that intellectuals ought to be defined not so much by responsibilities like thinking, teaching, and writing as by the ensemble of social relations in which these activities took place. Consequently, in his analysis of civil society he distinguished between the roles of traditional intellectuals and what he called "organic intellectuals," by which he meant the stratum of intellectuals that was organic or intrinsic to each social class and gave its members an awareness of their own function in economic, social, and political terms (AGR 301–4). Above all, it is through the richly variegated representation of intellectuals in the Neapolitan novels that Ferrante dramatizes the rise and fall of the Gramscian project. Whereas the first two novels of the series recount the coming of age of Lila and Elena's generation in Gramsci's shadow, the last two chronicle the gradual withering of the Marxist philosopher's ideals and the ascendancy of the culture industry in Italy. The subaltern characters who stand out for their intelligence such as Elena, Lila, or Nino produce no accomplishments that withstand the test of time. What instead prevails in the background of the story is the form of cultural hegemony that Silvio Berlusconi achieved through the transmutation of mediatic control into political power, as if hijacking Gramsci's theory for perverse ends. Although Ferrante never mentions Berlusconi in the tetralogy, hinting in a letter reprinted in *Frantumaglia* at an aversion toward such literal-mindedness, the catastrophic effects of Berlusconi's rise to preeminence in Italy are easy to recognize in *The Story of the Lost Child*.[55]

One of the first intellectual figures that we encounter in the narrative, however debased he may be, is Donato Sarratore. In the two friends' neighborhood, he enjoys a literary reputation thanks to his contributions to the daily newspaper *Il Mattino* and published verses, putting into caustic perspective Gramsci's credo that "all men are intellectual . . . but not all men have in society the function of intellectuals" (AGR 304). He dedicates a volume of his own poetry entitled *Attempts at Serenity* (*Prove di sereno*) to his mistress Melina Cappuccio, causing her in Lila's words "to suffer more than she's suffered till now" (1:129). The title of this magnum opus strikes a comic note in Italian because it yokes together two incongruous nouns, namely *prove* (literally, "tests" or "trials"), which portentously suggests a formal analysis or experiment, and *sereno* (properly, "clear skies" or "clear weather"), which grandiloquently connotes either meteorological or mental calm. From a rhetorical point of view, the turn of phrase enacts a figure of anticlimax, shying away precisely from the sort of passionate bombast that the book's dedication leads us to expect. In this context, Sarratore sounds less like a sentimental or erotic poet than an inept disciple of modernist abstraction. Readers of modern Italian poetry indeed may find it easy to hear in the name of his book an homage to Giuseppe Ungaretti, the founder of the poetic school of hermeticism, who in 1918 published a lyric bearing the title "Sereno."[56] That Sarratore evidently strains to imitate Ungaretti substantiates Gramsci's contention that in Italy "the subaltern classes try to speak like the dominant classes and the intellectuals" (SCW 181). Elena makes a similar gesture when at the age of twenty-three she goes to meet with the editor of her first book and finds herself resorting instinctively to "mimicking perfectly the tones of Professor Galiani, of her children, of Mariarosa" (2:452).

The obvious candidate for the role of organic intellectual in the novels at first glance would appear to be Sarratore's son, Nino. Revealing an interest in hard economic data even as a teenager, he cuts a very different figure from the idealist philosopher who, according to Gramsci, exemplified the traditional Southern intellectual, namely Benedetto Croce. Encountering Nino while in high school at a party at Professor Galiani's residence, Elena is enchanted by his air of competence as he talks about the future of the world: "He said that the world had the technical capability to eliminate colonialism, hunger, war from the face of the earth" (2:159). Yet for all his utopian rhetoric in adolescence, he manifests an increasingly conservative, technocratic aspect over the years, exactly corroborating Gramsci's definition of the traditional intellectual as a "specialist in applied science" who represents a class in Southern Italy that is "democratic in its peasant face; reactionary in the face turned towards the big landowner and the government; politicking, corrupt and faithless" (AGR 179). As a scholar,

Nino specializes in what he describes alternately as "economic geography" and "urban geography" first as a lecturer in Milan and then as a professor in Naples (3:33, 356). At the age of forty, he may be observed still writing the odd essay about "work and the automation at Fiat" as if trying to reassert his credentials as an organic intellectual (4:235). However, his opinions have already firmly established him as a darling of the culture industry, who writes biweekly columns for *Il Mattino*, sits on the editorial board of a journal in Turin, and even becomes a consultant to an American foundation (4:231).

Nino's insistence on dissociating the movements of capital from moral or political questions leads to a ruthless pragmatism that makes him scornful of "not only every subversive statement but also every ethical declaration, every display of purity" (4:227). To the dismay of his friends, as well as of Elena, he adopts the positions of the political right, declaring that the fascists are not always wrong, that justice should be "subordinated" to the interests of the ruling class because judges are "loose cannons," and that wages should be frozen to control the cost of labor (4:227–28).[57] Ultimately, he winds up siding not with the subaltern classes to which he belongs but rather their hegemonic oppressors, avowing a desire to "end the childish aversion to power: one has to be on the inside in the places where things are born and die: the parties, the banks, television" (4:229). As the saga nears its conclusion, he follows his ambition into a political career as a one-time deputy of the Socialist Party, which seemingly comes to a crashing halt in 1992 when his lack of principles lands him "in jail like an ordinary inhabitant of the neighborhood" (4:435). With almost ludicrous inevitability, however, he rebounds a couple of years later to reclaim a seat in Parliament as a right-wing official (4:442).

While still a young woman, as we know, Elena must face the knowledge that for her, unlike her male counterparts, the door to a university professorship is closed (2:431–32). At the age of twenty-three, she publishes her first book, which immediately becomes a commercial success. When she finishes her second manuscript, which actually represents the third of her published titles, she gives it to Lila to read. Forced by Elena to voice an opinion, Lila describes it in tears as an "ugly, ugly book" that isn't true to the author's personality, because the writing in the end only mirrors "the disgusting face of things" without awakening "the imagination" (3:272, 274). When she finally submits the manuscript for publication some nine years later, Elena feels vindicated by the editor's judgment, which he expresses in a turn of phrase by now familiar to us, that her book exemplifies "pure pleasure of narration" (4:258). He specifically enthuses over her achievement of what he takes to be "a sort of autobiography . . . in novel form" that is "masculine, but paradoxically also delicate, in other words a real step forward" (4:259). Yet Lila's anguished repudiation of the story implicitly returns to haunt Elena when the book's success prompts the Solaras to threaten her and Lila for "talking shit" and, as a result, Elena has to admit that "the relationship between truth and fiction must have gone awry" in the telling of her tale, so that "the neighborhood ceased to be, as it had always been for me while I was writing, an invention" (4:282–83).

The self-contrariety of the editor's verdict on the book slyly points up the arbitrariness of the publishing industry, but we may surmise as well some hint of self-referential irony on Ferrante's part, as critics often toil to define the pleasures of her writing, especially in the Neapolitan Quartet. The author and narrator's viewpoints appear to converge in a moment of the narrative when the temptation to read the story of the two friends as a sort of autofiction exerts a stronger than usual pull. Elena's third book, whose publication is greeted with excited press coverage thanks to its subject matter, indeed represents a real step forward in her career, as her editor suggests. By way of contrast, even the translations of her first novel into French, German, and Spanish strike her as "ugly books" adorned with tacky covers that feature "women in black dresses, men with drooping mustaches and a cloth cap on their head, laundry hung out to dry" (3:347). One may wonder whether on this score Ferrante does not comment on the perils of being associated wrongly with autofiction and her own contribution to the exotification of Italian literature. The covers of the Neapolitan novels in both Italy and the U.S. have adhered to a similar pastel-blue color palette, while other countries' editions have sported different styles of cover art. However, almost all these designs illustrate narrative scenes through pictorial representations of the two friends, often walking a fine line between fidelity to the local, historical circumstances of Lila and Elena's lives in Naples and rehearsal of globally consumable, ahistorical stereotypes about Southern Italian women.

Success leads Elena to a role like Nino's as a regular contributor to the daily *Il Mattino*, a column of her own in the feminist magazine, *We Women*, phone calls from well-known authors, and even discussions with a famous director who wants to turn the book into a film (4:290). Yet literary celebrity does not facilitate productive action. Although Elena, compared to Nino, can claim to be "a sensitive soul" of the sort he holds in contempt, she comes to see herself in the long run as an author whose writings have been tainted by commerce, whose books "had come out quickly and with their minor success had for decades given me the illusion of being engaged in meaningful work" (4:227, 461). Perhaps one of the saddest lessons of the series is that, despite her moral and political instincts, Elena is not immune to the temptations of money and fame, even if she never espouses corporate feminism along the lines of the "lean-in" dogma. Mariarosa's amiable bohemian circle has its charms, and Elena's theoretical collectives in Florence obviously ignite her critical intelligence, but any larger hopes of a feminism that can overturn the hegemony of patriarchal capitalism are dashed by the end of the story. Elena succumbs to the pressures of the culture industry by writing her last novel, *A Friendship*, which recounts the events of Tina's disappearance and triggers Lila's own desertion of Elena and the neighborhood. The book revives its author's fortunes and "still sells well today," as she tells us while adding one terse caveat: "But I hate it" (4:339).

Pietro fares somewhat better as a conventional intellectual figure, appearing to be less of a hypocrite than either Nino or Elena in a career of writing about topics such as Bacchic rites from the cozy perch of an "over-cultivated courtesy" (2:411). In due course, Elena neatly sums up his virtues when she acknowledges him as "a kind man, careful not to cause embarrassment with his role as a prestigious professor" (4:391). Of all the characters in the tetralogy, though, only Lila truly nurtures the potential of an organic intellectual throughout life, albeit in the completely unorthodox form of "intelligence without purpose" (4:462). According to Elena, only Lila may claim as she advances in age that "the qualities that we had attributed to her would remain intact, maybe they would be magnified," thus possibly enabling her to produce "a book whose success she would never enjoy, as I instead had done with mine, yet that nevertheless would endure through time" (4:403, 461). Indeed, Lila stands without equal in the narrative when it comes to resisting a subaltern attitude through sheer force of intellect. However briefly, she even breathes life into the project of educating her neighbors' children, the most touching of her many enterprises. In *Those Who Leave and Those Who Stay*, Elena wrenchingly describes Lila during the period of her job at the Soccavo salami factory as "coming home to devote herself to her son, and also to the children Gennaro played with. . . . She thought: I mustn't call him Rinuccio, that would drive him to regress into dialect. She thought: I also have to help the children he plays with if I don't want him to be ruined by being with them" (3:106–7). Later in the same volume, Enzo recounts how, when he and Lila are both busy working for IBM, she nevertheless persists in "helping Gennaro with his homework and, one way or another, . . . helping Rino's children, too, and all the children who happened to be around" (3:300).

At the same time, Lila always maintains a cool-eyed view of the distribution of power that underlies her social relationships. When Elena expresses shock at the news that Lila is working for Michele Solara as the head of his family's IBM data-processing center, Lila responds that she would rather work for Michele than for "that shit Soccavo," gets paid more than Enzo, and, unlike Elena, avoids empty arguments about "the revolution, the workers, the new world, and that other bullshit," which rely on rhetorical claims of writing "truthfully" (4:316–17). A prodigious student, shoe designer, factory worker, spokesperson for the worker-student collective in Via dei Tribunali, computer programmer, entrepreneur, and scholar of Neapolitan history, Lila assumes all her roles with fearlessness and virtuosity if not limitless determination. Refusing to abandon the neighborhood until the story nears its end, she comes closest of all the characters to the ideal of the organic intellectual. Up to the moment that she cuts off contact with Elena, Gennaro, and the rest of her loved ones, Lila stays attached to a specific idea of her local place and community and, after the youthful error of her marriage to Stefano, shows little desire for the upper-middle-class life that she could afford. Unlike Elena, she does not aspire to live in a wealthy district of Naples with a panoramic view of the sea. One of her more appealing tendencies is her indifference to the lures of travel and tourism. This is why, after she drops out of sight, we can hardly imagine her free of her "confines," as Elena does, and roaming the world with restless curiosity (4:473). We can admit, as Elena cannot bring herself to do, that Lila truly has vanished because in the spectacularized, commodified, and patriarchal space of contemporary culture there is no place for someone like her.

In Gramsci's theory, the organic intellectual exerted her influence as a critic in the civil society of the nation-state. We now live in times when the borders of this imagined community perpetually come into question as a result of globalization and the society of spectacle. Gramsci meant the adjective *organic* to convey the sense of an intrinsic, active complementarity between subaltern social groups and their intellectual vanguards. The Neapolitan novels in this connection may be thought to represent Ferrante's melancholic valediction to a dream of social and political justice that no longer seems tenable in the world because we have abandoned socialist revolutionary ideals without due reflection on the meaning of their loss. In Italy the twin experiments of the Historic Compromise (*Compromesso storico*), which would have united the Italian Communist Party and Christian Democracy in political alliance, and Eurocommunism, which sought to establish the autonomy of European socialist democracies from the Soviet Union, failed before getting started with Aldo Moro's kidnapping and murder in 1978. The historical debacle of East Germany, which in many respects is epitomized by Christa Wolf's tragic attempt to play the organic intellectual, delivered an enduring lesson that must not have been lost on Ferrante. In this light, the very transnational-popular success of the Neapolitan Quartet itself ironically raises questions about the prospects for survival of the last specters of Gramscian thought in our culture. Even Ferrante's pseudonymity gains new urgency in relation to the novels' focus not only on women's friendship and love but also subaltern forms of life. As useful a strategy as it may be for keeping the media at bay, her ongoing refusal to declare her identity of course disrupts any possible virtuous circle linking her organically to a specific social group. Paradoxically, her pseudonymity encodes a gesture both of resistance to the society of spectacle and of resignation to a postsocialist world. Perhaps Ferrante's greatest political merit in this context is her avoidance of any cruel optimism of the will, encouraging only a ferocious pessimism of the intellect.

Chapter Four

GENIUS LOCI

THE CITY WITHOUT LOVE: DARKNESS

Naples has long seized the literary imagination as a site of supernatural and even demonic vitality. According to both Homer in the *Odyssey* and Virgil in the *Aeneid*, the entrance to the underworld was located near Lake Avernus (Lago d'Averno), which is a volcanic crater in the Phlegraean Fields (Campi Flegrei) to the west of Naples.[1] In an essay published in 1923, the adoptive Neapolitan philosopher Benedetto Croce evoked a well-known saying of the seventeenth and eighteenth centuries that defined the city paradoxically as "a paradise where the devils live." Although he felt that, by his time, this description no longer applied, Croce's citation makes clear that in popular myth Naples customarily has represented a devilish urban locus. In the grand narrative of Elena and Lila's friendship, Lila's Mephistophelean role is an homage to this tradition, among other things.

Of course, Naples plays a central role in Ferrante's fiction as a whole, providing the setting of her debut novel, *Troubling Love*, as well as a magnetic, if distant, figure of the past for the protagonists of *The Days of Abandonment* and *The Lost Daughter*, whose quasi-exilic relation to the city allows them to reencounter its presence only as an uncanny intruder in their memories. As the author depicts them in the Neapolitan Quartet, Naples possesses not only deeply personal significance for the characters of the novels but a dazzling abundance of cultural and historical implications for readers as well. In Lila and Elena's experiences and opinions of the streets, *piazze*, monuments, and neighborhoods of the city, we encounter a Naples that cannot be distinguished from its reflected images in the writings of such authors as Goethe, Giacomo Leopardi, Walter Benjamin, Croce, and Anna Maria Ortese, to name only the most prominent. Of course, Goethe's *Faust* ironically provides the symbolic blueprint for the entire friendship between Lila and Elena, as I have noted in previous chapters. In what follows, I maintain that it is through Benjamin's sensibility more than any other writer's that Ferrante filters our view of Naples's meaning as a city in the quartet. Her evocations of the city's porosity in relation to present and past, labyrinthine mystery, magic to the gaze of a child, richness of meaning to the scholar, nocturnal splendor to the flaneur, and funereal spectrality all are debts owed to the German Jewish philosopher's writings.

THE EAST SIDE

Along both geographical and sociological lines, Naples may be divided into three main sections: a residential and prosperous west side, which includes Vomero, Chiaia, and Posillipo; the Historic Center (Centro Storico), which encompasses both elegant streets and tightly packed districts such as Rione Carità and Forcella; and the east side between Poggioreale and the sea, which, since the eighteenth-century reign of the Bourbon monarchs, developed into the area that drew more upwardly mobile members of the working class. The eastern edge of Naples abuts the congested, more newly built suburbs of San Giovanni a Teduccio and Barra, which lie outside its official perimeters but are considered to be natural extensions of the city.

Naples is furthermore split into east and west by Corso Garibaldi, which runs vertically from the Bourbon Hospice for the Poor (Real Albergo dei Poveri) in the north to the Via Marina in the south, and diagonally from northeast to southwest by the so-called Rettifilo or Corso Umberto I, which links the Piazza Garibaldi adjoining Napoli Centrale train station to the Piazza della Borsa, also known as Piazza Giovanni Bovio. The eastern quarters of the city were built to address problems of hygiene associated with the overpopulated stretches of the Historic Center, where the lower classes, whom Ferrante's Maestra Oliviero derisively would have called the plebs, lived. Beginning in the nineteenth century, officials proposed numerous plans to try to improve the stark conditions of the *bassi*, the cramped, windowless, street-level chambers that many poor Neapolitans still inhabit today.

Moving from west to east, the scale of the city noticeably diminishes. Whereas a typical thoroughfare in Mergellina on the west side may span forty meters in width like some of those in Paris, most streets on the east side measure around a mere eight meters wide, and only the main arteries exceed twelve meters. The city shrinks as we head east, nurtures fewer and fewer green spaces, offers to the eye mostly nondescript *piazze*. In a proposal to renovate the east side of the city that dates back to 1886, Adolfo Giambarba, the head of Naples's municipal engineering board, planned a grand, tree-lined boulevard (stradone) measuring eighty meters wide to separate residential buildings from factories in an area that at the time was swampland. As Sergio Stenti observes, the stradone promised to open the city's confines to air and sunlight, offering some relief from the unhealthy overcrowding of a city prone to cholera epidemics.[2] However, the boulevard was eliminated from a subsequent plan devised in 1906 and ultimately was never realized. In the Neapolitan Quartet, the Italian term for the "road" that cuts through Elena and Lila's neighborhood is, in fact, *stradone*. Ferrante's judicious choice of word to define a central feature of the novels' main setting thus subtly resonates with a long-standing public debate surrounding the hopes and failures of modernization in Naples.

Elena and Lila's neighborhood (rione) in Naples is located on the city's east side and is not characterized by the bassi of the Historic Center's most forsaken recesses. Ferrante herself has said that she drew on the Rione Luzzatti as one historical model, although she adds that her descriptions of the two friends' rione ultimately resulted from an imaginative commingling of several different districts. It is important to distinguish the neighborhoods that she had in mind from the desolate suburban ghettos of Rome that are called *borgate*. A *borgata* in the Roman sense may refer to a handful of illegally built, single-story shanties, whereas the combination of bourgeois aspiration and scarcity of space in Naples meant that rioni generally consisted of a large number of four- or five-story buildings, which often were grouped together in a series of square blocks. This is the case of the Luzzatti, where each block was organized around a central courtyard, and the complex as a whole included a "green plaza" (*piazza verde*).

Built on Via Taddeo da Sessa between 1914 and 1925 from a design by the engineer Domenico Primicerio and further enlarged over the next three years, Rione Luzzatti by the end of this period comprised thirty-nine buildings that housed a mix of residential apartments, ground-level retail stores, and an elementary school. Each apartment was made up of two or three rooms plus a kitchen and a bathroom, the last of which, according to Stenti, was variously defined as a "latrine" (*latrina*) or "water closet" (*stanzino da cesso*). The only element in the bathroom, in other words, was a toilet with neither a sink nor a bathtub.[3] During the fascist era, the rioni on the east side of the city were consolidated and enlarged. After World War II, a new scheme proposed in 1946 and enacted through 1952 gave rise to a disorderly effort to develop the eastern periphery of the city, resulting in the rapid disappearance of green spaces and a frenzy of new construction activities.

Named after the former prime minister Luigi Luzzatti (1841–1927), the Rione Luzzatti posed some distinct advantages and disadvantages to its residents in comparison with the other districts of the east side. Considering the dearth of available public transportation, getting from the Luzzatti to the city center took much longer than from Poggioreale, for example, and this inaccessibility, coupled with the swampiness of its surroundings, made the neighborhood a less desirable choice. Then again, the spaces of the Luzzatti were less compressed than those of other districts, as the planners eliminated some buildings from the neighborhood's design in order to make room for the interior courtyards where small gardens were planted.[4] All in all, the rione was neither a squalid nor threatening place. However, it gave the impression of being somewhat isolated, a suggestion that Ferrante reinforces in the quartet by means of repeated references to the tunnel and the stradone that divide the neighborhood from the rest of Naples.

If Lila and Elena as young girls believe that they can reach the waterfront only by setting out on an epic journey, their sense of the difficulty is not due simply to youth. When they decide to play truant and venture beyond the neighborhood's environs for the first time, Elena admits that never before has she attempted such an adventure: "As far back as I could remember, I had never left the four-story white apartment buildings, the courtyard, the parish church, the public gardens" (1:73). Yet their everyday reality no longer impresses the two girls, whose imaginations have been enflamed by reading about things they have never seen and who now get "excited by the invisible" (1:74). The two friends resolve to visit the sea, which Lila has heard about from her brother Rino, but which neither girl has experienced firsthand, because their families "didn't have time, they didn't have money, they didn't have the desire" (1:74). To depart the neighborhood for Lila and Elena, in other words, is to revolt against constraints placed by their own families on their class and gender. After three hours of walking, however, they find nothing more than a "landscape of ruins: dented tanks, burned wood, wrecks of cars . . . rusting scrap iron" (1:76). We might surmise that the moral of the girls' unsuccessful flight from the mundane material conditions of home is that "the sea does not bathe Naples" ("il mare non bagna Napoli"), to borrow an evocative turn of phrase from the Neapolitan writer Anna Maria Ortese, or to put it more precisely, the sea in Elena and Lila's case is not in reach of the rione.

The ruined wasteland in which the two friends end their excursion is an early example of the city's industrialization. It resembles or may be the location to which the teenage Elena and Antonio steal away for their dates, where they explore sexual pleasure together inside an abandoned canning factory that she portrays as "all iron beams and fragments of metal" (2:25). Nearby the factory, the terrain consists of grassy fields bordering ponds that give off "the odor of moss and putrid earth" (2:25). Indeed, Elena calls these bodies of water *stagni* in Italian, using a word that is etymologically related to the adjective *stagnante* or "stagnant" in English. *Stagno* customarily refers to a shallow body of still water of smaller dimensions than a lake. Whereas a pond may be either naturally formed or artificially constructed, there is no doubt that the stagni by the old canning factory are wild outgrowths of nature. True to their name, their waters are choked and fetid to the point of implying at least a latent threat to visitors (hence Elena's remark on their "putrid" smell), as stagni represent sites that can breed diseases and cause epidemic outbreaks when not reclaimed. In other words, these are not the sort of "ponds" that Henry David Thoreau visits in *Walden* on his quest for "the essential facts of life" and that, regarding Walden Pond itself, he memorably defines as "an amphitheatre for some kind of sylvan spectacle." Perhaps Ferrante's stagni could be more accurately designated as "swamps." At any rate, they make a suitable backdrop for Elena and Antonio's uneasy adolescent relationship, which is mainly sexual in appeal and, due to lack of depth, perpetually at risk of stagnating.

The rione in which Elena and Lila grow up is defined by, among other things, its relation to the stradone, which Elena initially describes as a "wide avenue that ran through the neighborhood" (1:40). Yet "avenue," according to the *Oxford English Dictionary*, conventionally signifies "any broad roadway bordered or marked by trees or other objects at regular intervals" (OED sense 3) and thus implicitly assigned the status of a landmark. By contrast, the stradone appears to have no other purpose than to be a conduit for traffic headed somewhere more important. It is clearly a prominent, unavoidable, and not especially pleasant feature of the environment. Large trucks continually rattle by on it, bringing noise, commotion, cargoes of shadowy substances "that can destroy us faster than the atomic bomb" (4:272), and "clouds of dust" (4:331). Most of all, the stradone ironically symbolizes the neighborhood's lack of civic or public identity, the tenuous sense of connection that its residents have to the world at large. When Lila angers Elena by calling her an idiot for taking up with Nino, Elena comforts herself with the thought of leaving Naples to see the world while Lila spends her life watching the trucks fade into the distance on the stradone (4:26). During a rare moment of solitude when Nino takes the girls for a ride in his car, Elena confesses that from her apartment "the image of the *stradone* . . . gave me a sense of anguish" because it forces her to confront the question "what was I doing in that place" (4:329). That the stradone also furnishes the setting of the most harrowing event of Lila and Elena's story, namely Tina's disappearance from the rione, in this light seems cruelly fitting.

Similarly, the neighborhood's small gardens (*giardinetti*) betray a menacing reality beneath their ostensible purpose of urban beautification. While taking a walk together in 2005, for example, Elena and Lila encounter, in one of these gardens next to the local church, the corpse of their murdered childhood friend, Gigliola Spagnuolo, whose final position indicates her struggling at the moment of death against "some pain or fear" (3:24). Already by the early 1980s, when Elena first moves back to the rione to raise her daughters, the gardens have become a den of criminality, where drug addicts strew their syringes and a knifing is not an unknown occurrence (4:261, 271, 278). Like the stradone, the giardinetti, at first glance, may give the appearance of being socially productive elements of the city's topography but quickly come to exemplify the degradation of communal space in the neighborhood.

What are the residences like? Elena hints that, although not as dismal as the Historic Center's worst sections, the living conditions of the rione can make for a chaotic atmosphere. During her childhood, Elena's family inhabits what in the United States would be categorized as a second-floor apartment in a four-story walk-up, while Lila's mad relative, Melina Cappuccio, lives on the third and the Sarratore family lives on the fourth. On the day that the Sarratores move out of the neighborhood to escape the scandal caused by Donato's seduction of Melina, all the women of the rione come to their windows to witness the spectacle of Melina screaming and throwing household objects at the departing family from her apartment (1:58–61). Lila's family lives on the second floor or *piano nobile* of another, similar building, where her father Fernando's violent outbursts during family arguments can be heard from the courtyard below. When she is still a "thin and delicate" child of ten, Fernando hurls Lila out of a window in a fit of rage, causing her to break her arm from the fall (1:82).

The interior quarters of the apartments give the nondescript impression of being organized mainly for utilitarian purposes. In her own home, Elena sleeps in one "little room" with her sister and two brothers, where she also does her homework at a table "riddled with worm holes" (2:132). Modern plumbing and conveniences clearly are unknown luxuries in the buildings. On Lila's wedding day, Elena helps her to bathe in a "copper tub full of boiling water" that apparently needs to be readied in advance, because it lacks a pressurized water supply (1:311). In the new zone close by to which Lila and Stefano move after their wedding, they equip their apartment with the latest household advances such as an "enormous bathtub, like the ones in the Palmolive ad," a bidet, inlaid furniture, a refrigerator, "and even a telephone" (1:288–89). At first, they disagree on where to live, since Lila prefers the homes of the old rione, which are "larger but dark" and lacking in views, whereas Stefano is "seduced by the new," but she eventually surrenders to the appeal of being "the mistress of a house of her own, with hot water that came from the taps" (1:288).

Stefano and Lila's new household initiates Elena into the novel experience of taking a bath, which turns out to be a surprisingly meaningful lesson for her in class privilege. Indeed, Elena as a girl is unfamiliar even with the habit of brushing her teeth, which she has to learn to do when she leaves home for the Scuola Normale in Pisa. After Lila returns from her honeymoon, Elena gets into a routine of going to Lila's place at the end of each school day. One afternoon, she asks Lila on a whim if she may try out the bathtub and quickly discovers what it means to be rich enough to afford consumer society's latest amenities:

> The warmth was an unexpected pleasure. After a while I tried out the numerous little bottles that crowded the corners of the tub: a steamy foam arose, as if from my body, and almost overflowed. Ah, how many wonderful things Lila possessed. It was no longer just a matter of a clean body, it was play, it was abandon. . . . Afterward, my skin was smoother than I had ever felt it, and my hair was full, luminous, blonder. Maybe the wealth we wanted as children is this, I thought: not strongboxes full of diamonds and gold coins but a bathtub, to immerse yourself like this every day, to eat bread, salami, prosciutto, to have a lot of space even in the bathroom . . . to have *this entire* house.
>
> (2:55)

Yet for all of the alluring material conveniences that its dwellings offer residents, the zone in which Lila and Stefano initially settle endures a precipitous decline only a few years after its construction. When Elena, on learning that her sister Elisa is engaged to Marcello Solara, returns to the vicinity from Florence in late 1973, she finds that "that whole part of the neighborhood appeared abandoned" and Lila's old building is marked by a dearth of surviving trees and a "crack in the glass of the front door" (3:321).

Modernity, in other words, fails to deliver meaningful advantages to the rione. Indeed, it is true that the voracious urban expansion fueled by the Economic Miracle resulted in rampant "building speculation" in Naples but little improvement in the circumstances of the general populace.[5] According to Antonio Ghirelli, at least three hundred thousand new housing units were built in the city between 1951 and 1961. However, they were located mostly in areas such as Posillipo, Vomero, and Colli Aminei that lay beyond the reach of the less wealthy. With the construction of the San Giuseppe-Carità district, a "metastasis" of development displaced much of the traditional population of the Historic Center's older precincts.[6] In this context, the abandonment of the new zone where Lila and

Stefano live after getting married reimagines in the starkest possible terms the historic reality of the boom years. Symptomatic of the virulence of Neapolitan housing schemes and cut off from the commercial activities of the old neighborhood, the new zone almost immediately mutates into a ghost town, expiring before a true economic revival can take hold.

The traditional iconography of Naples, which at its most basic consists in the gulf (or bay), Mount Vesuvius, and the umbrella pine tree (Pinus pinea), is for the most part unknown to the people of Elena and Lila's district. Ferrante takes pains to depict their neighborhood as relatively modern, hence situated in a more mediated relationship to Neapolitans' collective memory than older communities. Poorer, more densely populated quarters of the city such as Forcella, Mercato, or Vicaria, which, as we have noted, were characterized by bassi or ground-floor dwellings, exposed their denizens to the circulation of people and traffic through the streets and thus contributed to dissolving the boundaries between the private and public worlds. By contrast, the rione of Ferrante's quartet exemplifies modern, rationalist architectural principles inasmuch as the apartments are relatively spacious compared to those of the new zone and bassi have been banished from street-level spaces. In their place, we find small, family-run businesses such as the Cerullos' shoe repair store, the Solaras' pastry shop, and the Carraccis' grocery. Commerce in the neighborhood for the most part takes place indoors in a city where selling goods to passersby outdoors has become something of an art.[7] It thus is plain that the rione represents a working-class enclave, not a "slum," as too many casual commentators on Ferrante's saga have called it.[8] The term more readily applies to the sections of Naples where we encounter high unemployment, substandard housing, poor sanitation, or even a lack of clean water.

One emblematic example of such a locality was the Palazzo dei Granili, the massive edifice in Pompeian red that was built beginning in 1779 on via Reggia di Portici. Ortese rehearses the history of the Granili in an essay entitled "The Involuntary City," which Ferrante mentions approvingly in a letter reprinted in *Frantumaglia*. Designed by the royal architect Ferdinando Fuga, the colossal structure stretched along the marina for 560 meters, had 87 windows on each floor, and was converted in succession from its original purpose as a granary into an arsenal for artillery storage, a prison, a hospital, and a barracks. The Granili suffered damage from Allied bombing in 1943, yet in spite of being partially ruined was adopted as a shelter by otherwise homeless families of squatters. Finally, the building was demolished in 1953 due to its advanced state of decay. Ortese met and interviewed many of the inhabitants, who described the Granili as a place of moaning walls, a site of pervasive affliction.[9] Reeking of unsanitary conditions, the long, dark hallways revealed the presence of children who inevitably were forced to witness their parents' sexual trysts and in countless other ways to grow up too soon, sadly becoming "little men" (*piccoli uomini*) and "little women" (*piccole donne*) as a result.[10] Ortese concludes the essay with a stirring description of their misery as she leaves the hellish, cavernous palace at night: "Night fell at the Granili, and the involuntary city prepared itself to consume its few goods in a fever that would last until the next morning, when the lamentations, the surprise, the mourning, and the inert horror of life begin again."[11]

Of course, the neighborhood of the Neapolitan Quartet is a far cry from Ortese's Granili or the city's most notoriously dangerous sections such as Forcella or the Spanish Quarter. By no means does Ferrante place her protagonists in the legendary "belly of Naples."[12] We ought to recall in this connection that the Luzzatti, which provides Ferrante with a historical model for her fictive rione, was built to help redistribute the city's teeming population along more rational lines. The argument in favor of such a reorganization actually dates back before the creation of the Luzzatti at least to 1884 when Italy's Prime Minister Agostino Depretis proclaimed during a visit that "Naples must be gutted" (*bisogna sventrare Napoli*). Both the avenue known as the Rettifilo that connects Piazza Municipio and Piazza della Borsa and the new districts that the municipal authorities created in previously less developed areas, such as the hills between Capodimonte and Vomero and the territory between Poggioreale and Granili roughly corresponding to the location of Lila and Elena's rione, were part of this plan.[13] In other words, the two friends' neighborhood belongs to a genealogy of urban planning in Naples aimed at solving the problems of public health and safety that besieged the city from the cholera epidemics of the late nineteenth century through the industrialization of the early twentieth.

Notwithstanding the hardship and violence that they face, Elena and Lila can dream as girls about being writers and read *Little Women* for inspiration in their rione rather than become little women prematurely, as in Ortese's portrait of the children of Granili. When Lila needs to relocate because she no longer can bear her loveless marriage to Stefano, the new lodgings that she takes first with Nino in Campi Flegrei and later with Enzo in San Giovanni a Teduccio both seem shabbier than her family's old home. The apartment in Campi Flegrei in fact does not have a bathtub and is dark and decrepit. The three-bedroom flat in San Giovanni a Teduccio also appears to be a step backward, and Lila shows no hesitation in abandoning it and returning to the neighborhood to rent an apartment that Elena finds for her and Enzo (3:177, 215).

We can also understand why Elena may decide to join Lila, with her daughters, in the old rione, once her relationship with Nino comes to an end in 1982. After much hesitation, she decides to take the apartment just above Lila's own, clearly reveling in the triumph of having been told by her editor that he will publish her third book: "I felt strong, no longer a victim of my origins but capable of dominating them" (4:260). Elena is aware that she is living in a "wretched apartment, situated in an increasingly run-down area" (4:271). When the photographer for the magazine *Panorama* goes to see her to prepare an article, she is struck by the "wretched place" too (4:279). The two friends are separated by only one layer of floor (4:329). Ferrante uses the nineteenth-century trope of the madwoman in the attic, only to subvert it. The ostensible madwoman, Lila, lives below Elena, as if she were her topological unconscious.[14] We can never know if the Solara brothers are responsible for Tina's disappearance or if, as a few witnesses suggest, the little girl chases a blue ball into the path of a speeding truck that runs her over in the stradone, leaving nothing in its wake. Lila's infatuation for her neighborhood comes to an end. In time she displaces her attachment onto the city itself, a city without love perhaps, like Dido's Carthage, but of epic beauty.

THE OTHER NAPLES: LIGHT

We first encounter the city beyond the rione when Elena, accompanied by her father, explores Naples for the first time. As she has to attend a *liceo* on Corso Garibaldi, her father wishes to acquaint her with the layout of the city, showing her its landmarks as if she were a tourist. Wandering more or less east to west and ending up at the waterfront, they visit Piazza Garibaldi, Corso Garibaldi, Piazza Carlo III, Via Toledo, Piazza Municipio, where her father works as a porter at the City Hall housed in Palazzo San

Giacomo, and Via Caracciolo, where she can finally contemplate the spectacle of the sea "full of light and sound" (1:138). When Elena tries to share the excitement of her discoveries with Lila, her friend dismisses her news of the attractions of Naples outside the neighborhood as "useless signs from useless spaces" (1:139). As their story progresses, however, Lila too eventually discovers the well-heeled locales and public sites of the city such as Via Toledo, Chiaia, Piazza dei Martiri, the former royal garden turned public park known as Villa Comunale, the seafront or Lungomare, and Santa Lucia.

Yet in their girlhood entering the more affluent districts is "like crossing a border" for the two friends (1:192). When Lila, Elena, Carmela, Pasquale, and Rino set out on a Sunday to see what wealthy Neapolitans are up to, they wind up walking in an increasingly bellicose mood down Via Chiaia, where the sight of a girl dressed from head to toe in green elicits their incredulous mockery. The girl's boyfriend insults Rino by calling him a "hick," and he responds by drawing blood with a punch to the boy's face. Retreating with his girlfriend at first, the boy returns a short time later with a group of four or five other well-dressed, burly young men wielding wooden clubs. The group attacks Rino and Pasquale in Piazza dei Martiri, savagely beating and kicking them until the Solara brothers, who happen to be driving past at the time, stop and help to repel the attackers. For Elena, the brutality of the encounter amounts to a grim lesson in the inescapability of class warfare as a way of life in Naples, leading her to feel "as if our neighborhood had expanded, swallowing all Naples, even the streets where respectable people lived" (1:197).

The party at Professor Galiani's home marks a symbolic turning point in the saga, as it is the first time that Elena and Lila split from each other. When Elena's high school professor invites her to a gathering organized by her children, Elena agonizes over the "unthinkable" prospect of entering what looks to her like a "royal palace" and exposing her "poor breeding" to the judgment of her teacher's more privileged guests (2:149). She overcomes her shame at the stigma of her lower-class upbringing and agrees to attend only when Lila, who wishes to know if the professor's house has a view of the sea, volunteers to go with her. The hostess's family, whose name evokes the famous eighteenth-century Illuminist thinker Ferdinando Galiani, lives in a spacious apartment on the fourth floor of an elevator building on Corso Vittorio Emanuele.[15] Crossing Naples northeastward for four-and-a-half kilometers from Piedigrotta in the southwest to Piazza Mazzini near the center, Corso Vittorio Emanuele was established in the nineteenth century under Ferdinand II of the Two Sicilies, unfurling through the hills rather than along the sea in an effort to protect the city's topography, especially the views along the shore of the gulf, from a flood of traffic. After the Risorgimento, the roadway was named for the first king of Italy.

The two friends discover that, indeed, one can look out on "the dark plane of the sea" from the Galianis' terrace as well as the city "sparkling with light" (2:154). The entire episode enacts a dialectic of darkness and light in which Elena's wide-eyed wonder at the "open and bright" ambience of the soiree symptomizes the opposition between the gloomy circumstances of the poor and the brighter conditions of the wealthy in Neapolitan society. Light in this sense is a by-product of class for the people of the city.[16] After Elena and Lila reach the apartment on foot, because they have never ridden an elevator and are wary of getting into trouble, the professor welcomes them into a big, high-ceilinged residence filled with "more books . . . than in the neighborhood library," where they encounter "young people dancing freely in a large, brilliantly lighted room" (2:154). As they climb the stairs to the party, Elena notices that every feature of the building is spotlessly clean and "gleaming" (2:153).

Like Cinderella at the ball, Elena experiences in this strange, luxurious setting a magical "sense of power," thanks to her teacher's high regard for her (2:153). She also encounters the handsome object of her affections, Nino Sarratore, as well as Professor Galiani's son, Armando, and sixteen-year-old daughter, Nadia, who is the "luminous" girl she once saw Nino kissing outside of school (2:156). Confronting Nadia's luminosity in the past forced Elena to admit her own "dullness," as she puts it (2:156). At the party, however, Elena realizes that the revelation of Nadia's identity as both Nino's girlfriend and Galiani's daughter unexpectedly reassures her because it confirms her own sense of "the natural order of things" and provides her with an image of perfect "symmetry" (2:156). Elena's perception of Nadia, when she stands next to Nino, as "a minor, but radiant divinity" comports with the idea that, by reflecting the luster of people and things around us, which in Nadia's case include not only Nino but her family and home, we may come to shine with our own light (2:159).[17] Surrounded by bright, educated people her own age, Elena for the first time can see "the world of persons, events, ideas" illuminated, recovered from the amorphous shadows of ignorance (2:158). In this milieu, she finds herself to be "more at ease than I did with my friends in the neighborhood," intuiting that her future belongs among the guests at the party rather than her more proletarian childhood peers (2:158).

Lila's customary brilliance, by contrast, never reveals itself at the party. Yet Elena at first fears that Lila's "beauty would explode like a star," making clear to the guests that "I was only Lila's pale shadow" (2:151). As Elena later learns from reading her journal, Lila instead feels "voiceless, graceless, deprived of movement, of beauty" in the unfamiliar atmosphere of the Galianis' household, where the hosts and their guests ignore her while pampering her friend (2:161). Concluding that the rest of her life will revolve around nothing more than "the grocery stores, the marriage of her brother and Pinuccia, . . . the petty war with the Solaras," she feels "irrefutably lost" and turns spiteful toward Elena (2:161). When Stefano picks up the two friends in his car to drive them home, Lila tells him in dialect that the party was boring, the hosts "don't have a thought that's their own," and that, in their company, Elena talks like "the parrots' parrot" (2:162). Lila's tirade has inevitable consequences, as Elena reports: "That night began the long, painful period that led to our first break and a long separation" (2:163). This turn of events is crucial because it dramatizes the radical difference between Lila and Elena's views of things in both a literal and figurative sense. Whereas Lila tends to focus her vision on an exact point by narrowing her eyes to a squint, Elena appears to respond to her surroundings with open eyes like Dante encountering the diffuse light of heaven in *Paradiso*. To borrow Roland Barthes's terminology in *Camera Lucida*, we may say that Lila seeks a *punctum* in the world, meaning a singular insight into each situation, whereas Elena aims to explore the *studium*, which is to say the all-encompassing context.

Even before she relocates to the aristocratic environs of Florence, Elena's penchant for light and space draws her to Naples' more luxurious precincts. For Lila's wedding dinner, for example, she chooses a restaurant on the very elegant Via Orazio and, when she returns to the city following her separation from Pietro, she decides at first to live on Via Tasso. As it winds up the hill of Posillipo, Via Tasso offers the eye some of Naples' most scenic vistas including the gulf, Mount Vesuvius, local woods full of pine trees, and the islands of Capri and Ischia in the distance. Both Via Orazio and Via Tasso possess an air of exclusivity that results from the mix of their distance from the city's clamor, imposing literary names, and an abundance of beautiful villas and estates built in the neo-Renaissance and late Liberty or Floreal architectural styles.[18] Both streets lie on the west side of Naples, in the opposite direction from the rione where Elena and Lila grew up. When Elena explains to Lila her rationale for moving to Via Tasso rather than their old neighborhood, arguing that her new residence has a view of the sea, her friend cynically replies: "What's the sea, from up there? A bit of color. Better if you are closer, that way you notice that there is filth, mud, piss, polluted water. But you who read and write books like to tell lies, not the truth" (4:131–32). The mocking note that Lila strikes in her response to Elena may be said to evoke Giacomo Leopardi, the nineteenth-century poet and thinker (1798–1837) who died and was buried in Naples. Schopenhauer praised Leopardi in *The World as Will and Representation* for his meticulous repudiation of philosophical optimism, extolling his eloquence on the theme of "the mockery and wretchedness of this existence."[19] In the sprawling collection of his personal writings that readers have come to know as *Zibaldone*, Leopardi famously debunks our romanticized ideas of nature in an entry of April 22, 1826, where he observes that beneath the beauty of a garden inevitably lie signs of destructive reality: the withering of a rose by the sun, a tree's destruction by insects, or the trampling underfoot of a grassy meadow by humans.

Although one can dismiss Lila's rebuke of Elena as mere envy, we also may regard it as a gesture of criticism in the vein of Leopardian pessimism that raises a serious question. For Lila's rebuke of Elena clearly hinges on the charge that writers such as she, who prefer to observe Naples from an artful distance, propagate lies. In this light, her fondness for streets named after poets such as Horace and Tasso looks like little more than obfuscation of her own egocentric impulses. Although urged on by both Michele Solara and Stefano, Lila instead refuses to move to the aptly named Piazzetta degli Artisti in the elegant, hilly neighborhood of Vomero. When her marriage falls apart, she does not hesitate to move with Enzo to the grimy, industrial quarter of San Giovanni a Teduccio rather than acquiesce to Michele and Stefano's plot (2:430). Unlike Elena, Lila knows all too well that the lofty street names of Naples's bourgeois districts can confer only the appearance of respectability on a *camorrista* such as Michele Solara. As she puts it, when contemplating Michele's interest in her separation from Stefano: "If I don't submit he'll make me pay, and he'll make anyone who's helped me pay" (2:428). It is telling that, in middle age, Michele, like Elena, chooses to settle in Posillipo. When Elena visits her old schoolmate Gigliola, whom Michele has married, she finds her in a beautiful if gaudily furnished apartment, which features a terrace that has been transformed into a floating garden full of flowers. Gigliola proudly boasts of the views that accompany her new upper-class home and compares her situation in Posillipo to the old rione: "Look, have you ever seen the sea like that? And Naples? And Vesuvius? And the sky? In the neighborhood was there ever all that sky?" (3:204). Elena does not answer the rhetorical question but finds herself "hypnotized" by the spectacle of Naples's beauty, while remaining aware that only "the defacement of the city" makes possible such "high-cost observatories of concrete" as Michele has purchased following his marriage to Gigliola (3:204).

PIAZZA DEI MARTIRI

Slightly beyond the end of Via Chiaia as one walks west and shortly before reaching the Lungomare, we find the most emblematic public space of the city in the Neapolitan Quartet. The square known as Piazza dei Martiri, which revolves around a monumental column topped by a bronze statue of Victory and encircled by four majestic stone lions commemorating the Neapolitan revolutionaries of 1799, 1820, 1848, and 1860, constitutes a symbolic crossroads for several of Ferrante's characters at different points in the narrative. By contrast, Lila and Elena's neighborhood represents an imaginative "non-place" that looks to the protagonists all the more stultifying for its meager gardens and nameless streets such as the stradone. French anthropologist Marc Augé first coined the term *non-place* to describe spaces where human beings cannot rise above anonymity, sites that are not anthropologically significant enough to merit classification as places.[20] When he defined the notion, Augé associated it with structures such as supermarkets, airports, and hotels, but we may easily imagine modern, low-cost public housing being included in the category. By comparison to the notorious slums of Naples such as Forcella, the city's more modern working-class neighborhoods such as the Luzzatti often appear to be lacking in historical particularity, to be deficient in what Clifford Geertz would have called the cultural "webs of significance" that elicit ethnographic "thick description." This semiotic poverty is a condition that Ferrante registers by resisting the use of place names and avoiding mention of all but the most rudimentary landmarks in her descriptions of the neighborhood.

Piazza dei Martiri instead represents a condensation—in something like the psychoanalytic sense of the word—of many of the disparate events and storylines of the two friends' saga. Especially for Lila, this location is where "for reasons that were obscure to her, every crucial development . . . had occurred" (2:345). A showcase of consumerist luxury, the square is bordered by some of the most fashionable streets for shopping in Naples such as Via Calabritto, which links the site to the Lungomare, and Via Filangieri. The piazza is where, after the attack on Rino and Pasquale by the young toughs in Via Chiaia, Lila resolves to find a way out of poverty, where the Solaras open the shop selling Cerullo shoes, where Lila transmogrifies her wedding portrait into an abstract collage, where she suffers the death of her first child during pregnancy, builds up the shop's affluent clientele through vivaciousness of personality, and momentarily finds happiness with Nino. In middle age, she studies the history of the piazza itself and teaches what she has learned to Elena's youngest daughter Imma in order to inspire the girl to develop an appreciation of Naples (4:438–39). We may even surmise an oblique historical model for the events concerning Cerullo shoes if we recall Lila's comment, after the death of her brother Rino, that he could have "surpassed Ferragamo" (4:359). Salvatore Ferragamo in fact was born in the town of Bonito near Naples and studied shoemaking in the city proper before establishing his own brand of women's shoes in Florence. We should hardly be surprised, then, that among the most prominent retail presences in Piazza dei Martiri are Ferragamo's two boutiques for women and men. Another commercial brand name that has become a fixture of the piazza ever since opening a branch there in 2001 is the Feltrinelli chain of bookstores. It is in this branch of Feltrinelli that Elena gives a reading in 2007 from her newly published book *A Friendship*, thus breaking her promise to Lila never to tell their story and causing Lila in turn to sever all ties between them (4:339).

The episode of Lila's desecration of her own bridal portrait is a pivotal moment. A gift to the seamstress who made Lila's wedding dress, the large photograph of Lila in her white finery initially goes on display in the dressmaker's store on the Rettifilo, but winds up in the shop in Piazza dei

Martiri when Stefano gives in to Michele Solara's demand. With a typical narrowed gaze of concentration, Lila attacks the image when she sees it in its new location, pinning strips of black paper over everything but an eye, a hand, the legs and shoes (2:119). All her companions react angrily at her supposed act of vandalism except Elena, who is thrilled by Lila's daring, and, ironically, Michele, who exclaims: "I like it, *signò*. You've erased yourself deliberately . . . to show how well a woman's thigh goes with those shoes" (2:121). Michele's characterization of Lila's defacement of the portrait inaugurates an important theme of the quartet, namely the idea of Lila erasing herself from her own life as a paradoxical means of self-preservation. The notion resurfaces crucially in *The Story of the Lost Child* when Elena imagines Lila defining her life as "the story of an erasure" and when Lila's fear of dissolving boundaries (smarginatura) during the Neapolitan earthquake of 1980 prompts Elena to observe that, at that moment, "Lila lost Lila . . . and she—so active, so courageous—erased herself and, terrified, became nothing" (4:25, 179).

Yet Lila's eventual refashioning of the black-and-white photo into a colorful visual patchwork enacts a wild vitality that suggests irrepressible artistic talent. After Michele praises her handiwork, Lila shuts herself with Elena in the shop for days, enabling the two friends to share "magnificent hours of play, of invention, of freedom" (2:121). Observing her friend's actions while pondering Michele's use of the word *erase,* Elena soon concludes that Lila's aim is to achieve "her own self-destruction *in an image*" (2:123). As the two friends continue to apply paper and paint to the display, Lila explains the origin of this drive to self-negation in her perplexity over being renamed "Rafaella Cerullo Carracci" as a married woman, which in her judgment signifies that "Cerullo *goes toward Carracci, falls into it, is sucked up by it, is dissolved in it*" (2:124). Eradicating her own likeness as a bride, she seems to hint, represents a means of counterbalancing the dissolution of her maiden name and identity by the rite of marriage. What Michele construes as a smart marketing ploy thus encodes a trenchant critique of the norms of married life.

If the collage upholds a pointed critical agenda, it also betokens a joyful visionary energy never again so fully expressed by Lila in the narrative, a "fierce happiness" that, according to Elena, culminates in her "laughing as I had never heard her laugh, a free, self-mocking laugh" when the work is completed (2:122, 124). As the camera depicts her, Lila appears to be sitting in a pensive attitude with her legs crossed, "her chin on the palm of one hand, her gaze . . . turned boldly toward the lens" (2:87). Her pose calls to mind the celebrated sequence of photographs of Marilyn Monroe dressed as a ballerina, which was shot by Milton H. Greene in 1954, only a few years before Lila's wedding in the quartet. In one photo, the actress leans forward while sitting in a chair and rests her chin on an upstretched finger as she gazes provocatively at the camera with a smile, her toes pointing inward toward each other and her gauzy white tutu billowing around her like a bridal dress. This depiction of Monroe's insolent seductiveness became so iconic that the editors of *Time-Life* named it one of the three most popular images of the twentieth century. It is possible that, after inviting comparisons to Princess Soraya and Jackie Kennedy (1:268, 273), Lila strikes Elena on an unconscious level as a Marilyn lookalike, perhaps as a consequence of sharing the actress's traits of vulnerability and self-destructiveness. While displayed in the store window on the Rettifilo, Lila's bridal portrait elicits interest from passersby including "the famous singer Renato Carosone, an Egyptian prince, Vittorio De Sica, and a journalist from the paper *Roma*, who wanted to talk to Lila and send a photographer to do a story on bathing suits" (2:87). Lila's mother, Nunzia, goes so far as to claim that her daughter would have had the opportunity to star in a film like *Marriage Italian Style* or become an Egyptian princess if it were not for marrying Stefano Carracci (2:88). It can hardly come as a surprise that, when the Solaras bully Stefano into giving them the picture to decorate their store in Piazza dei Martiri, Lila reacts in anger.

Whatever popular impulse may underlie the portrait of Lila in her wedding dress, the "visual synthesis" of photographic snippets, paper scraps, and splashes of "midnight blue and red" paint that she and Elena ultimately concoct represents a creative production of an entirely different order (2:122, 124). We might say, in fact, that the collage epitomizes the principles of difficulty and antirepresentationalism associated with the Abstract Expressionist movement of modernist art. It is true that Lila's eradication of every trace of her own visage from the photo except a single "very vivid eye" suggests a reimagining of the titular subject of Odilon Redon's nineteenth-century symbolist painting *The Cyclops* (1914) in female form (2:124). Yet her embrace of fragmentation and randomly applied colors places her squarely in modernist genealogy, raising the possibility of redefining artistic creation in terms of a woman's genius, hence in terms of a feminist reimagining of

modern culture. Elena's portrayal of Lila evokes the predilection for frac-
tured forms and collage techniques of Picasso or Braque in their Cubist
phases as well as the exuberantly experimental approach to color and line of
Pollock. Lila, in other words, appropriates methods identified with some of
the most celebrated male artists of the twentieth century and enlists them in
the service of feminine aesthetic and political concerns. Ironically, once
again Michele registers the importance of Lila's project, complimenting her
abstract store display with the pronouncement that "when you do a thing
you do it right" ("quando fai una cosa la fai a regola d'arte"; 2:121 E, 2:119 IT).
In the original Italian, the assertion literally praises her for performing her
task "according to the rule of art" ("a regola d'arte"), thus explicitly designating the field of her achievement.

By inviting Elena to collaborate on this endeavor, Lila breaks with
received wisdom regarding the solitary nature of artistic labor and instead
affirms a sharing of responsibility and purpose between women that exhila-
rates her friend: "Those moments were thrilling . . . I was suddenly happy,
feeling the intensity that invested her, that flowed through her fingers"
(2:119). Elena's admission of happiness suggests that, in the two friends' early
adulthood, Piazza dei Martiri denotes for them the operations of the pleasure principle as opposed to the workings of the reality principle, which are
signified by the rione, Campi Flegrei, and San Giovanni a Teduccio. When
Lila becomes pregnant in 1963 from her trysts with Nino, she indeed decides
that she must end "the deception of Piazza dei Martiri" and abandon the
store where they blissfully meet during the hours of *siesta* (2:349).

As the years advance, however, Piazza dei Martiri continues to occupy
a position of symbolic privilege not only for Lila and Elena but also for
Alfonso, who, while working in the store, undergoes a process of self-
discovery that eventually leads to his cross-gender transformation into
Lila's lookalike. His metamorphosis, which Elena at first marvels at without understanding its significance, ironically serves to keep Lila's image
associated with the place. After the closing of the store, the loss of Tina,
and the death of Alfonso, the piazza makes one last, crucial appearance in
the quartet. Nearing the age of fifty, Lila teaches Imma the history behind
the site's name and monuments, which Elena's youngest daughter recounts
in a breathless mix of fact and fantasy when she and her mother go shopping one morning in the famous square. During this period, Elena learns
from her daughter that Lila has become engrossed night and day in

reconstructing the story of "Naples in its entirety," while avoiding any mention of her "enormous project" to Imma's mother (4:437–38). Lila draws on the knowledge she has gained from this undertaking to elucidate for her young pupil the origin of the four stone lions in the center of Piazza dei Martiri that memorialize the Neapolitan patriots who died in revolt against the Bourbon monarchy. According to the girl's summary of this explanation, the sculptor Enrico Alvino "put at the base of the column these four lions, which symbolized the great moments of revolution in Naples: the lion of 1799, mortally wounded; the lion of the movements of 1820, pierced by the sword but still biting the air; the lion of 1848, which represents the force of the patriots subdued but not conquered; finally, the lion of 1859, threatening and avenging" (4:438–39). At the top of the column stands a bronze sculpture of a young woman representing Victory in tribute to the martyrs of Naples's historical struggles and replacing a sculpture of the Madonna from an earlier era.

Of all the places that Lila visits with Imma in her phantasmagorical quest to grasp Naples in its "entirety," only Piazza dei Martiri plays a prominent role in her own personal history. It is in this location that Lila's spirit finds its fullest and most genial expression. We may recognize in the lions of the square her own propensity for rebellion, her own strength and vulnerability. After all, Lila is not only devilish, cynical, and spiteful in personality but also remarkably courageous, as Elena and other characters remark throughout the quartet. As a child, she shows this courage when she takes Elena's hand and leads her up the stairs of the terrifying Don Achille's apartment building to demand that he return their dolls. As an adult, she demonstrates courage again when she braves the hazardous, dehumanizing conditions of the Soccavo salami factory and defies Marcello and Michele Solara's efforts to scare her into silence. Her determination to bring them to justice spurs her to submit an incendiary exposé of their criminal ventures and deeds for publication in *L'Espresso* under Elena's name. When Tina disappears from the neighborhood, the possibility arises that the brothers either kill or abduct her in revenge, but the reality is never made clear. Enzo indeed accuses them of taking Tina away because he and Lila refused to surrender a share of their business to the Solaras (4:341). However, little Tina's fate forever remains an unresolved enigma for Enzo and Lila, with excruciating consequences for both of them, as he explains to Elena, but most especially for her: "For

Lila . . . in all these years, the world collapsed as if it were hearsay, and slid into the void left by her daughter, like the rain that rushes down a drain-pipe" (4:411).

NEAPOLITAN ARCADES

In ancient Rome, the word *genius* referred to a presiding deity that accompanied one everywhere like a personal genie. For Elena, Lila represents a genius along these lines because she seems like a supernatural force. Indeed, her spirit is so vital that Elena at moments throughout their story symbolically entrusts her life to Lila, albeit occasionally with some ambivalence. At the same time, a specific site or locale in classical Roman culture could be understood to have a kind of living essence as well—what literally was called the *genius loci* or "spirit of place." Lila's long-standing, and eventually agonizing, imaginative connection to the two friends' native city in this sense makes her the genius loci of Naples in Ferrante's quartet. She herself explicitly acknowledges this role when, toward the end of the series, she sets out to research the city's cyclical history of destruction and renewal. From Elena's narration, we know that Lila never forsakes Naples for another city, never travels to a foreign country, never even visits Rome. She makes her home in the strictly Neapolitan environment of the rione and only ever ventures out of it for the neighboring settings of Amalfi (during her honeymoon), Ischia, and San Giovanni a Teduccio.

Elena is more peripatetic, living for stretches of time in Naples, Pisa, Florence, Milan, and finally Turin and traveling around the world to visit France, Germany, Austria, and the United States. With her young daughters Dede and Elsa in tow, she moves back to Naples in 1979, but quits the city for good in 1995 because, as she retrospectively puts it, she "no longer believed in its resurrections" (4:335). She may be said to represent what Erri De Luca labels the condition of being "Naplesless" or *napòlide*, which punningly evokes the Italian *apolide* or "stateless." As De Luca uses it, the neologism connotes a Neapolitan exile's loss of birthright, which results in an anxiously tenuous sense of connection to the rest of the world.[21] If we view Lila by contrast as the genius loci of Naples, we nonetheless may feel her association with the role is more than somewhat paradoxical. As Elena puts it in the closing sentences of her chronicle, Lila is "always in the same place and always out of place" (4:471). Yet this sense of being at odds with her situation is precisely what qualifies Lila to serve as the city's animating principle, its guardian angel. Her adroit mobility, caustic wit, cynicism, anarchic sympathies, capriciousness as a "waggish knave," and faith in ghosts call to mind well-established notions of what is most idiosyncratically Neapolitan. Ever since childhood, Elena admires Lila's nimbleness, noting for example that she "had slender, agile legs, and was always moving them" (1:46). No less an observer than Walter Benjamin remarks, in the celebrated essay on the city that he coauthored with Asja Lacis, that the main characteristic of life in Naples is the sense of vitality conveyed by the city's perpetual motion: "So everything joyful is mobile: music, toys, ice cream circulate throughout the streets."[22]

We may conclude that Lila's cynicism stems from her instinctive suspicion of the order of things, which at times rises to an almost cosmological level of mistrust. As we know, she refers to her fear of unstable foundations by the name *smarginatura*, surrendering to its pull in the face of random events such as a childhood recognition of her relative Melina's madness, a New Year's Eve display of fireworks, the toll of working at the Soccavo factory, or the earthquake of 1980 that roils "the churning guts of the earth" in Naples (4:174). Her skepticism toward claims of a rational universe diverges from Elena's stoicism and ultimately leads to a moral position hearkening back to the ancient Greek Cynics' practice of *askesis* or the ascetic renunciation of everything worldly. Whereas Elena seems to believe that the highest good is pursuit of knowledge in order to overcome the suffering of the passions, Lila inclines toward acts of "erasure" or self-denial that evoke the doctrines of cynicism in the classical philosophical sense. Although as a young woman she is enticed by promises of wealth and freedom, the happiness of her marriage to Stefano soon unravels to the point that she abandons him and sets off with Gennaro and Enzo to carve out a bluntly proletarian existence, continuing in later years to shun the trappings of prosperity even after the success of Basic Sight. Her cynicism, in other words, consorts with a drive to repudiate the fallacies of bourgeois consumerism that sets her apart from her fellow Neapolitans. The sort of cynicism historically associated with Naples instead perhaps originates in a more defensive impulse: the mistrust of a people accustomed to centuries of imperial domination by Normans, Swabians, and Bourbons, among others.[23]

When it comes to her scornful wit, Lila may well appear to be more typically Neapolitan. In *Italian Journey*, Goethe stresses the importance of wit in the cultural economy of the city, emphasizing its residents' "shrewd and cutting" temperament.[24] Citing the prologue of Goethe's *Faust* in the front matter of *My Brilliant Friend*, Ferrante, as I note earlier, implicitly assigns to Lila the role of the derisively mocking Mephistopheles while giving Elena the part of the scholarly Doctor Faust. Examples abound throughout the series of Lila's knowing and acerbic jibes; for example, when Marcello Solara tries to express his desire to marry her, she curtly and decisively puts him in his place. He recounts to her a dream in which he gave her an engagement ring, which prompts her to ask him: "In that dream I said yes?" When he confirms the outcome, she snaps in reply, "Then it really was a dream, because you are an animal" (1:185). Her irreverence, in other words, springs from a contempt of decorum that makes her fearless in the face of power. In some episodes, Lila's iconoclasm asserts itself as an unflinching disregard for the law. Not only is she firmly convinced, as she tells Elena, that the law is effective only "when you're dealing with people who pay attention if you merely say the word 'law'" (4:274), but she insists that the lessons of Naples's history validate her own hostility toward social conventions and institutions. On one of her strolls through the city with Imma, she regales her young protégé with tales of the anarchic exploits of Masaniello, the Neapolitan fisherman who led a revolt against the Spanish Habsburgs in 1647. She concludes her account of his feats by declaring that in Naples such dynamic personalities can effect change "openly, without the pretense of making laws and decrees" (4:442).

With her irrepressible vitality, Lila herself may be said to resemble Masaniello, whom Ghirelli credits with being the first personage to exemplify fully the city's attitude of irreverence, which the historian likens to the sly, transgressive character of Pulcinella in *commedia dell'arte*.[25] Charismatic and impertinent, Masaniello's astonishing success in mustering the "little people" (*popolino*) of Naples against the imposition of new taxes ended in tragedy with his betrayal and murder at the hands of an embittered faction of merchants. Lila's account of Masaniello's adventures tellingly focuses on an apocryphal episode that highlights the similarity between the story's hero and herself, namely his comic vandalism of paintings of his enemies by decapitating their portraits with his sword (4:441–42). In this light, Lila's disfiguration of her bridal photo by papering over her own head underscores her imaginative affinity with the seventeenth-century revolutionary whom she calls a "funny and terrible spirit" (4:441).[26] The epithet she bestows on Masaniello suggests that she sees him less as a real historical figure than as a supernatural presence, perhaps as her own magical benefactor. On this score, she appears to share a traditional Neapolitan fascination with ghosts, a popular weakness for superstition and fabulous lore. Erri De Luca finds a symptom of this predilection for the fantastic in what he calls Neapolitans' "effervescent and tropical" animism; and surely there is something effervescent about the stories of spirits that Lila spins for Imma.[27] In Lila's narratives, the souls of the dead haunt the ruins found in neighborhoods such as Posillipo or Santa Lucia, where an especially menacing ghoul named Faccione ("Big Face") hurls stones at anyone who bothers him. The ranks of these shades include "many spirits of dead children" whom she movingly describes as dwelling not only in the city's derelict sites but "in people's ears, in the eyes when the eyes looked inside and not out . . . because words are full of ghosts but so are images" (4:441). Finally, she insists that the past's phantoms may be encountered even at "the museum, the painting gallery, and, especially, the Biblioteca Nazionale" (4:441), perhaps dropping a hint that she has studied Naples's spectral inhabitants in the library by reading Benedetto Croce's *Neapolitan Stories and Legends* (*Storie e Leggende Napoletane,* 1919), which rehearses at length the stories of Faccione and other spirits.[28]

The emphasis Lila gives to the way that Neapolitans envision the phantoms of their city "when the eyes looked inside and not out" echoes in nearly verbatim terms Ferrante's praise of Walter Benjamin for epitomizing the attitude of critical watchfulness toward the metropolis in the chapter titled "Tiergarten" in *Berlin Childhood Around 1900*: "I am not going to talk here about Benjamin's gaze, the extraordinary gaze of eyeballs that are pupils in their entire spherical surface, and which therefore see not only before, not only outside, not the afterward that is in store but the ahead behind, the inside-outside, the after in the then-now, without chronological order. I wish to emphasize, rather, the marvelous opening that goes: 'Not to find one's way around a city does not mean much. But to lose one's way, as one loses one's way in a forest, requires some schooling'" (F 143). Ferrante's playful denial of the intention to admire Benjamin's uncanny style of observation in his book on Berlin of course only succeeds in calling our attention all the more insistently to its originality. The surreal figure of eyeballs that consist wholly of pupils and can look in all spatial and temporal dimensions at once suggests a mode of seeing that is not so much visual as visionary.

A moment later she elaborates this implication when she defines Benjamin's critical method as an attempt to reach "the difficult to express, what is deep down and barely visible," which is to say to recover from the figurative or fictional the hard truth that resists a superficial gaze (F 143). We may suspect that Benjamin's childhood images of Berlin are not so distant in fact from the girlhood views of Elena and Lila's Naples with which their story begins. Ferrante's encounter with Benjamin, in other words, implies a passage from the Naples of Lila and Elena's poverty through the labyrinth of urban childhood to the Berlin of Benjamin's bourgeois upbringing, full of Fräuleins, carousels, loggias, and imperial panoramas. Both cities—Naples and Berlin—look to the child like enchanted forests that are populated by fairy-tale characters. In Benjamin's we discover a hunchback, whereas in Ferrante's we find the ogre, Don Achille, while in both there are dangerous cellar holes from which extraordinary creatures may emerge.[29]

Lila's enthusiasm for the city's revenants emerges in the next-to-last division of *The Story of the Lost Child*, "Old Age: The Story of Bad Blood," which comes after the traumatic narrative break that coincides with Tina's disappearance. In the wrenching penultimate section of the quartet, as we noted briefly in chapter 2, "Working Women," Elena grows obsessed by the thought that Lila, with her typical brilliance, may write a book that will turn out to be the definitive history of Naples. Grief-stricken at the loss of her daughter, Lila begins to escape intermittently from home and work as she becomes convinced that "going out, wandering around, was now the solution to all the tensions and problems she struggled with" (4:384). She apparently makes a habit of her *flâneries* through the city even at night, persuading Imma that in Naples "what was beautiful and solid and radiant was populated with nighttime imaginings" (4:441). In this manner, Lila takes refuge from despair. Under Lila's mournful gaze, Ferrante's Naples, in the end, appears as a phantasmagorical city, a dream city in which we recognize the present as a distillation or condensation of the past.[30] Just as Benjamin made visible Paris's dreamlike texture through Baudelaire's eyes, so Ferrante brings to life Naples's shadowy grandeurs in Lila's reports of her nocturnal strolls, as if the city has become for her a sunken and chthonic underworld (4:422). Whatever comfort she finds in such diversions may be ephemeral, however, as she perhaps lets slip her stubborn longing for a sign of Tina when she claims that "a child could often be seen at night in the neighborhood of Porta Nolana" (4:441). Although Elena never learns anything from Lila about her book, during a conversation with Pietro on one of his rare visits after their divorce, she discovers that Lila has confessed to him her passion for researching Naples's past in the Biblioteca Nazionale. Elena surmises that Lila already has written down the anecdotes and oral histories she rehearses for Imma and herself, that these fables secretly belong to "a vast text whose structure, however, escaped me . . . a book of Neapolitan curiosities" (4:448).

When, in the process of moving to Turin with Imma in 1995, Elena makes her final departure from Naples by train, she looks back one last time at her native city and Vesuvius receding in the distance. Suddenly, she has a piercing intuition that Lila's book about Naples would be for its author a way of writing about Tina "and the text—precisely because it was nourished by the effort of expressing an inexpressible grief—would be extraordinary" (4:452). Paradoxically, Elena's epiphany at once reasserts the two friends' splendid interdependence and signifies the beginning of its end. After moving to Turin, as we know, Elena is the one who writes about Lila and Tina in her last book, *A Friendship*, thus provoking Lila to cut off all contact with her (4:339). We get no indication that Lila ever completes her magnum opus, but beneath her tales of the city's landmarks, characters, and events we may detect the underlying contours of an encyclopedic groundwork that could be called Lila's Neapolitan Arcades Project, given its similarity in ambition to Walter Benjamin's unfinished *Arcades Project*.[31] Through sweeping accumulation and condensation of images, fantasies, and anecdotes, Lila constructs a dreamlike image of the city of Naples, at least from the evidence of Imma's testimonials.

Ferrante is particularly fond of Benjamin's reading in "Tiergarten" of the figure of Ariadne as the personification of the hope of finding a way out of the urban maze (F 144). For young Imma, Lila becomes her Ariadne. Lila's enthralling stories reanimate Naples's history with such energy that even the distant past begins to look modern, suggesting a metamorphic fluidity that may remind us of Benjamin's characterization of Baudelaire's dynamic mode of modernity. According to the German critic's line of reasoning, the creation of a kind of dream-space in Paris originates in the architecture of the *passages couverts*, which enables instantaneous transitions between internal and external space. A similar logic evidently informs his perception of the topography of Naples insofar as he declares that the city's anarchic conflation of inside and outside, which he dubbed "porosity," represents for him the quintessential Neapolitan form of life.[32] We may surmise that the kinetic sprawl of the city's expanses, both horizontally from east to west and vertically from Vomero, Posillipo, and Vesuvius down to the tunnels and catacombs below the surface, only serves to amplify this impression. The primary process of the dream, which in Freud's theory is characterized by condensation and displacement, is therefore organic to the city's historical and geographical layers. With its Greek origins and volcanic terrain, ancient Naples, even more than modern Paris, may be said to look like "the breeding ground of mythology."[33] The fact that it is through Imma's reports that Elena learns of Lila's engagement with the city adds a further layer of transferential fantasy and condensation, which perhaps accounts for the dreamlike quality that Naples acquires in the final volume of the tetralogy. In a sense, the phantasmatic allure of the book that Elena attributes to Lila recapitulates the tantalizing appeal of the idea of Benjamin's *Arcades Project*, which scholars for decades have sought to reconstruct definitively from its fragments. The inclusiveness of Lila's notional magnum opus indeed evokes Benjamin's labyrinthine montage of writings, which aimed to bring to light the ur-history (*Urgeschichte*) of nineteenth-century Parisian experience at the moment of its collision with the commodifying forces of modernity by irradiating the ephemera of the city's arcades.

Ferrante achieves something like the amalgamation of present and past that Benjamin's illuminations and dialectical images enact in Lila's explanation to Elena of the history of the gladiatorial games called *ioco de carbonara* that apparently were inaugurated by Virgil in what since has become the neighborhood of San Giovanni a Carbonara. Lila recounts to Elena the violent vicissitudes of this district between Forcella and the Tribunali, which the two friends have crossed countless times. Prompted by the name *Carbonara* (coal carrier), she believed the locale was for storing coal until she learned it was in reality a dump for the city's waste: "dirty water ran in it, animal carcasses were tossed into it" (4:446). Looking back over millennia, Lila recounts how the games evolved from at first nonlethal contests of gladiatorial skill to increasingly mortal confrontations. The dangerous sport of *prete* or stone throwing, played by the two friends in their childhood, originated in these competitions. She remarks that the ancient spectacles of violence aroused the bloodlust of people of all classes and walks of life: "When some handsome youth fell, pierced by a blade beaten on the anvil of death, immediately beggars, bourgeois citizens, kings and queens offered applause that rose to the stars. Ah, the violence: tearing, killing, ripping" (4:447). Hovering in a mood between fascination and horror, Lila envisions the cruelties perpetrated at the Carbonara in terms of "a lot of human blood" and a "chaos of broken limbs and dug-out eyes and split heads," which time has obscured all too conveniently as buildings have been raised, such as the church of San Giovanni a Carbonara or a monastery of "Augustinian hermits" with a treasured library (4:447).

Elena notices that Lila relates this chronicle in a farrago "of dialect, Italian, and very educated quotations" (4:447), implying that she must have consulted a wide array of sources in order to piece together the history of the place. Indeed, Lila's account moves through historical and cultural epochs at hallucinatory speed until she reaches the apocalyptic and characteristically cynical conclusion that "the entire planet . . . is a big Fosso Carbonario" (4:447). After Lila goes missing, Elena wonders whether, among other alternatives, her friend may have retreated into "an ancient garbage pit, one of those she devoted so many words to" (4:472). Yet Lila also depicts Naples as a sublime natural phenomenon, as a wellspring of transformative energy that fuels a continuous cycle of life and death: "What a splendid and important city: here all languages are spoken, Imma, here everything was built and everything was torn down, here the people don't trust talk and are very talkative, here is Vesuvius which reminds you every day that the greatest undertaking of powerful men, the most splendid work, can be reduced to nothing in a few seconds by the fire, and the earthquake, and the ash, and the sea" (4:440). The adjective *splendid*, which here Lila employs twice in a short paragraph, is an especially resonant word in the two friends' shared lexicon. Toward the end of their saga, Elena uses the term to sum up their relationship to one another in all its vitality and ambivalence: "Every intense relationship between human beings is full of traps, and if you want it to endure you have to learn to avoid them. I did so then, and finally it seemed that I had only come up against yet another proof of how splendid and shadowy our friendship was, how long and complicated Lila's suffering had been, how it still endured and would endure forever" (4:451).

Both friends evidently grant the designation of *splendid* only to things that in some way are self-contradictory or oxymoronic. In Lila's case the label encapsulates the city's oscillation between greatness and futility, whereas in Elena's it applies to the two friends' veering between love and hate for each other. As they use it, the word does not name a static state of being but rather a dynamic quality of grandeur or brilliance. Like the Kantian sublime, what is splendid for the two friends is not made for serene contemplation. In the quartet, only one character is so naive as to define Naples as simply and without qualification *beautiful,* namely the pubescent Marcello Solara, when he tries to persuade Lila and Elena to join him and his brother in his new car to see "the most beautiful city in the world" (1:134). Both Lila and Elena instead regard the city as at once horrendous and delightful; both, similarly, are seized by the ambivalent feeling that "in the Neapolitan facts . . . there was always something terrible, disorderly, at the origin, which later took the form of a beautiful building, a street, a monument, only to be forgotten, to lose meaning, to decline, improve, decline, according to an ebb and flow that was by its nature unpredictable" (4:439). For her part, Elena appears to suffer more distress from the shock of everyday experience in Naples than Lila does, although, interestingly, she voices no special preference for her living situations at different moments in Florence or Turin. On what is no more than a brief visit to the city with her daughters, after she learns from Lila that her sister Elisa has taken up with Marcello Solara, she claims that "as soon as we . . . were in the chaotic traffic of Naples, I felt gripped by the city, ruled by its unwritten laws. . . . The noise seemed unbearable, I was irritated by the constant honking, by the insults the drivers shouted" (3:319).

Not even sweeping political change succeeds in undoing or amending these "unwritten laws" of Neapolitan life. Despite the city's election of Maurizio Valenzi to be its first-ever Communist mayor, nothing really changes during the years of his administration from 1975 to 1983, as Elena ruefully attests: "The city had not improved at all, its malaise wore me out immediately . . . I struggled to meet the endless demands of daily life" (4:114). Over time, she witnesses a proliferation of new, modern buildings throughout the city, only to see these soaring edifices quickly plunge into obsolescence and decay. From the "dull tower" that rises above Via Novara, in what looks like a parody of the skyscrapers she encounters in New York, to the failed architectural experiments of Scampia, Arenaccia, Via Taddeo da Sessa, and Piazza Nazionale, only the cosmetic "powder of modernity" reaches Naples (4:335).[34] Like Lila, Elena regards Naples in a pessimistic light as a synecdoche for the ills of the world or, at least, for those of the West. It is in Naples, she feels, that the historically optimistic faith in technology and rational progress decisively reveals itself to be an illusion, a charade that, as I have observed earlier, she defines as "a nightmare of savagery and death" (4:337). However, while the world for Lila may be one big Fosso Carbonario, her cynicism in the end is counterbalanced by her excitement at the vitality of Naples, where she remains at the end of the quartet, if only in memory, as the genius loci. By contrast, Elena internalizes in the first-person voice of her own narrative the pessimism she ascribes to Lila, clearly reflecting the sense of disenchantment that eventually compels her to leave the city for good.

We should notice that Elena's view of Naples contrasts markedly with that of one of the most influential Italian artists and thinkers of the twentieth century, namely Pier Paolo Pasolini. A celebrated film director, poet, and novelist, Pasolini was also a gifted and in many ways prophetic cultural critic, who introduced terms such as *anthropological mutation*, *homologation* (*omolagazione*), and *cultural genocide* into Italy's intellectual debates of the 1970s.[35] He felt that the dominance of neoliberalism resulting from the boom years of the Economic Miracle after the Second World War threatened to destroy the authenticity of the proletariat, which increasingly was becoming a slave to consumerist impulses. Naples, in his eyes, was the only place in Italy that managed to resist this trend, "the last plebeian metropolis."[36] In a long essay, "Genariello," that he published serially in 1975, he imagines himself as the teacher of an idealized Neapolitan boy whose name gives the treatise its title. Pasolini depicts his subject as embodying a type of working-class youth that was disappearing rapidly from Italian society outside of Naples: lively, joyful, and sexually appealing. With one bold declaration, the critic voices his emphatic predilection for the city's energy and exceptionality: "In Naples, both the poor boy and the bourgeois boy are full of vitality."[37]

According to Ghirelli in his tract, *La napoletanità* (1976), Pasolini also held the belief that native residents of the city over time eventually came to "extinguish" themselves in order to remain truly Neapolitan, which is to say inimitable, to their end. From Ghirelli's fleeting reminiscence, it may be difficult to pin down exactly what Pasolini meant by this notion of extinguishing oneself. Yet the implications of the idea, however cryptic they may be, allow us to consider a potential explanation for Lila's final desertion of the rione and Elena at the end of the saga. It is as if, like a genie dissolving back into its locus, her withdrawal constituted the ultimate, wordless proof of loyalty to her city. *Pace* Pasolini, Elena determinedly refuses to romanticize Naples as a utopia where somehow the plebs may survive the ceaseless aesthetic and political assaults of consumer culture in Italy. As a young woman, Lila, to the contrary, notably responds with enthusiasm to a talk by Pasolini she attends with Nino in the early 1960s (2:358–59). Perhaps for this reason, she diverges at the end of the two friends' story from Elena's repudiation of the mythical image of the city that the Friulian writer and filmmaker famously proposed.

That most visitors from other places tend to represent Naples as a "third-world city" may explain to some degree why the Neapolitan Quartet occupies such a strange place in the literary market.[38] On the one hand, Ferrante's chef d'oeuvre can be seen as an alternative to the risk of neocolonialism raised by works of so-called world literature, writings that publicize the stories of marginalized communities in non-Western countries by translating them into the homogenized vernacular of global consumerism. Although some may admire the quartet for its protagonists' feminism, other readers seem to view the series as a fairy tale about Elena and Lila's rise from the working class set against the exotic backdrop of the poverty of Southern Italy. To resist such touristic shallowness, we may surmise that the ideal mood of encountering the Neapolitan novels is one of appreciation for the specificity of Ferrante's characters, their language, and their story's settings as a means of exploring the city's historical and global economic particularity. On the other hand, if Naples may be said to symbolize a transnational plebeian space in the narrative, the two friends' epic tale can be interpreted as the latest instance of a politically engaged Weltliteratur that unveils the material realities of the world—its dirt, slums, and violence—as the inescapable historical legacy of Fosso Carbonario.

According to this view, Elena and Lila cannot be said to complete the journey from subaltern singularity to hegemonic universality. The story of the two friends instead may be regarded as giving voice to a tantalizing, unfulfilled wish for personal and political emancipation. In this case, we may feel that Ferrante's Neapolitan Quartet is best read as a tragedy of the impossibility of lasting entrustment between women. If the narrative memorably attests to its two protagonists' hard-won victories, it even more pointedly brings to light the immeasurable costs that Elena and Lila must bear in the loss of their friendship.

NOTES

QUESTIONS OF IDENTITY

1. These pronouncements are, respectively, the opinions of James Wood, "Women on the Verge," *New Yorker*, January 21, 2013, https://www.newyorker.com/magazine /2013/01/21/women-on-the-verge; Rachel Cusk, "The Story of the Lost Child," *New York Times*, August 26, 2015, https://www.nytimes.com/2015/08/30/books /review/the-story-of-the-lost-child-by-elena-ferrante.html; and Judith Shulevitz, "The Hypnotic Genius of Elena Ferrante," *Atlantic*, October 2015, https://www .theatlantic.com/magazine/archive/2015/10/the-hypnotic-genius-of-elena-ferrante /403198/.

2. David Kurnick, "Ferrante, in History," *Public Books*, December 15, 2015, 4, https:// www.publicbooks.org/ferrante-in-history.

3. See, for example, the front matter of Elena Ferrante, *Frantumaglia: A Writer's Journey* (New York: Europa, 2016), 1. All subsequent citations of *Frantumaglia* in English are noted in the body of the argument by page number following the abbreviation F.

4. "When I say I'm a storyteller, I go back to a very Italian tradition in which writing is one with the story and is 'good' because it has the energy to create a world, not because it strings together metaphors" (F 301). Ferrante has written about the specific importance that Boccaccio's *Decameron* held for her as an adolescent: "The 'Decameron' by Giovanni Boccaccio (1313–1375) made a great impression on me. In this work, which is at the origin of the grand Italian and European narrative traditions, 10 youths—seven women and three men—take turns telling stories for 10 days. At around the age of 16, I found it reassuring that Boccaccio, in conceiving his narrators, had made most of them women. Here was a great writer, the father of modern story, presenting seven great female narrators. There was something to

hope for." Elena Ferrante, "A Power of Our Own," *New York Times*, May 17, 2019, https://www.nytimes.com/2019/05/17/opinion/elena-ferrante-on-women-power .html.

5. See Elena Ferrante, "Adolescence: The Story of the Shoes," in *My Brilliant Friend*, trans. Ann Goldstein (New York: Europa, 2012), especially 116, 164, 202, 240–41, 304–6, 316, and 331. All subsequent citations of the Neapolitan Quartet in English are noted by volume and page number followed by the abbreviation EN when necessary: *My Brilliant Friend* (2012) being volume 1, *The Story of a New Name* (2012) volume 2, *Those Who Leave and Those Who Stay* (2014) volume 3, and *The Story of the Lost Child* (2015) volume 4. Similarly, all citations in Italian refer to the novels published by Edizioni e/o and are noted by volume and page number followed by the abbreviation IT: *L'amica geniale* (2011) being volume 1, *Storia del nuovo cognome* (2012) volume 2, *Storia di chi fugge e di chi resta* (2013) volume 3, and *Storia della bambina perduta* (2014) volume 4. It is noteworthy as well that Ferrante strategically organizes the entire narrative of her latest novel, *The Lying Life of Adults* (*La vita bugiarda degli adulti*; 2019), around the circulation of a golden bracelet.

6. Claudio Gatti, "Elena Ferrante: An Answer?," *New York Review of Books*, October 2, 2016, https://www.nybooks.com/daily/2016/10/02/elena-ferrante-an-answer/.

7. On the day after the news broke, Deborah Orr declared in the *Guardian* that Gatti had trampled on a "perfectly satisfactory contract between writer and reader." Deborah Orr, "The Unmasking of Elena Ferrante Has Violated My Right Not to Know," *Guardian*, October 3, 2016, https://www.theguardian.com/books/2016/oct /03/unmasking-elena-ferrante-italian-journalist-claudio-gatti. Alexandra Schwartz of the *New Yorker* added along similar lines that "to fall in love with a book . . . is to feel a special kinship with its author . . . that Ferrante has chosen to be anonymous has become part of this contract, and has put readers and writer on a rare, equal plane." Alexandra Schwartz, "The 'Unmasking' of Elena Ferrante," *New Yorker*, October 3, 2016, https://www.newyorker.com/culture/cultural-comment/the-unm asking-of-elena-ferrante.

8. Claudio Gatti, "The Story Behind a Name," *NYR Daily*, October 10, 2016, https:// www.nybooks.com/daily/2016/10/02/story-behind-a-name-elena-ferrante/.

9. Tiziana de Rogatis, *Elena Ferrante: Key Words*, trans. Will Schutt (New York: Europa, 2019); published in Italian as *Elena Ferrante. Parole Chiave* (Rome: Edizioni e/o, 2018).

10. That the monograph boasts a cover by Emanuele Ragnisco, whose illustrations adorn the Neapolitan novels themselves, does little to quiet our doubts.

11. Dayna Tortorici, "Bluebeard," *n+1*, October 2, 2016, https://nplusonemag.com /online-only/online-only/bluebeard/.

12. Lisa O'Kelly reported in 2018 that Naples had become a tourist destination "thanks to the huge popularity of the enigmatic author Elena Ferrante" in "Naples: Elena Ferrante's Brilliant City," *Guardian*, February 25, 2018, https://www.theguardian .com/travel/2018/feb/25/naples-elena-ferrante-brilliant-city-travel. In the summer of 2019, Laura Rysman noted that the number of visitors to Naples had more than doubled since 2010 and declared that "Elena Ferrante's beloved Neapolitan novels . . . has roused [sic] curiosity about a destination long considered little more than a steppingstone to Capri, Ischia, and Amalfi" in "36 Hours in Naples, Italy,"

New York Times, July 11, 2019, https://www.nytimes.com/2019/07/11/travel/what-to
-do-36-hours-in-naples-italy.html.

13. As Ferrante writes in a letter to her publisher that is collected in *Frantumaglia*: "I
believe that books, once they are written, have no need of their authors" (F 15).
Later in the same volume she declares: "The author, who outside the text doesn't
exist, inside the text offers herself, *consciously adds herself* to the story, exerting
herself to be truer than she could be in the photos of a Sunday supplement, at a
presentation in a bookstore, at a festival of literature, in some television broadcast,
in the spectacle of a literary prize" (F 274). Still further on she adds: "Our singularity as authors is a small note in the margin" (F 345).

14. See Christopher L. Miller, *Impostors: Literary Hoaxes and Cultural Authenticity*
(Chicago: University of Chicago Press, 2018) for a more comprehensive statement
of this position.

15. Rebecca Falkoff amusingly divides her critical reception in Italy into two camps,
the "self-flagellating" and the "snidely condescending," and perceptively links the
gender politics of Ferrante's reception to public debates in Italy about the value of
her novels and her pseudonymity in "To Translate Is to Betray: On the Elena Ferrante Phenomenon in Italy and the US," *Public Books*, March 25, 2015, https://www
.publicbooks.org/to-translate-is-to-betray-on-the-elena-ferrante-phenomenon-in
-italy-and-the-us/.

16. Ferrante's stories often feature Neapolitan situations and characters that appear to
revise and comment on those of Starnone's novels. For example, the character of
Donato Sarratore in the Neapolitan Quartet bears more than a passing resemblance to the protagonist of Starnone's *Via Gemito* (2000). More broadly, it might
be said that Ferrante and Starnone share a fascination with questions of education,
which both writers demonstrate recurrently in their writings. However, Ferrante
also strategically distances herself from Starnone at times, as she does with her
amusing representation of Edmondo De Amicis's novel *Heart* (*Cuore*, 1886) in *My
Brilliant Friend*. In fourth grade, we may recall, Maestra Oliviero gives Lila a copy
of *Little Women* and Elena a copy of *Heart,* and Lila, who immediately reads both
books, proclaims *Little Women* by far the superior novel, while Elena labors to get
through *Heart.* Ferrante's staging of this battle of the books sheds a slyly unflatter-
ing light on the nationalistic pieties of De Amicis's tale, which in its current Italian
edition appears with a long preface by Starnone. Finally, we may find it noteworthy
that Starnone's fiction seems to have evolved in response to Ferrante's ideas in
recent years. His celebrated novel *Trick* (*Scherzetto*, 2016), which was nominated
for a National Book Award in Jhumpa Lahiri's English translation, is heavily
indebted to Ferrante's *The Days of Abandonment*. The crucial scene of *Trick,* in
which the protagonist Daniele is shut out on a balcony overnight by his grandson
Mario, bears a striking resemblance to the central episode of Ferrante's second
novel, in which Olga and her children temporarily are trapped in their apartment.

17. Judith Thurman, "What Brings Elena Ferrante's Worlds to Life," *New Yorker*,
August 24, 2020, https://www.newyorker.com/magazine/2020/08/31/what-brings
-elena-ferrantes-worlds-to-life.

18. Carla Benedetti, *The Empty Cage: Inquiry Into the Mysterious Disappearance of the
Author*, trans. William J. Hartley (Cornell: Cornell University Press, 2005), 212.

19. Toni Morrison put the argument persuasively when she stated, "I can accept the labels because being a black woman writer is not a shallow place but a rich place to write from. It doesn't limit my imagination; it expands it. It's richer than being a white male writer because I know more and I've experienced more." As reported by Hilton Als, "Ghosts in the House," *New Yorker*, October 27, 2003, https://www.newyorker.com/magazine/2003/10/27/ghosts-in-the-house.

20. Rebecca Solnit, *Whose Story Is This? Old Conflicts, New Chapters* (Chicago: Haymarket, 2019), 17.

21. Among many other examples on this score, see in particular Joshua Rothman, "Knausgaard or Ferrante?," *New Yorker*, March 25, 2015, https://www.newyorker.com/culture/cultural-comment/knausgaard-or-ferrante; Gaby Wood, "How Karl Ove Knausgaard and Elena Ferrante Won Us Over," *Telegraph*, February 28, 2016, https://www.telegraph.co.uk/books/what-to-read/how-karl-ove-knausgaard-and-elena-ferrante-won-us-over/; Liesl Schillinger, "The Hottest Trend in American Literature Isn't From the U.S.," *Atlantic*, November 11, 2018, https://www.theatlantic.com/ideas/archive/2018/11/ferrante-knausgaard-translation-rise/575482/; and Charles Finch, "What Tweets and Emojis Did to the Novel," *New York Times*, November 29, 2019, https://www.nytimes.com/2019/11/19/books/review/charles-finch-emoji-autofiction-knausgaard-ferrante.html.

22. John Williams, Entry #3 ("Me, myself and I") of "33 Ways to Remember the 2010s," *New York Times*, November 24, 2019, https://www.nytimes.com/interactive/2019/11/24/arts/2010s-decade-end.html.

23. "As Simon During states convincingly: 'The interest in world literature obviously follows the recent rapid extension of cross-border flows of tourists and cultural goods around the world, including literary fiction.'" Simon During, *Exit Capitalism: Literary Culture, Theory and Post-Secular Modernity* (London: Routledge, 2009), 57–8, as cited in Emily Apter, *Against World Literature: On the Politics of Untranslatability* (London: Verso, 2013), 2.

24. The importance of Greek tragedy and classical Sanskrit, as David Damrosch suggests, helped to define *Faust* as one of the major works of world literature. See Damrosch's prefatory note to the excerpt from Goethe's "Conversations with Eckermann on *Weltliteratur* (1827)," in David Damrosch, ed., *World Literature in Theory* (Oxford: Wiley, 2014), 15.

25. She also notes that the reality predictably has fallen short of this promise. Apter, *Against World Literature*, 7–8. Cf. Goethe's "Conversations" and John Pizer, "The Emergence of *Weltliteratur*: Goethe and the Romantic School," in Damrosch, 15–34.

26. "We need to bear in mind, however, that if our reception of transnational, emergent, diasporic literatures is mediated only through English, not only linguistic but also cultural differences and specificities will be lost in translation." Azade Seyhan, *Writing Outside the Nation* (Princeton: Princeton University Press, 2000), 157.

27. Lorna Finlayson, "Travelling in the Wrong Direction," *London Review of Books*, July 4, 2019, 7, https://www.lrb.co.uk/v41/n13/lorna-finlayson/travelling-in-the-wrong-direction.

28. "A relation of cruel optimism exists when something you desire is actually an obstacle to your flourishing. It might involve food, or a kind of love: it might be a fantasy

of the good life, or a political project. It might rest on something simpler, too, like a new habit that promises to induce in you an improved way of being. These kinds of optimistic relation are not inherently cruel. They become cruel only when the object that draws your attachment actively impedes the aim that brought you to it initially." Lauren Berlant, *Cruel Optimism* (Durham: Duke University Press, 2011), 1.

29. Kurnick, "Ferrante, in History," 7.

30. Kurnick, 9.

31. "Semiotically, the 'concrete detail' is constituted by the *direct* collusion of a referent and signifier; the signified is expelled from the sign, and with it, of course, the possibility of developing a *form of the signified*, i.e., narrative structure itself. (Realistic literature is narrative, of course, but this is because its realism is only fragmentary, erratic, confined to 'details,' and because the most realistic narrative imaginable develops along unrealistic lines.) This is what we might call the *referential illusion*. The truth of this illusion is this: eliminated from the realist speech-act as a signified of denotation, the 'real' returns to it as a signified of connotation; for just when these details are reputed to *denote* the real directly, all they do—without saying so—is *signify* it . . . it is the category of 'the real' (and not its contingent contents) which is then signified; in other words, the very absence of the signified, to the advantage of the referent alone, becomes the very signifier of realism: the *reality effect* is produced, the basis of that unavowed verisimilitude which forms the aesthetic of all the standard works of modernity." Roland Barthes, "The Reality Effect," in *The Rustle of Language*, trans. Richard Howard (Berkeley: University of California Press, 1989), 147–48.

32. Berlant, *Cruel Optimism,* 81.

33. Kurnick, "Ferrante, in History," 5.

34. Elena Ferrante, "Elena Ferrante on *Sense and Sensibility*," *Guardian*, October 16, 2015, https://www.theguardian.com/books/2015/oct/16/sense-and-sensibility-jane-austen-elena-ferrante-anonymity.

35. Thurman, "What Brings Elena Ferrante's Worlds to Life."

36. These essays have been collected in Elena Ferrante, *Incidental Inventions*, trans. Ann Goldstein, illus. Andrea Ucini (New York: Europa, 2019).

37. The exact lines in German are:

> Du darfst auch da nur frei erscheinen;
> Ich habe deinesgleichen nie gehaßt.
> Von allem Geisten, die verneinen,
> Ist mir der Schalk am wenigsten zur Last.
> Des Menschen Tätigkeit kann allzu leicht erschlaffen,
> Er liebt sich bald die unbedingte Ruh;
> Drum geb ich gern ihm den Gesellen zu,
> Der reizt und wirkt und muß, als Teufel, schaffen.
> (LINES 336–43)

I have revised somewhat the lineation of the Italian translation so that it is easier for the reader to follow the correspondence between the original German and the English and Italian versions.

38. See Johann Wolfgang von Goethe, *Faust*, trans. Barbara Allason (Turin: De Silva, 1950), reissued with an introduction by Cesare Cases (Turin: Einaudi, 1965); *Faust*,

trans. Franco Fortini (Milan: Mondadori, 1970); and *Faust/Urfaust*, trans. Andrea Casalegno (Milan: Garzanti, 1994). For a helpful analysis of the history of translation of *Faust* into Italian and Cases's influence on all three of the most important twentieth-century renderings, see Michele Sisto, "Cesare Cases e le edizioni italiane del *Faust*. Letteratura, politica e mercato del Risorgimento a oggi," *Studi Germanici*, no. 12 (2017): 107–78.

39. Given the significance of this gesture, it is unfortunate that Ann Goldstein has selected Bayard Taylor's 1870 translation of Goethe's *Faust* as the source of the epigraph for *My Brilliant Friend* rather than a more recent version such as David Luke's rendering of 1987, but questions of copyright may be at stake.

40. The use of language is never a trivial question for Ferrante's protagonists. When her middle-school teacher meets with her mother, Elena somewhat drolly remarks on the spoken Italian of her *professoressa*, which "slightly resembled that of the *Iliad*" (1:95). At any rate, Ferrante takes pains to present *Faust* as something other than a stilted or forbidding museum piece. Allason translates the first line of the epigraph—"Du darfst auch da nur frei erscheinen"—as follows: "Be anche in tal caso potrai venirmi davanti liberamente." Fortini instead opts for "avrai solo anche allora, da mostrarti liberamente come sei," whereas Casalegno renders it as "vieni anche allora liberamente." In Ferrante's handling, the line becomes almost conversational in tone: "Ma sì, fatti vedere quando vuoi." Her version of the second line of God's rationale for the devil's existence confirms her preference for simplicity as she settles on "non ho mai odiato i tuoi simili" to translate "ich habe deinesgleichen nie gehaßt" in contrast to Allason and Casalegno's uniform rendering, which starts with the complement—"i tuoi simili, io non li ho mai odiati"—and more in line with Fortini, who starts with the subject. For the verb *reizt* in the penultimate line of the epigraph, Ferrante uses *pungoli,* which subtly revises Fortini's rendering of the verb as *punga* along even more demotic lines while eschewing both the sexualized overtone of Allason's "lo eccita e irrita" or Casalegno's flatter, less specific "lo stimola."

41. "Psychologically, present-day cynics can be understood as borderline melancholies, who can keep their symptoms of depression under control and can remain more or less able to work. Indeed, this is the essential point in modern cynicism: the ability of its bearers to work—in spite of anything that might happen, and especially, after anything that might happen. The key social positions in boards, parliaments, commissions, executive councils, *publishing companies*, practices, faculties, and lawyers' and editors' offices have long since become a part of this diffuse cynicism. . . . They (i.e., cynics) know what they are doing, but they do it because, in the short run, the force of circumstances and the instinct for self-preservation are speaking the same language, are telling them that it has to be so. . . . Thus, we come to our first definition: Cynicism is *enlightened false consciousness*. . . . Well-off and miserable at the same time, this consciousness no longer feels affected by any critique of ideology; its falseness is already reflexively buffered." Peter Sloterdijk, *The Critique of False Consciousness*, trans. Michael Eldred (Minneapolis: University of Minnesota Press, 1987), 5.

42. Michel Foucault, *The Courage of Truth (The Government of Self and Others II): Lectures at the Collège de France, 1983–1984*, ed. Arnold I. Davidson, trans. Graham Burchell (London: Palgrave Macmillan, 2011).

43. Fredric Jameson, *Allegory and Ideology* (New York: Verso, 2019), 335.

44. Mephistopheles is described as a genius in the *Urfaust*. In his introduction to a reprint of the first part of Goethe's epic drama, Julius Goebel notes that for poets from the sixteenth through the eighteenth century the terms "demon, genius and angel" were synonymous and the notion of "genius" represented "an object of actual belief, and not merely a figure of speech." Johann Wolfgang von Goethe, *Faust, Erster Teil*, rev. 2d ed., ed. and intro. Julius Goebel (New York: Holt, 1910), xlvii.

1. CRUEL SEXUALITY

1. James Wood, "Women on the Verge," *New Yorker*, January 21, 2013, https://www.newyorker.com/magazine/2013/01/21/women-on-the-verge.

2. Rachel Cusk, "The Story of the Lost Child," *New York Times*, August 26, 2015, https://www.nytimes.com/2015/08/30/books/review/the-story-of-the-lost-child-by-elena-ferrante.html.

3. Jacqueline Rose, *Mothers: An Essay on Love and Cruelty* (New York: Farrar, Straus and Giroux, 2018), 151.

4. Ferrante's latest novel, *The Lying Life of Adults* (New York: Europa, 2020)/*La vita bugiarda degli adulti* (Rome: Edizioni e/o, 2019), is no exception, although it is the first of her works to depict sexual acts between women.

5. Elena Ferrante, *The Days of Abandonment*, trans. Ann Goldstein (New York: Europa, 2005), 16, 57, 106. All subsequent citations of this title are noted in the body of the argument by page number following the abbreviation TDA. Similarly, all subsequent citations of Ferrante's *Troubling Love* refer to Europa's 2006 edition of Goldstein's translation by page number following the abbreviation TL. Quotations of the same translator's rendering of *The Lost Daughter* cite Europa's 2008 edition of this title by page number following the abbreviation TLD.

6. One of the most interesting, and interestingly mimetic, responses to the originality of Ferrante's representation of female friendship in the Neapolitan novels is the anthology of critical essays by Sarah Chihaya, Merve Emre, Katherine Hill, and Jill Richards, *The Ferrante Letters: An Experiment in Collective Criticism* (New York: Columbia University Press, 2020).

7. The language and tropes of Ferrante's *The Days of Abandonment* may remind us at times of Austrian writer Elfriede Jelinek's passionate and, for some, pornographic writing in novels such as *Women as Lovers* (*Die Liebhaberinnen*, 1975), *The Piano Teacher* (*Die Klavierspielerin*, 1983), and *Lust* (1989). Yet the women that Jelinek portrays in her novels tend to be intellectually and emotionally more static than those in Ferrante's, who for her part generally places more emphasis on her protagonists' dynamism and potential to change. Ferrante also does not emulate Jelinek's perpetually biting tone.

8. The name Lena is uncommon in Italian. We find the name Lena as one half of the pairing of names that gives Georg Büchner's play, *Leonce und Lena* (1836), its title.

9. Sigmund Freud, *Beyond the Pleasure Principle*, ed. and trans. James Strachey (New York: Norton, 1961), 18–25.

10. *Larousse* gives two definitions of the verb from which *délimitation* derives: "1.) Fixer, tracer les limites d'une étendue; en constituer la limite: Délimiter les

frontières. Le mur délimite le cour. 2.) Déterminer précisément les limites de quelque chose; circonscrire: Délimiter un sujet thèse." See the entry for *delimiter* at https://www.larousse.fr/dictionnaires/francais/délimiter/23104.

11. See *Duden* senses 1a: "(in einer Flüssigkeit) zerfallen, zergehen lassen (z.b. Tabletten in einem Glas Wasser auflösen)"; 4a: "die Lösung von etwas finden (z.b. ein Rätsel, eine mathematische Gleichung auflösen)"; and 5b: "(eine Dissonanz) zur Konsonanz fortführen (z.b. eine Dissonanz auflösen)," https://www.duden.de/rechtsch reibung/aufloesen#Bedeutung-4.

12. The *Oxford Spanish Dictionary* website gives the primary meaning of *desbordamiento* as "Acción de desbordarse un liquido u otra cosa contenida en un recipiente, o un río de su cauce: La lluvia provocó el desbordamiento de los torrentes y el corte de seis carreteras en el norte de la isla"; https://www.lexico.com/es/definicion/desbordamiento.

13. "1. L'operazione, il lavoro di smarginare; il risultato di tale operazione. 2. In botanica, leggera incisione all'apice di un organo (per es., nelle foglie dell'abete bianco." http://www.treccani.it/vocabolario/smarginatura.

14. Given the lasting influence of Jacques Derrida's deconstruction of metaphysics through intense critical attention to the margins of philosophy, it is hard to regard Ferrante's use of the word *smarginatura* as theoretically naive. After all, she herself highlights the importance of contemporary philosophy on her writing when she acknowledges Jean-Luc Nancy's notion of abandonment as a source of inspiration for her second book, *The Days of Abandonment*.

15. Lauren Berlant argues that trauma theory too quickly adjudicates the modalities and temporalities of crises that instead may be lived according to different "styles" of being overwhelmed. See Lauren Berlant, *Cruel Optimism* (Durham: Duke University Press, 2011), 81.

16. The looming presence of Vesuvius over the paroxysm of smarginatura that Lila experiences during the earthquake reminds the reader of the fact that Naples's very geology is *smarginato*, as the phenomenon of *bradidismo* in Pozzuoli and Campi Flegrei even more literally illustrates. A periodic raising or lowering of ground level, *bradidismo* may be regarded as the geological manifestation of *smarginatura*.

17. Sara Ahmed, *Living a Feminist Life* (Durham: Duke University Press, 2017), 59–60.

18. In a poetry roundtable organized by the *New York Review of Books*, Ferrante discloses that her favorite poem is Amelia Rosselli's "Well, so, patience to our souls," which is reprinted in the collection entitled *Sleep. Poesia in Inglese*, ed. Emmanuela Tondello (Milan: Garzanti, 1992). In an interview with Deborah Orr, Ferrante also admits that when it comes to provocative narration, she takes her cues from what she regards as Rosselli's literary manifesto "What black deep activism there is in my menstruation" (F 361–62).

19. See Jennifer Scappettone's introduction to Amelia Rosselli, *Locomotrix: Selected Poetry and Prose of Amelia Rosselli*, ed. and trans. Jennifer Scappetone (Chicago: University of Chicago Press, 2012), 5; and Emmanuela Tondello, *Amelia Rosselli. La fanciulla e l'infinito* (Rome: Donzelli Editore, 2007), 5.

20. Ahmed, *Living a Feminist Life*, 13–14.

21. By my reckoning, Lila speaks of sexual experience with pleasure only once in the Neapolitan Quartet, and even in this case only through Enzo's eyes. When she is pregnant with Tina and finally feels good about herself, she confides to Elena with "a trace of vulgarity" that "Enzo . . . likes me pregnant even more" (4:190).

22. See Gilles Deleuze, "Desire and Pleasure," in *Foucault and his Interlocutors*, ed. and intro. Arnold I. Davidson (Chicago: University of Chicago Press, 1997), 183–92. In the Neapolitan novels, this form of desire is described as the ability "to make connections between very different things" (2:359), a skill that Lila repeatedly demonstrates.

23. Similarly, we may read Lila's reluctance to leave Naples—her extraordinary disinterest in ever boarding a plane or even a train throughout the saga—as perhaps revealing her own need to check her natural tendency to follow the potentialities of desire.

24. "Basic Sight was earning her a growing reputation for innovation and for profit. . . . The business was going so well—people said—that Enzo was looking for a space for a proper office and not the makeshift one that he had installed between the kitchen and the bedroom. But who was Enzo, clever though he might be? Only a subordinate of Lila. It was she who moved things, who made and unmade. So, to exaggerate just slightly, the situation in the neighborhood seemed in a short time to have become the following: you learned either to be like Marcello and Michele or to be like Lila" (4:129–30).

25. Interestingly, Elena's mother's name is not revealed until a relatively late moment in the series, when Elena has to explain why she is not naming her second daughter after her (3:268). Elena's mother finally gets her wish when Elena names her third daughter Immacolata (4:195).

26. Deleuze, "Desire and Pleasure," 189–90.

27. Deleuze, 189.

28. Elena and Nino's affair begins shortly after their reunion on March 9, 1976, and continues until June of 1982 (3:355, 4:257).

29. Ferrante stages another scene of grueling sex *more ferarum* in *The Days of Abandonment* when she depicts the coupling of Olga and the musician Carrano (TDA 84–85). In his famous case study, *The Wolfman*, Freud speculates that the patient experiences a trauma when he witnesses his parents' *coitus a tergo*, as he shows signs that parental intercourse represents for him a pathogenic "primal scene." Ferrante's fascination with images of heterosexual copulation in which the man is posterior to the woman seems to imply a sort of feminist "primal scene." She evidently ascribes to this sexual position an almost symbolic meaning when it comes to revealing the crude, animalistic, and disappointing nature of straight sex for many women.

30. Olga seems obsessed with Carla's beauty, focusing in particular on her neck and smooth hair (TDA, 69). Olga also repeatedly envisions Carla's genitalia while fantasizing about her having sex with her husband Mario: "She (Carla) opened her thighs, she bathed his prick, and imagined that thus she had baptized him, I baptize you with the holy water of the cunt. . . . (Mario) was spreading Carla's thin legs, letting his gaze rest on her cunt half covered by underpants, lingering, his heart pounding, on the obscenity of that position" (TDA, 71, 83).

31. Massimo Fusillo has observed that the complicated libidinal entanglement of Lila, Nino, and Elena during their summer vacation on Ischia suggests a sort of polyamorous utopia. See Massimo Fusillo, "Sulla *smarginatura*. Tre punti-chiave per Elena Ferrante," *Allegoria 73*, 28, third series, no. 73 (January–June 2016): 151. The issue of *Allegoria 73* is one of the best volumes of literary criticism on Ferrante's works that has been published.

32. The importance of the verb *becoming* in the Neapolitan novels may have something to do with Gilles Deleuze and Félix Guattari's influential concept of "becoming woman," which they set out in their landmark treatise, *A Thousand Plateaus: Capitalism and Schizophrenia*, trans. Brian Massumi (Minneapolis: University of Minnesota Press, 1987). Among Ferrante's many other merits is her ability to bring to life philosophical or theoretical concepts by exploring their implications in her characters' feelings and actions. While her storytelling is often praised for its realism, her writings are evocative of contemporary philosophical notions and often seem charged with the speculative excitement of thought experiments. Aside from the importance of "becoming" in the Neapolitan Quartet, other examples of Ferrante's fascination with philosophical ideas include her professed attachments to Freud, Melanie Klein, and Luce Irigaray, her admission of a deep affinity between her second book, *The Days of Abandonment*, and Jean-Luc Nancy's notion of "being abandoned," and her clear evocation of Guy Debord's *The Society of the Spectacle* when she speaks of "the permanent spectacle in which we are immersed" (F 122, 210, 243).

33. See Judith Butler, *Undoing Gender* (New York: Routledge, 2004).

34. I allude to the title of Kaja Silverman's *Male Subjectivity at the Margins* (New York: Routledge, 1992).

35. As Judith Butler famously argues, gender is neither a name nor an attribute but rather is a performance, which is to say a "doing." Butler, *Gender Trouble: Feminism and the Subversion of Identity* (New York: Routledge, 2006), 24–25.

36. Fusillo, "Sulla *smarginatura*," 148.

2. WORKING WOMEN

1. Among Ferrante's earlier novels, *Troubling Love* in particular is an important point of reference for the Neapolitan Quartet. Although the style of the earlier works differs from that of the quartet, Ferrante in *Troubling Love* constructs a relationship between the mother-daughter protagonists, Amalia and Delia, that foreshadows the relationship between Lila and Elena. Like Amalia, Lila vanishes from the sight of those closest to her, who regard her as both charismatic and untrustworthy. Like Delia, Elena is more guarded and restrained. In *Troubling Love*, we encounter several devices that Ferrante revisits and transforms in the quartet. Amalia's photo is displayed in a shop window like Lila's wedding portrait, and the neighborhood where Delia spent her childhood appears to be the same as that of Elena and Lila's childhood, as it is situated near the railway station of Piazza Garibaldi and features numerous four-story buildings that all exemplify "the same unimaginative geometry" (TL 110). In Delia's father's apartment, we even find the same octagonal floor tiles that adorn the bathroom of Lila's childhood apartment (TL 111).

2. See Vivian Gornick, *The End of the Novel of Love* (Boston: Beacon, 1997). In her article "The Essential Ferrante," which appeared in the *Nation* on November 2, 2016, Gornick dismisses Ferrante's writing as "premodernist" and even "neorealist." Her criticism of the Italian writer, which conveys a degree of hostility that is rare among American readers of the Neapolitan novels, comes off as petty and self-serving. She laments the characters' lack of evolution, for example, in spite of the fact that Ferrante is at her best in the quartet describing moments of transition from adolescence to old age when everything changes. She also takes pains to dispute Ferrante's feminism. See https://www.thenation.com/article/archive/the -essential-ferrante/.

3. Benedetto Croce, "I lazzari," in *Un paradiso abitato da diavoli* (Milan: Adelphi, 2006), 83–95.

4. As cited by Croce, 105.

5. Johann Wolfgang von Goethe, *Travels in Italy: Together with His Second Residence in Rome and Fragments of Italy*, trans. Charles Nisbet (London: George Bell, 1885), 337.

6. On the difference between labor and work, see Hannah Arendt's *The Human Condition,* 2d ed., intro. Margaret Canovan (Chicago: University of Chicago Press, 1998), 79–174. Arendt famously distinguishes between the classical idea of labor, which in antiquity amounted to a futile activity of self-preservation aiming at mere reproduction, and that of work, which represented a means of instrumental reasoning that connected the beginning to the end of a process. According to Arendt, the third category that separated the *vita activa* from *vita contemplativa* was that of action: the public, shared domain of political life.

7. The origin of this saying in Italian is not clear. In the Christian tradition generally, work appears to coincide with the penance needed to make redemption from original sin a possibility. In Paul's writings, work—or more properly labor— specifically represents a necessary condition of survival. See in particular 2 Thessalonians 3:10, which the KJV gives as "For even when we were with you, this we commanded you, that if any should not work, neither should he eat." Yet the Benedictine monks, whose principle of *ora et labora* ("pray and work") defined their order, insisted on the essential nobility of working.

8. Given Anita Raja's family background, it is hard not to wonder whether the horrific propagandizing of "work" in Nazi Germany does not supply a historical justification for Ferrante's withering skepticism toward the value of industrialized or professionalized toil.

9. Arendt, *The Human Condition,* 126–27.

10. Aristotle regards the condition of the laborer as closer to that of the slave than to those of the craftsman and merchant. Arendt contends that the laborer has become the paradigm of work in modernity as the imperatives of production and consumption have rendered all other activities obsolete (Arendt, 126).

11. I discuss Ortese's remarkable book at greater length in the chapter 4, "Genius Loci," this volume.

12. Pier Paolo Pasolini, "Il PCI ai giovani!," in *Bestemmia. Tutte le poesie* (Milan: Garzanti, 1993), 1851.

13. As Weil remarked in a celebrated sentence, "The effect of exhaustion is to make me forget my real reasons for spending time in the factory, and to make it almost

impossible for me to overcome the strongest temptation that this life entails: that of not thinking anymore, which is the one and only way of not suffering from it." Rather than invoke the hope of future class redemption, Weil's journal focused on workers' quotidian duress. Simone Weil, *Formative Writings, 1929–1941*, ed. and trans. Dorothy Tuck McFarland and Wilhelmina Van Ness (Abingdon: Routledge, 2009), 123.

14. Simone Weil, *Notebooks*, vol. 2, as cited in the Milan Women's Bookstore Collective, *Sexual Difference: A Theory of Socio-Symbolic Practice*, ed. Teresa de Lauretis (Bloomington: Indiana University Press, 1990), 23. For the epigraph in the Italian edition of this landmark book, see Libreria delle Donne di Milano, *Non credere di avere dei diritti. La generazione della libertà femminile nell'idea e nelle vicende di un gruppo di donne* (Turin: Rosenberg & Sollier, 1987), 7. All subsequent citations of these texts are noted in the body of the argument by page number respectively following the abbreviations SD and NC for the English and Italian titles.

15. Adriana Cavarero, *Relating Narratives: Storytelling and Selfhood*, trans. Paul A. Kottman (New York: Routledge, 2000), 3–4. The English title represents a somewhat anemic translation of the original edition's more dramatic Italian title, *Tu che mi guardi, tu che mi racconti* ("You who look at me, you who tell my story"; Milan: Feltrinelli, 1997).

16. Cavarero, 55.

17. Cavarero, 55.

18. On the limits of Elena's success, see Elena Ferrante, *Frantumaglia: A Writer's Journey* (New York: Europa, 2016), 359. See also how Ferrante does not consider writing to be a job (F 380).

19. Ferrante leaves some tantalizing clues for the reader regarding Tina's disappearance. For example, when the Solara brothers finally are murdered in 1986 on the steps of a church, in the same place where Pasquale's father had been assaulted decades before, we are left to draw our own conclusions. When Elena visits Pasquale in prison, he seems to be on the verge of confessing his responsibility for killing the Solaras in revenge for Tina. Even more significant is Lila's reaction to the news of the Solaras' murder. She is at the hospital for a fibroma. Carmen claims that Tina is "encysted" (*incistata*) in Lila's body, and we may not be surprised when she says that she feels like Tina came out of her stomach to kill the Solaras (4:355).

20. Giorgio Agamben, *Idea of Prose*, trans. Michael Sullivan and Sam Whitsitt (Albany: SUNY Press, 1995), 64.

21. When Agamben analyzes the idea of study, he frames it in terms of the role of the Talmud in the Jewish tradition and the messianic redemption of potential (63–65).

22. Sigmund Freud, "Mourning and Melancholia," in *The Standard Edition of the Complete Psychological Works*, vol. 14, trans. James Strachey in collaboration with Anna Freud, assisted by Alix Strachey and Alan Tyson (London: Hogarth, 1971), 251.

23. Indeed, to cite two of many examples, James Wood calls *My Brilliant Friend* "a large, captivating, amiably peopled Bildungsroman," while Elissa Schappell calls the tetralogy as a whole "an unnervingly clear-eyed bildungsroman." James Wood, "Women on the Verge," *New Yorker*, January 21, 2013, https://www.newyorker.com

/magazine/2013/01/21/women-on-the-verge; Elissa Schappell, "The Mysterious, Anonymous Author Elena Ferrante on the Conclusion of Her Neapolitan Novels," *Vanity Fair*, August 27, 2015, https://www.vanityfair.com/culture/2015/08/elena -ferrante-interview-the-story-of-the-lost-child.

24. On the topic of Elena's disenchantment with her own career, see her description of her "crisis" in the winter of 2002 (4:456–59), especially the last sentence: "My entire life would be reduced to a petty battle to change my social class." I discuss more substantially Elena's interest in the concept of "becoming" in the next chapter.

25. In fact, there is very little in Ferrante of Balzac's worldlier notion of Bildung, which he envisioned as a process culminating on a hill from which the protagonist, in full possession of power and riches, gazes down at the city.

26. In Italian a *zibaldone* is a hodgepodge or miscellany. The term may refer to a commonplace book. It also provides the title of the great nineteenth-century poet Giacomo Leopardi's sprawling collection of personal reflections on literary and philosophical topics, which ran to over four thousand pages and was never published in his lifetime.

27. Walter Benjamin, "On the Concept of History," in *Walter Benjamin: Selected Writings,* vol. 4: *1938–40,* ed. Howard Eiland and Michael W. Jennings, trans. Edmund Jephcott and others (Cambridge, MA: Belknap/Harvard University Press, 2006), 389. All subsequent citations of this essay are noted in the body of the argument by page number following the abbreviation OCH.

3. POLITICAL COSMOLOGIES

1. Gayatri Chakravorty Spivak, "Can the Subaltern Speak?," revised from the "History" chapter of *A Critique of Postcolonial Reason: Toward a History of the Vanishing Present* (Cambridge, MA: Harvard University Press, 1999), 198–311, and reprinted in *Can the Subaltern Speak: Reflections on the History of an Idea,* ed. Rosalind C. Morris (New York: Columbia University Press, 2010), 21–78.

2. Ann Goldstein's translation on a few other occasions normalizes speech that in the original is deliberately unusual or problematic. A case in point is her rendering of *ricchione* with the word *queer,* which at least since the early 1990s has come to acquire a positive, defiant value, at least in American English. The Italian term instead is crudely derogatory and probably would be better translated as *faggot.* Consequently, the English-language edition softens the force of Alfonso's confession of his true sexual identity to Elena. He tells her, "Lenù, sono ricchione, le femmine non mi piacciono" (3:191 IT), which the translation gives as: "Lenù, I am queer, I do not like girls" (3:212). Far from being at ease with his identity, Alfonso declares that "life is an ugly business" (3:212) and depicts himself as occupying a position of subalternity (*subalternità*) to Lila, which in this case Goldstein translates as "inferiority" (3:210 EN; 3:189 IT).

3. Spivak, "Can the Subaltern Speak?," 48.

4. Antonio Gramsci, *Selections from Cultural Writings,* ed. David Forgacs and Geoffrey Nowell-Smith, trans. William Boelhower (Cambridge, MA: Harvard University Press, 1985), 294. All subsequent citations of this collection are noted in the body of the argument by page number following the abbreviation SCW.

5. In one of the most dramatic images of the series, when Elena's teenaged boyfriend Antonio realizes that he has not received an exemption from military duty, he falls to the earth and begins putting dirt in his mouth like the eponymous hero of Pasolini's film *Accattone* (2:71).

6. Stefano's subservience is especially evident in his willingness to "sell" Lila to the Solaras, at least in symbolic terms. In addition to giving Marcello her prototype of the Cerullo shoe design, he allows the Solaras to display Lila's photo in their store in Piazza dei Martiri and then, after their separation, encourages Lila to live in an apartment belonging to Michele Solara.

7. Recent feminist philosophers have reevaluated the importance of the thinking of difference, eschewing simplistic charges of essentialism. See, for example, Linda M. G. Zerilli, *Feminism and the Abyss of Freedom* (Chicago: University of Chicago Press, 2005), in particular the third chapter, "Feminism Makes Promises: The Milan Collective's *Sexual Difference* and the Project of World Building," 93–123.

8. See Sheryl Sandberg, *Lean In: Women, Work and the Will to Lead* (New York: Knopf, 2013). For sharp critiques of Sandberg's book and claims to feminism, see Linda Burnham, "1% Feminism," *openDemocracy*, April 8, 2013, https://www.open democracy.net/5050/linda-burnham/1-feminism; and Dawn Foster, *Lean Out* (London: Repeater, 2015).

9. Julia Kristeva discusses the same painting in her celebrated essay "Stabat Mater" (1977), which is collected in *The Julia Kristeva Reader*, ed. Toril Moi (Oxford: Basil Blackwell, 1986), 160–86.

10. Zerilli, *Feminism and the Abyss of Freedom*, 94.

11. Zerilli, 96.

12. Zerilli, 98–102.

13. Elena's insistence in this context on the importance of the word *become* suggests that Ferrante may be thinking of the French philosopher Gilles Deleuze's famous notion of "becoming-woman"; see note 32, chapter 1.

14. Carla Lonzi, "La donna clitoridea e la donna vaginale," in *Sputiamo su Hegel* (Milan: et al./Economica, 2010), 61–113.

15. The expression "the mother of us all" comes from a work by Gertrude Stein on the American feminist Susan Anthony (SD 113–14).

16. For a political interpretation of Melvile's short story, see Giorgio Agamben, "Bartleby, or On Contingency," in *Potentialities: Collected Essays in Philosophy*, ed. and trans. Daniel Heller-Roazen (Stanford: Stanford University Press, 1999), 243–71.

17. Peter Fenves brilliantly defines "the shape of time" in Benjamin's thought by emphasizing "the tension between the nondirectionality of time and the unidirectionality of history." See Fenves's *The Messianic Reduction: Walter Benjamin and the Shape of Time* (Stanford: Stanford University Press, 2010), 4.

18. Walter Benjamin, "Paralipomena to 'On the Concept of History,'" in *Walter Benjamin: Selected Writings*, vol. 4: *1938–40*, ed. Howard Eiland and Michael W. Jennings, trans. Edmund Jephcott and others (Cambridge, MA: Belknap/Harvard University Press, 2006), 402.

19. In the 1976 general election, Christian Democracy received 38.71 percent of the vote or about 14.2 million votes while the PCI received 34.37 percent of the vote or about 12.6 million votes. See https://en.wikipedia.org/wiki/Italian_general_elec tion,_1976.

20. It has to be noted that the PCI was the only major party that was not found guilty of any corruption; its eventual dissolution came about in response to the fall of the Berlin Wall and the global mutation of political conditions.

21. See https://www.asymptotejournal.com/special-feature/anita-raja-on-christa-wolf/. The essay was first published in Italian as "Parole contro i guasti del mondo. Riflessioni sul linguaggio di Christa Wolf," in *Prospettive su Christa Wolf. Dalle sponde al mito*, ed. Giulio Schiavoni (Milan: Franco Angeli, 1998), 96–102.

22. Wolf's standing in the German Democratic Republic (GDR) was complicated. She belonged to the state political party, which was known as the Socialist Unity Party of Germany (Sozialistische Einheitspartei Deutschland or SED), but over time distanced herself from Marxist orthodoxy, supporting dissenting voices and heretical writers such as Wolf Biermann.

23. Christa Wolf, *Cassandra*, trans. Anita Raja (Rome: Edizioni e/o, 1990), 153.

24. Dwight Garner, Parul Sehgal, and Jennifer Szalai, "The New Vanguard," *New York Times*, March 5, 2018, https://www.nytimes.com/2018/03/05/books/vanguard-books -by-women-in-21st-century.html.

25. Stefano Jossa, "Non si deve studiare la Ferrante all'Università" in *doppiozero*, May 20, 2017, https://www.doppiozero.com/materiali/non-si-deve-studiare-la-ferr ante-alluniversita.

26. As cited in Laura Benedetti, "Elena Ferrante in America," *Allegoria 73*, 28, third series, no. 73 (January–June 2016): 112.

27. We encounter more tiresome examples of Italian male critics' reflexive misogyny in the interviews included in the DVD release of Roberto Faenza's cinematic adaptation of *The Days of Abandonment* (*I giorni dell'abbandono*, 2005), as I note in my introduction.

28. Christa Wolf, *Premesse a Cassandra*, trans. Anita Raja (Rome: Edizioni e/o, 1984), 161. At the same time, we should observe that Ferrante makes an effort to advance beyond the example of Bachmann's *Ways of Dying* (*Todesarten*), the Austrian writer's cycle of novels including *Der Fall Franza* (1966), *Malina* (1971), and *Requiem für Fanny Goldmann* (1972) about women whose only possible fate is either to die or to disappear. In her first two novels, *Troubling Love* and *The Days of Abandonment*, Ferrante imposes a sort of minimalist happy ending on her protagonists' ethical and psychological conflicts. However, she apparently grows dissatisfied with this strategy in her later works, as she undertakes to complicate or problematize her characters' responses to their situations in *The Lost Daughter* and the novels of the Neapolitan Quartet.

29. Christa Wolf, *The Quest for Christa T.*, trans. Christopher Middleton (New York: Farrar, Straus and Giroux, 1970), 3. All subsequent citations of this novel are noted in the body of the argument by page number following the abbreviation QCT.

30. Perhaps the most renowned example of this genre in modern German literature is Thomas Mann's *Doctor Faustus,* which revisits the life of the world-weary musical genius Adrian Leverkühn through the narration of his friend Dr. Serenus Zeitblom. Leverkühn embodies the figure of the genius who performs superhuman creative feats with effortless charm yet is doomed to descend into madness and nihilism, as recounted by his calmer counterpart, the aptly named Serenus. Mann's novel was important to Wolf, as we may deduce from her speeches and diaries. For instance, see Christa Wolf, "Strati Temporali. Su Thomas Mann," in *Parla, così ti vediamo.*

Saggi, discorsi, interviste, trans. Anita Raja (Rome: Edizioni e/o, 2015). We may suspect that Mann's retelling of the Faust legend was no less significant to Ferrante. A crucial event in *Doctor Faustus* is Adrian's loss of his beloved little nephew, Echo, as a condition of his pact with the devil for twenty-four years of creative genius. Underscoring this requirement, the devil tells Adrian, "You may not love." When Lila loses Tina, who represents both an echo of herself and her most beloved, she tragically assumes a more Faustian than Mephistophelean role in the narrative.

31. "She was always, to her own way of thinking, a person with prospects, latent possibilities" (QCT 136). "Christa T. said she did not like things to be fixed: that everything, once it's out there in existence . . . is so difficult to get moving again, so one should try in advance to keep it alive while it's still in the process of coming to be, in oneself" (QCT 167). "She was trying out the possibilities of life until nothing should be left: that much was understandable" (QCT 170).

32. Christa Wolf, *Un giorno all'anno 1960–2000*, trans. Anita Raja (Rome: Edizioni e/o, 2006).

33. "Cara Christa, quando ho letto il tuo *Ricordi di Christa T.* ero a metà del manoscritto di questo libro. Spero che capirai perché l'uno e l'altro (*Cassandra!*) sono stati così importanti. La tua Raja." Wolf, 338.

34. Wolf, 338–39.

35. Anita Raja compiles (or approves) a revealing entry for herself in *Un giorno all'anno*: "Librarian in Rome; her mother, a German Jew, migrated to Italy. Translator of C. W.'s books in Italian, a close friend of the Ws" ("Bibiotecaria a Roma; sua madre, ebrea tedesca, emigro in Italia. Traduttrice dei libri di C.W. in italiano, molto amica dei W. Wolf, 567.

36. Claudio Gatti, "The Story Behind a Name," *NYR Daily*, October 10, 2016, https://www.nybooks.com/daily/2016/10/02/story-behind-a-name-elena-ferrante/.

37. When it comes to Wolf's collaboration with the Stasi, we ought to remember that refusal to cooperate was impossible in the GDR, as many critics have observed. Wolf never provided any useful information to the authorities and ultimately wound up as the object of surveillance herself, along with her husband. See Margit Resch, *Understanding Christa Wolf* (Columbia: University of South Carolina Press, 1997), 164.

38. Wolf, *Auf dem Weg nach Tabou*, 75, as cited in Resch, 161.

39. For a clear-eyed account of the rise and decline of the Italian left, see the chapter entitled "Italy" in Perry Anderson's *The New Old World* (London: Verso, 2009), 278–351.

40. David Forgacs and Geoffrey Nowell-Smith remind us that in the 1950s "neorealism" along with "social realism" often were regarded as practically synonymous with the national-popular (SCW 196). From the 1960s onward, hostile critics in Italy hammered on the risks of populism that were implicit in Gramsci's theories, causing his influence on the Italian intelligentsia steadily to decline. For a useful analysis of this debate, see Marco Gatto, *Nonostante Gramsci: Marxismo e critica letteraria nell'Italia del Novecento* (Macerata: Quodlibet, 2016).

41. David Forgacs provides helpful exposition of Gramsci's concept of the national-popular in his "National-Popular: Genealogy of a Concept," in Simon Durling, ed., *The Cultural Studies Reader* (London: Routledge, 1993), 209–19. Joseph Buttigieg meticulously analyzes Gramsci's view of civil society and the role of the intellectual in "Gramsci on Civil Society," *boundary 2*, 22, no. 3 (Autumn 1995): 1–32.

42. In the aftermath of the Second World War, Italian writers and intellectuals for the most part agreed gradually to discredit the very possibility of cultural and political emancipation, preferring more static and idealist aesthetic models à la Croce; see Forgacs and Nowell-Smith's commentary, SCW 91).

43. Henry A. Giroux, "Rethinking Cultural Politics and Radical Pedagogy in the Work of Antonio Gramsci," in Carmel Borg, Joseph A. Buttigieg, and Peter Mayo, eds., *Gramsci and Education* (Lanham, MD: Rowman and Littlefield, 2002), 55.

44. For more on this topic, see Cecilia Schwartz, "Ferrante Feud: The Italian Reception of the Neapolitan Novels Before and After their International Success," *Italianist*, May 5, 2020, https://www.tandfonline.com/doi/full/10.1080/02614340.2020.1738122.

45. Dayna Tortorici, "Those Like Us," *n + 1* 22 (Spring 2015), https://nplusonemag.com /issue-22/reviews/those-like-us/.

46. Some critics, especially those in Italy, hold in higher regard Ferrante's early novels, with their narrower focus on middle- and upper-middle-class women. The *écriture féminine* of these novels, so the thinking goes, guarantees the satisfaction of certain formal preoccupations that otherwise seem to go unattended in the tetralogy. At times, the label of *écriture féminine* that James Wood first applies to Ferrante's writing has seemed useful for a stylistic rescue of her project. Yet is this label really useful in defining her style? It is true that Ferrante writes in a passionate, generous voice, yet her controlled energy of storytelling and eclectic use of genres seems to diverge fundamentally from the fluid absence of boundaries and privileging of feminine difference in language that characterizes the narrative mode first defined by Hélène Cixous. Cixous's evocative coinage has been crucial in conferring authority on women's writing, even if the charge of gender essentialism, which certainly was never Cixous's own intent, has been leveled against the category's proponents.

47. Reviewing *The Story of a New Name*, Joseph Luzzi observes that, whereas Manzoni famously went "to rinse his laundry" in the Arno ("risciaquare i panni in Arno") by recasting his work in the normative Tuscan language, Elena instead tosses Lila's notebooks into the Arno to drown them. Notwithstanding Ferrante's symbolic riposte to Manzoni's idealization of the birth of Italian literature, Luzzi is convinced that Ferrante, like Manzoni, has created a "general tragedy" that allegorically expresses the historical fate of its subjects. Joseph Luzzi, "It Started in Naples," *New York Times,* September 27, 2013, https://www.nytimes.com/2013/09/29/books /review/elena-ferrantes-story-of-a-new-name.html.

48. James Wood, in his review of *My Brilliant Friend,* invokes the neorealist films of Vittorio De Sica and Luchino Visconti as well as Giovanni Verga's novels as reference points for the Neapolitan Quartet. Although there may be some faint resemblance between these works, the setting, sociology, and gender of Ferrante's characters are notably different. Visconti's *The Earth Trembles* explores life in a fishing village and, although De Sica's neorealist films such as *The Bicycle Thief* or *Umberto D.* are more urban in setting, they focus almost exclusively on male protagonists. Wood, op. cit.

49. Paolo Mauri, "Torna Elena Ferrante tra i segreti di Napoli," *La Repubblica*, August 10, 2011, https://ricerca.repubblica.it/repubblica/archivio/repubblica/2011 /10/08/torna-elena-ferrante-tra-segreti-di-napoli.html. We should note that Pratolini's choral personae are denizens of a dignified *quartiere* in Florence, as the title of one of his novels makes clear, rather than the sort of anarchic rione that Ferrante depicts in the Neapolitan novels.

50. Gramsci regarded Dante's *De Vulgari Eloquentia* (c. 1303–1305) as a pivotal event in Italy's national and cultural history and the continued use of Latin throughout the Renaissance as highly problematic (SCW 197).

51. See David Forgacs and Geoffrey Nowell-Smith's commentary (SCW 164).

52. See the section "Intellectual and Education" in Gramsci, *An Antonio Gramsci Reader: Selected Writings, 1916–1935*, ed. David Forgacs (New York: Schocken, 1998), 300–22. All subsequent citations of this collection are noted in the body of the argument by page number following the abbreviation AGR.

53. Benedetto Fontana, *Hegemony and Power: On the Relation Between Gramsci and Machiavelli* (Minneapolis: University of Minnesota Press, 1993), 106–7.

54. Benedetto Croce, a Southern philosopher, was responsible for the cultural hegemony in Italy of the school of idealism, which held that poetry had its own strictly formal domain that categorically distinguished it from "nonpoetry" or writing about social and historical concerns. See Croce, *Poesia a non poesia. Note sulla letteratura europea del secolo decimonono* (Bari: G. Laterza, 1923).

55. "If I were capable of writing about our Berlusconian Italy not through allegories, parables, and satires, I would like to find a plot and characters that could represent the mythology within which the symbol Berlusconi is dangerously encysted. I say symbol because the man will disappear, his personal troubles and those of his management have their power, one way or another the political struggle will remove him from the scene, but his ascent as supreme leader within democratic institutions, the construction of his figure as a democratically elected economic-political-television duce, will remain a perfectible, repeatable model" (F 93).

56. It is useful to recall that Gramsci notoriously disliked Ungaretti's poetry, which he found to be incomprehensible and disconnected from the concerns of the Italian people (SCW 272–73).

57. Nino's criticism of judges should be understood in context of the *Mani Pulite* scandal of the early 1990s in Italy, when several judges indicted politicians of the center right and center left for corruption and thereby brought the status quo of the post–World War II era to an abrupt end.

4. GENIUS LOCI

1. Benedetto Croce, *Un paradiso abitato da diavoli* (Milan: Adelphi Edizioni, 2006 [1923]), 11.

2. Sergio Stenti, *Napoli moderna. Città e case popolari (1868–1980)* (Naples: CLEAN Edizioni, 1993), 16.

3. Stenti, 20.

4. Stenti, 71.

5. Francesco Rosi's film *Le mani sulla città* (1963) exposed the abuses of the *speculazione edilizia* or real estate speculation in Naples.

6. Antonio Ghirelli, *Storia di Napoli* (Turin: Einaudi, 2015), 540.

7. As a child, Enzo still sells fruits and vegetables from a horse-drawn cart, but as a young man he turns his attention to technical schooling and the trade of computer programming.

8. Cf. Judith Shulevitz, "The Hypnotic Genius of Elena Ferrante," *Atlantic*, October 2015; Vivian Gornick, "The Essential Ferrante," *Nation*, November 2, 2016; and Ruth Franklin, "Who's Afraid of Claire Messud," *New York Times*, August 10, 2017.

9. Anna Maria Ortese, *Il mare non bagna Napoli* (Milan: Adelphi Edizioni, 1994 [1953]), 80.

10. Ortese, 93.

11. "Cominciava la notte, ai Granili, e la città involontaria si apprestava a consumare i suoi pochi beni, in una febbre che dura fino al mattino seguente, ora in cui ricominciano i lamenti, la sorpresa, il lutto, l'inerte orrore di vivere." Ortese, 97.

12. Matilde Serao's *Il ventre di Napoli* (1884) is a famous novel, written during the historically worst outbreaks of cholera in the city, that describes the miserable condition of Neapolitans who were forced to live in *quartieri popolari*.

13. Ghirelli, *Storia di Napoli*, 314.

14. Ferrante has used the same conceit in *The Days of Abandonment* where the character of the poverella, an abandoned and fragile woman, is supposed to live immediately above Olga in Naples. Instead Carrano, the musician with whom she eventually settles, lives in the apartment below hers.

15. Ferdinando Galiani (1728–1787) was an economist who also wrote a treatise on the Neapolitan language. It is Lila who makes the explicit connection between Galiani's apartment and a cultural heritage that may date back a full three centuries. Although none of Ferrante's characters make explicit reference to Ferdinando Galiani, it is clear that the professor's name implicitly evokes several layers of Neapolitan culture, including a notional connection from Italian illuminism to the modern-day political left. To Lila, however, this heritage is nothing but a burden: "There is not a thing here, an object, a painting, that was acquired by them directly. The furniture is from a hundred years ago. The house is at least three hundred years old. . . . They've read and studied in that house, father, grandfathers, great-grandfathers. . . . But in their heads they do not have a thought of their own" (2:162).

16. Elena describes the apartment in Genoa that belongs to her in-laws, the Airotas, as giving "an impression of light" (4:71). Even more than Professor Galiani and her children, the Airotas stand for the refinement of the haute bourgeoisie in the quartet.

17. See Stefano Petrosino, *Piccola metafisica della luce* (Milan: Jaca, 2004).

18. See Renato de Fusco, *Il floreale a Napoli* (Naples: Edizioni Scientifiche Italiane, 1989).

19. Arthur Schopenhauer, *The World as Will and Representation*, vol. 2, trans. E. F. J. Payne (New York: Dover, 1966), 588.

20. Marc Augé, *Non-Places: Introduction to an Anthropology of Supermodernity*, trans. John Howe (London: Verso, 1995).

21. "And if I do not have the right to call myself stateless, I can claim to be Naplesless, one who has scraped the origin from the body to consign himself to the world" ("E se non ho il diritto di definirmi apolide, posso dirmi napòlide, uno che si e raschiato dal corpo l'origine, per consegnarsi al mondo"). Erri De Luca, *Napòlide* (Naples: Edizioni Dante e Descartes, 2006), 6.

22. Walter Benjamin and Asja Lacis, "Naples," in *Walter Benjamin: Selected Writings*, vol. 1: *1913–1926*, ed. Marcus Bullock and Michael W. Jennings (Cambridge, MA: Belknap/Harvard University Press, 1996), 417.

23. In an entry of May 28, 1787, Goethe reasoned that cynicism, meant in the classical philosophical sense of the practice of renouncing all worldly impulses, would occur more naturally in a climate such as Southern Italy's, which satisfies all wants with its abundance. Goethe, *Travels in Italy*, 337.

24. Goethe, 337.

25. "Masaniello di Amalfi, il primo personaggio storico che riassuma intensamente . . . l'essenza della napoletanita, ossia il primo napoletano che si presenti in un preciso contorno storico con una personalita fortemente caratterizzata da quello stesso ambiente di cui sulle scene, Pulcinella e stato e sara la maschera emblematica." Ghirelli, *Storia di Napoli*, 49.

26. The affinities between Lila and Masaniello may go well beyond a shared taste for decapitating portrait pictures. According to Ghirelli, Masaniello was a vulnerable man, notwithstanding his fame, and was known to swoon in public. Like Lila, he seems to have suffered from his own strain of dissolving margins. Ghirelli, 60.

27. De Luca, *Napolide*, 41.

28. Benedetto Croce, *Storie e leggende napoletane* (Milan: Adelphi Edizioni, 1990 [1919]), 325–26.

29. Walter Benjamin, *Berlin Childhood Around 1900*, in *Selected Writings*, vol. 3: *1935–1938*, ed. Howard Eiland and Michael W. Jennings, trans. Edmund Jephcott, Howard Eiland, and others (Cambridge, MA: Belknap/Harvard University Press, 2002), 384.

30. Benjamin in the *Arcades Project* describes the dialectical image as the actualization of a moment from the past in the "now of recognizability" (*Jetzt der Erkennbarkeit*). Walter Benjamin, *The Arcades Project*, trans. Howard Eiland and Kevin McLaughlin, prepared on the basis of the German volume edited by Rolf Tiedemann (Cambridge, MA: Harvard University Press, 1999), xii.

31. Another trait that Lila's notional book appears to share with Benjamin's *Arcades* is its reliance on "quotations" that its author has learned by heart (4:447). Benjamin's text, like Lila's, relied heavily on a collage of quotations.

32. While visiting Naples with Asja Lacis, Walter Benjamin conflates the city with the African Kraal, as it seems to him that private life in Naples has become utterly public, given the density and porosity of its architecture and social life. Benjamin and Lacis, "Naples," 419.

33. Benjamin, *The Arcades Project*, 82.

34. Scampia is the complex of modern buildings that Neapolitans call *le vele* for the buildings' resemblance to the sails of a sailboat. Roberto Saviano made it famous in his book *Gomorra* (Milan: Mondadori, 2006). It is an area dominated by the Camorra and disfigured by the consequences of drug trafficking.

35. Pasolini used each of these three terms to describe a somewhat different, albeit related, aspect of what he regarded as Italy's catastrophic postwar social and cultural decline. In an essay published in *Il Corriere della Sera*, June 10, 1974, he warns readers that Italy's middle classes "have radically—I would say anthropologically—changed" to embrace consumerist hedonism and "the American type" of tolerance. In the same paper on June 24 of that year, he distinguishes between "the anthropological mutation of Italians" and their "complete homologation to a single model" of power. Finally, in a reflection on his 1961 film *Accattone*, published on October 8, 1975, he decries the cultural "genocide" of the young boys of the

working class, which he claims has transformed them into "Hitler SS." See, respectively, "Studio della rivoluzione antropologica in Italia," "Il vero fascismo e quindi il vero antifascismo," and "Il mio *Accattone* in TV dopo il genocidio," in *Saggi sulla politica e sulla società*, ed. Walter Siti and Silvia de Laude (Milan: Mondadori, 1999), 308, 315, and 676.

36. "Napoli è ancora l'ultima metropoli plebea. . . ." Pier Paolo Pasolini, "Gennariello," in *Pier Paolo Pasolini. Saggi sulla politica a sulla società*, ed. Walter Siti and Silvia De Laude (Milan: Mondadori, 1999), 553.

37. "A Napoli sono pieni di vitalità sia il ragazzo povero che il ragazzo borghese." Pasolini, 553. The translation is mine.

38. Assessing what they describe as Naples's "serious tourism crisis" from the 1960s to the early 1990s, Maria Immacolata Simeon and Elèna Lucariello observe that in newspaper articles and tourist guides published between 1980 and 1992 "the city is announced as a 'nightmare' for tourists and Naples is described as a 'Third World city'" before concluding that stories published in the *Economist*, the *Daily Telegraph*, the *Herald Tribune*, the *New York Times*, *El Pais*, *Le Monde*, and *Le Nouvel Observateur*, among others, represent the city as "a picture of civil and urban decay." Maria Immacolata Simeon and Elèna Lucariello, "Naples, City of Art and Culture: Tourism Policy and a New Image for the City in the 1990s," *Journal of Tourism and History* 10, no. 1 (2018): 68. Stereotyping of Naples as a third-world city surely predates the period studied by Simeon and Lucariello; one might even consider Benjamin and Lacis's aforementioned comparison of the city to the African Kraal (see this chapter's note 32) as an early example of the trope.

INDEX